T0308514

I dedicate this book to my daughters Leila, Lexi, Liz, and Leah who are my greatest teachers. I hope my actions prove my love for you.

Please don't ever forget how precious you are!

And to my wonderful husband Aubrey, thank you for always taking care of me. It is because of you I have the confidence and strength to pursue my dreams.

Acknowledgments

"Both the experts and the word-of-mouth savants on the street agree: Marci Barker's book, The Accountability Code, provides a clear and reliable formula that helps people turn their lives around. And Marci puts a smile on your face as she does it! She's fun!"

Dr. Ivan Misner, *NY Times* Bestselling author and Founder of BNI.

"Seriously nothing quite like this book. I mean totally comprehensive with life hacks to live your BIG life. From beginning to end the learning point density is unreal. And QR codes to scan for quizzes and videos. #1AwesomeBook. Bravo Marci."

David M. Corbin, Mentor to Mentors, Speaker, Two-time *Wall Street Journal* Best Selling Author

"Success in C-suite and life results from an individual's accountability formula. The book breaks down this proven formula. Read and implement its teachings to start succeeding today."

Marshall Goldsmith, Author of *What Got you Here Won't Get You There*.

ISBN: 978-1-954759-35-0 (Ebook)
ISBN: 978-1-954759-36-7 (paperback)
ISBN: 978-1-954759-37-4(hardcover)

TABLE OF CONTENTS

Introduction   **1**

Chapter 1 - Reflection   **7**

Doubt Yourself No More   12
Born With It   16
Meditation Practice   19
Creating A Vision   22
Abuse Cycle   27
Look Inward First   31
Must Be Trained   35
Getting Help   39

Chapter 2 - Humility   **43**

Shut Down The Negativity   47
Judgment   47
Fixing Mistakes   54
Standing Up   58
Shared Control   63
Adversary   66
Humble Help   70

Chapter 3 - Planning   **75**

Your Path Is Correct – for *You*   78
Our Own Story   84
Foolproof Plan   88
Broken Record   92
From Pain to Plan   97
Choose Your Struggles   100
Plan for Growth   104
Planned Productivity   110

Chapter 4 - Implementing   **115**

Freedom   119
Health Basics   123
Positive Mindset Affirmations   126
Comparison Is Not A Thief of Joy   132
Life Is Unfair   135
Implementing Contributions   138
Fear Can Motivate   143
Urgency   147
Single Tasking   151

Chapter 5 - Commitment 155

Fresh Start 159
Anxiety-Calming Habits 163
What's Most Important 167
Burn-Out Cure 171
Always Ready 175
Stability 179
Brain—Body Connection 182

Chapter 6 - Feedback 187

How To Turn Your Weakness Into A Strength 191
Behaviors 194
Shift Intentions 197
Recognize Patterns 202
Feed Your Focus 205
Listen Up 209
Check Ins 212
Results Determine Shift 215

Conclusion 219

Boundaries 219
Charity 223
Once The Gift Has Been Given 226
Listen and Act 229

Introduction

All right, you just picked up this book, *The Accountability Code: Wake Up and Show Up*. You likely were interested because you want to be clearly accountable to values you already strongly believe in. You were drawn by the idea of finally being able to clearly identify and do the things you know you should be doing to be happy with your life.

Before we dive in, let's define what The Accountability Code is, what it is used for, and how it has the power to change your life.

The word "accountable" means "required or expected (of a person, organization, or institution) to justify actions or decisions; responsible." Like many vital personal skills, the ability to be accountable isn't something we are born with. It is something we develop systematically, over time, in order to be happy, independent, and successful.

When I asked my clients what they thought of when hearing the word "accountability," they answered with an interesting variety of responses:

follow through

extreme ownership

doing something hard

dread and forgetfulness

shutting down

having someone to answer to other than myself

someone to help me in a loving way to achieve my goals by 'staying on my case'

That last client response is the best. All of us want to justify our actions in pursuing success, and oftentimes that is hard to pass on to someone else in a friendly,
loving manner.

The Accountability Code is a 6-step process that helps you transform your uncertainties about your goals and methods into confident activities that fulfill your values and ensure your success as a happy, independent, and thriving achiever.

When you develop the skills for increasing your self-accountability, you'll find that many problems just melt away. In this book, I often use my negative relationship with my dad to illustrate how the Accountability Code can reverse a strongly negative experience into a positive achievement.

My dad and I have had a really tough relationship for the past few years, and it has hindered my ability to be happy or to create a feeling of success in my life. I finally realized that I needed a process to change how I interacted with him, because our relationship constantly tore me down, dissolved my feelings of happiness, created overflowing confusion, and made me feel depressed about my whole life.

I reversed all that by using the six steps of The Accountability Code, transforming how I think, speak, and act. Because of The Accountability Code (TAC), I am a better parent and a better person, my body is healthy, I enjoy life, and I am more available to help others.

Using TAC is a journey of fulfilling progression. Throughout this book, you will see how I have used TAC to change negative issues in my life so that I could reach a high level of happiness. And I show you how you can, too, because, as a life and fitness expert, I have successfully helped many clients create their own happiness with the same process.

These are the six steps of The Accountability Code:

    1. Reflection — feeling and thinking on your values, goals, problems

    2. Humility — a modest view of one's importance, related to who you can be

    3. Planning — making a detailed proposal for achieving success

    4. Implementing — putting into use your desired skills or values

    5. Commitment — dedicating yourself to a person or cause

    6. Feedback — information used as a basis for improvement

Each step is vital to developing your own self-accountability. With each step, I explain how to plug in your own custom action steps, making it simple and natural to follow through with what you know you need to do to fulfill your own strong values.

Applying your customized TAC as often and as deeply as needed is exactly how you will wake up to what is really needed in your life. And I will show you how to show up so that your ability to be accountable to the values that matter to you will give you peace and happiness to take on the next day as your best self.

Time to Wake Up

I once had a dream that I was going to commit suicide. In my dream, I was running through town, trying to get away from the police, and Aubrey (my husband) was helping them. He wanted to save me, but I was convinced he was helping them catch me.

I ran into a building and began climbing the stairs until I got to the top floor. I went to the window and out onto the ledge, hoping the police wouldn't see me. I could hear them talking about how I must have hit a dead end.

The only way for me to escape getting caught was to jump to my death. That thought was comforting, and I was ready to end it all because it would free me from the pain and the sorrow I felt. I had no regrets, and I thought I finally had a way out.

As I closed the window behind me, it suddenly locked from the inside. I didn't care that I couldn't get back in. I was ready to jump. I didn't imagine myself plastered on the ground. I saw myself, instead, going up to heaven to be free. Then Aubrey appeared at the window and opened it. He had a plate of food in his hand. He understood I was exhausted from running, and he was offering me something he knew I couldn't refuse.

I reached out and accepted the plate, but, in an effort to situate myself on the ledge to eat, I accidentally dropped the food. My sorrow enveloped me again, and I felt as if this small mistake was exactly the reason my life continued to result in failure. It reaffirmed my need to jump. But because the window was open and Aubrey was there, he reached out to take hold of me and pulled me back inside. And then I woke up.

Upon waking, I remember feeling scared. I do sometimes worry about my mental health, due to my turmoil with my parents and family, and the mental illness that runs deep in my family. And although I've never had suicidal thoughts in my waking life, I fear not being understood and thus not getting the help I need.

The image of my grandmother Hulda's headstone came to mind. She died in a mental hospital after having a breakdown while her husband was at war, and she was raising several children alone. Her headstone reads, "Let no person ever again be wrongly removed from the community by reason of disability." She was left without the resources she needed to return to a normal, healthy life.

My commitment to staying mentally stable is reinforced by my drive to stay well in all aspects of health. Since I place such a major focus on mental

3

health, I was incredibly grateful to dream of finding peace with the act of ending one's life. I know that God gave me the gift of empathy and a deeper understanding of how to help those around me.

I don't claim to know what being suicidal is actually like. However, that dream gave me the wisdom to know what those who choose suicide may feel like. I knew that the dream was all about choice. In the dream, I made the choice to run away. I started the painful street chase in the first place. But the dream was also about opportunity. Aubrey showed up in my time of need. He offered me what I needed, which was nourishment. I wasted that opportunity when I dropped the plate of food, and then, ultimately, I was saved.

That ever-so-real-feeling dream allowed me to again have the opportunity to wake up and show up. I have a major responsibility to share what I felt and what I have worked so hard to know. I know that as I continue sharing and talking about the hard things, that I become a vessel of aid for others and a very good gauge of my own mental well-being.

I was given the gift of clarity to know that I am still here for a reason. I have work to do, and even though life isn't perfect, we need to keep going. I must continue to work on my mental health for myself and for others. I will never judge anyone for choosing to take their own life or even just trying to do so. Instead, I will do everything I can to prevent that situation from happening in the first place.

As you continue to deepen the connection between your mind and body, my hope is that you keep purpose at the forefront of your thoughts. **YOU HAVE A PURPOSE FOR BEING HERE**, and connecting your mind and body is the key to keeping you interested in fighting and living on!

As you read *The Accountability Code: Wake Up and Show Up*, keep your precious life at the forefront of your mind. This journey is about becoming the best version of yourself. I have put this content together for the sheer purpose of helping and teaching you to absolutely love what you see when you look in the mirror.

What message have you been given that you know others need to know, too? I know that true health is not even about the way you look, but how you feel about yourself and how you prove it through your actions. That is a major part of the message I am here to share with you.

That frightening dream was eye-opening. I have had many dreams that have given me important insight, but that one topped them all! I was surprised at how confident I felt at the decision to end my life. Each person who commits suicide has a thought process and experience that is entirely their own, and we may never know what that is. What revelations have you had that allow you to be more empathetic to others?

You have so much to contribute to the world, and you can make a larger, more positive impact than you realize. I hope that each person I come in contact with knows how amazing they are. I want them to love all of what they see when they look in the mirror and to know they are not just seeing their physical reflection. If you could pick one thing that people would come to know because of your influence and example, what would it be?

The ability to "wake up and show up" allows us to catch a glimpse of where we are going and what our true purpose is in life. I know that as we experience life-changing moments, we have the power to extract meaning and purpose to help us grow as individuals. These insights put things into proper perspective. What perspective do you have that helped you improve as a person?

If we don't change, then we don't grow. And if we don't grow, then we're barely living. Aren't you here for more than that?

I believe that I experienced that dream for a reason. I had that dream right after Mental Health Awareness Day, and I know for a fact that someone out there needed to hear my experience. I will never know if I saved someone from suicide or just gave them a glimpse of hope, but I believe without a doubt that I had to act upon what I had been given. My words have impacted others, and yours do, too. What message do you need to share that can help others in profound ways?

As a personal trainer, I learned that I needed to share deeper messages than just improving your physique. How many times do people read weight and body mass index during eulogies? Life isn't about how you look! It's about who you are on the inside. My message to others is one of overall health, and mental health and strength are central to that message. Can you put into words how your message helps others improve their life in important ways?

That dream of a suicide attempt is one that I will remember forever, especially as I read back through what I have written about the experience. In order to continue learning and growing, I must not forget that dream. It focuses on and reiterates why I want to help others to use their physical bodies to increase their awareness, to make conscious choices, and to seize life-saving opportunities. As a reminder of this message, take a deep breath and say, "I am worthy of life in every moment."

You'll find that utilizing *The Accountability Code* will help you honor your life today and seize every joyful opportunity.

When we make mental progress, our bodies are better able to go through the physical actions needed to live our truth. Having a deeper awareness also helps us understand when we may be moving backwards.

As always, we must bring this awareness to a physical standpoint because we live within our material bodies. How can you ensure that your body is as healthy as possible so that you are healthy enough to share your message with those who need to hear it?

And when you are having a rough day, place your hand over your heart. Do you feel your heartbeat? It's an embodiment of your purpose.

You are alive for a reason! So don't ever give up!

Get ready for massive amounts of clarity, progress, and success as we journey together!

Let's get started!

Throughout this book you'll find special QR codes that go along with what you read here. I invite you to take action and scan the codes to enhance your experience. Simply hover your phone over the QR code as if you were going to snap a picture. Then, wait for your phone's camera to read the image and you'll receive a prompt from your browser. Follow the link and see what's in store! I am here for you during this entire process. :)

Chapter 1 - Reflection

Reflection – Feeling and thinking on your values, goals, problems

The first key to successfully using your Accountability Code is engaging in daily Reflections about your values, goals, and problems — and, yes, it's a bit like meditating.

One day, my daughter asked me, "Mom, did you know that you have never seen your own face? Did you know that you've only seen it in a mirror, pictures, or in a video?" After pausing for a second, I realized my daughter was right — in order for us to see ourselves physically, we need the help of an external resource, such as a mirror, a pool of still water, a photograph, or a video.

And the same is true of seeing and understanding our internal lives of feeling and thinking — we need the help of some sort of source that is external to ourselves.

Isn't it interesting that all our values, goals, or problems in our lives originally came from outside sources? If, for instance, we have friendship as one of our values, we first saw examples of it in other peoples' lives (or in books, movies, or in-person telling of stories, either fiction or real-life stories), and somebody used that word, friendship, to label it. And we said to ourselves something like, 'Yeah! That's good! I feel good about that! I want that in my life! I will pursue that in my life!'

And we do the same sort of thing with every value and goal in our lives. It all begins with recognizing something external to ourselves as being desirable, being good for us to have in our lives, and we try to get it, to have it, to cultivate it in our lives, usually without any good plan for doing so — at first, anyway.

And those without a plan, or with a weak plan, usually don't succeed very well in obtaining those values and goals. Those with a good plan often do succeed. Reflection has helped me in pursuing values and goals, and it has worked for my clients, as well. I will share many such real-life stories about how they are continuously succeeding using Reflection, as well as all the elements of TAC and further values that I teach.

The following brief list probably has many of your own sought-after or cherished values:

Love	Virtue	Compassion	Reliable
Friendship	Courage	Diligent	Punctual
Loyal	Creative	Humble	Wise
Honest	Patient	Preparing	Intelligent
Honorable	Kind	Helpful	Generous
Grateful	Educated	Fair	Efficient
Planning	Commitment	Perseverance	Courteous
Wealth	Feedback	Reflection	Implementing

How do you obtain them, how do you cultivate them, how do you grow them in your life?

Answer: By Reflection, which trains your mind and soul in having them in your life. That training then gets triggered when you come upon similar circumstances in your daily life. We'll get into that in detail, shortly.

So here is an outline of how to start and practice your personal process of Reflection:

1. Arrange time away from distractions.

Distance yourself from people, voices, noises, obligations, and work.

You could get up very early in the morning, at a time when you know others are not going to be up and about, starting their day. I often get up around 6:00 AM, and I go into my office to reflect and meditate.

Sometimes, in the middle of the day or even late at night, I drive to a secluded spot near a small lake or a bit of woods; I stay in my car, with all the doors locked, and I reflect and meditate on how my values, goals, and problems are going in my life.

2. Focus on one value or goal you want in your life.

Focus clearly on one value at a time.
As you focus on that one value, think of it first in terms of very positive, specific images and feelings you have already learned to associate with it.

At first, just think of a word or words closely associated with the value or goal.

Notice what images, thoughts, and feelings pop up.

When it feels natural, start visualizing, as discussed in the next step.

3. Visualize yourself role-playing the motions and feelings of living that value or goal.

Visualize yourself in one specific situation living, feeling, and thinking that value.
Actually imagine SEEING and FEELING yourself in the situation.
Focus on positive feelings. If you ignore any negative feelings that may pop up, they will go away as you replace them with positive feelings and thoughts.

Make it as lifelike as you can without working too hard on it. And be sure not to obsess about details.

4. Celebrate your successful completion of the role-playing scene.

At the end of your role-playing scene, emotionally celebrate your successful completion of the imaginary scene.

Do what feels natural for you.

You might want to jump up and shout something, like "Yayyy! I did it! Way to go!"

Or you might want to sing, or even to dance.

And imagine someone you respect congratulating you on implementing your value or achieving your goal.

5. Focus on role-playing about solving one problem.

Do the same sort of role-playing with confronting one specific problem in your life or at work, from time to time.

Do the same sort of visualizing/role-playing that has you solving the problem, being the hero.

Celebrate.

Imagine being congratulated for your achievement by someone you know and respect.

6. Journaling.

Writing about what's happening in your life can help you reflect.

When you put your feelings, thoughts, and experiences down on paper, save them onto a computer screen, or save them in a short video, you separate them from yourself and from the constant, ever-overflowing chaos of reality — you can see them better, and you can let yourself experience positive feelings better.

As part of the commitment I made to the Reality TV show I was in, every day I had to record a recap of my day that was less than 1 minute long. I got really good at summing up in a 60-second video, because I had taken time throughout the day to reflect on what was most important.

When you journal, you will find inspiration, strengthen your memory, and improve your communication skills. When you don't, you keep all of your stress and worries in your body to accumulate. It also becomes difficult to see and measure progress.

7. Talk with people you trust.

Reflection includes comparing what we think to what is or has been.

Talking with people you trust has the power to immediately shift your directions and can be the difference between going down the rabbit hole to failure or putting on the right armor for the next worthy battle.

When I talk with people I trust, I feel secure and validated. I feel supported and cared for.

When I don't, I start to tell myself untrue stories and feel depressive thoughts more often.

Reasons for resistance to Reflection —

1. Overstimulation

This is when you are surrounded by more experiences, activities, and noise than you can handle well. This can come from too much social media, screen time, an excessive amount of stuff around the house, or even stress. It may feel that you have a hard time shutting off distractions because you are constantly surrounded by them.

In order to beat this resistance and practice reflection effectively, rid yourself of unnecessary sources and distractions.

With a computer programmer husband and an excessively techy world targeted at children, I find that too many screens stop not only me, but also my family from necessary reflection.

I counteract this by unplugging devices around the house and hiding them for a while.

2. Rebellion

Rebellion is a resistance to an authority, leader, or ruler. Like many, you probably don't like being told what to do, and that can cause you to focus on what you don't want to do instead of on what will benefit you.

In order to beat this natural resistance to reflection, give yourself permission for this path to be your own and no one else's. Understand that you can reflect on what YOU want and how you want to act.

Ignore and forget an agenda coming from someone else.

Even as I tell you that you need to reflect, the fact is that unless someone is forcing you to read this book, you have already made a strong choice to obey yourself.

That is awesome! You're on the right road — and for the right reason!

Reflection with the intent to improve is all that is needed in this first step, and you already have that.

3. Doesn't seem worth the effort

Whether you want to believe it or not, you are constantly reflecting on your life. It's a gift we all have been given by the Gods, but we've learned to ignore the deepest parts of ourselves.

Why not develop that skill so that it actually benefits you? Forget what you think should happen, and let it help you determine what comes next in your life.

In order to beat this resistance, keep your expectations low at first.

When I started reflecting and meditating, I just had to practice being still for 5 minutes with my eyes closed. I put on some soft music and literally challenged myself not to give into an impulse.

Even though I didn't get a life-changing revelation from the heavens, I had, in fact, overcome my ability to resist impulses for 5 minutes! Now that I knew I could do 5 minutes, I knew I could increase that to 10. Knowing I can resist impulses has helped me with my impulsive food choices, my impulsive comments to my family, and my impulse to overreact to many things.

Make reflection worth your effort by allowing yourself to make progress one step at a time.

As you practice taking time to reflect, you'll be inexplicitly hit with new information that's been making its way to you through that part of the universe that knows what new experiences you are having, and knows how to supplement them. Through that new information, you may very well find the answers to some important questions, such as,

'What have I been avoiding?'

'How am I being a light to others?'

'What behaviors are holding me back?'

'What do I need to do better?'

By engaging in Reflection, you are setting many forces in motion that will help you.

Doubt Yourself No More

When it comes to leveling up in life and becoming the person you want to be, you have to try new things.

In high school, I got into an argument with a girl on my soccer team who was also a cheerleader. I was a 16-year-old know-it-all, and I started trash-talking the cheerleading team because, as I said, "Their stunts always fail and most of them don't even try to tumble!"

My teammate angrily said, "It's hard work, and you can't do what we do."

I impulsively said, "Watch me!"

Well, then I had to prove that I could, in fact, do what they did. I convinced a friend to join me for cheerleader tryouts, and we went to a tumbling gym in hopes of learning how to do a back handspring. But on tryout day, my friend skipped out! I'm no quitter, so I stayed. I worked really hard learning to tumble (even if it was only a spotted back handspring, so far) and wanted to know what it was like to do stunts.

I remember watching the other hopefuls getting ready. They were practicing, some of them had their moms with them, and there was a LOT of glitter! As audition numbers were handed out, I heard one girl after another shriek with glee. Each audition number was assigned to three candidates, and, once you received yours, you had to find the two people who shared your number.

I got my number and went looking for my matches, and I discovered that a girl my younger sister's age and the only boy trying out were in my tryout group. A captain yelled out to head into the wrestling gym, where mats were waiting for us to warm up our tumbling. Yikes! I had never tumbled on mats before. I was used to springboards and tumble tracks, so I was nervous, but I figured the captains could spot me.

But as I began to warm up on the mats, I found I could not throw my back handspring! Disappointed, I told myself it was okay, that I just wasn't ready, and that maneuver wouldn't be part of my audition. I walked away from the mats to the side gym, continuing to work on my cheers. While I waited, the butterflies in my stomach were swarming, but I found comfort knowing that at least one person on my team (the boy) looked more awkward than me. I'm embarrassed to admit that I pridefully drew power from knowing that I wasn't the suckiest person trying out that day.

Little did I know that boy had some tricks up his sleeve! The judges asked if he had anything he wanted to show in his audition, and he said, in his pumped up voice, "Yes. I'm going to do sixty pushups in sixty seconds," and then he did! It was really cool, and I realized I needed to do something cool, too.

"3B, do you have anything you'd like to show us as part of your audition?"

With my heart pounding, I said, "Yes. I'm going to do a roundoff back handspring." I walked to the end of the gym, knowing I might have more luck accomplishing a back handspring if I could run into it instead of a two-stride power step to gain momentum.

In fact, I needed the entire length of the gym to sprint into this tumbling pass, and that's what I did. I successfully landed my first ever tumbling pass without assistance! I felt so happy that I said a little cheer to myself, but I tried not to show the surprised and pleased shock on my face. Then I returned to my position among my peers, looked at the judges, and told them I had one more thing I wanted to show them.

Ladies and gentlemen, I did the worm (a popular dance move where you lie facedown on the ground and then whip your feet upward you use that momentum to move your entire body forward the way a worm does)! I performed my most popular move from youth church dances, and I did it so well that I heard oohs and ahhs from the judges. So I decided to go for broke: I made my worm go in zigzags and circles! When I finished, I ignored the growing bruises on my knees and stood up to enjoy my accomplishment. Whether or not I was going to make the team, I had that move in the bag!

At the end of tryouts, I headed home feeling proud, but expecting that it was the last of my cheerleading efforts. I had taken on a challenge and had fun while doing it. I knew I didn't fit the typical mold of a cheerleader. I didn't come from a rich family, hadn't been tumbling since I was little, and did not have a lot of support for my athletic ambitions. But I was happy that I had experienced something exciting that taught me new things about myself.

But, hey, then I made the team! So did the boy from my team.

This experience greatly enriched my life. I learned I could be so much more than I was. I could open up to new experiences, and it shaped how I view myself and others. That's priceless: Don't let who you are now hold you back from becoming who you're supposed to be!

Nobody expected me to make the cheerleading squad, myself included. But I did it because I wanted to prove to myself and others that I was capable.

Whatever your goals may be, they'll require you to try something unexpected and to love the process. I want to share with you a pattern for success so that this concept becomes second nature to you.

That is exactly how The Accountability Code has come to be. It's the exact process of executing new things that are going to help you grow into and become the person you are supposed to be.

At sixteen, I wanted to stunt like the cheerleaders did. I seized the opportunity, even though I didn't have much hope of succeeding, and I adapted in order to meet the demands.

You have endless opportunities in front of you to achieve your dreams. It's time to tap into your potential. This isn't something you do one time and then it's over. We'll work at this process throughout our entire lives.

Before you dive deep into this book, I want to give you a little taste of how interactive it will be. Let's do a simple exercise to help you practice making The Accountability Code work for you.

First, think of three things you'd like to accomplish that you haven't quite succeeded at, as yet.

Now do some research. Head to Pinterest, YouTube, or find a Facebook group for ideas. The Internet is full of information on every topic you can think of. You'll find tutorials and classes online, even basic kits to get started. Great news: If your goals are related to improving your health, then you are in the perfect place.

Your brain is actually capable of learning more than one thing at a time. Learning a fun new skill will keep you humble, motivated, and conditioned for continual growth. After all, the Accountability Code follows six crucial and easy to follow steps: reflection, humility, planning, implementing, commitment, and feedback.

As you begin exploring your new goal and accompanying skills, ask yourself why you find this interesting? For me, I found joy in challenging my body and growing stronger. Throwing my friends into the air without dropping them? Yeah, I was sure I could do that and have fun with it!

Your three new fun goals are not the limits to what you can do. You're destined for much more.

I continue to use my cheerleading skills with my daughters. I've taught them how to stunt and they are each in tumbling classes. Not only do I use my skills to teach others, but that ability to challenge myself only grows with each phase of my life. My love for moving and challenging my body became the very path I pursued to help others with their fitness and now life goals.

How will your new skills fit into your future? How will they enhance your personality?

I didn't expect to make the cheerleading team back in high school, but I did want to be known as someone who follows through. Ultimately, my placement on the team was in God's hands. But the ability to grow and the dedication to follow through (a.k.a. accountability) — that's what keeps you alive!

I had the grit to make the team, but I had to develop the talent to remain on it. It was a journey with many unexpected turns, but I know that my dedication opened the doors to many life lessons. I can't wait to share them with you in this book.

You've already been successful in many areas of your life. Think about new jobs you started, new friends you made, or tasks you had to wing your way through. You figured it out, and you can continue using that confidence to take on your next challenge.

Sign up for that class. Schedule time with a coach. Get going with your goals. Remember, if you make a plan, you're more likely to achieve your dreams. The only person holding you back — is *you*!

Born with It

All my life, I wanted to follow in my mother's footsteps. She had eight children by age 30, and I wanted a big family, too. In fact, in high school I was named "Most Likely to Have the Most Kids!" And, true to course, I was engaged by 18 and ready to fast-track my plans of being a wife and mom.

My husband, Aubrey, and I were blessed with our first pregnancy just four months into our marriage. I was so excited! I couldn't wait to pop all those babies out, and I told everyone about the big, happy family we were starting.

Everything went according to plan — until it didn't.

My first baby, Leila, ended up in the NICU with fluid in her lungs. Instead of seeing and holding my baby immediately after birth, she was whisked away, and I was left alone in a hospital bed with nothing to do and no baby to cuddle. That first day, I had to rely on family members who could visit my daughter to tell me how cute she was.

Baby Leila was allowed only two visitors at a time, and I wasn't one of those visitors until the following day. That's when I learned she had developed an infection, and I had to return to my room, miserable and all alone. I was so young, I had no idea how to operate the breast pump, and nobody came to talk to me. I'd never been taught how to communicate when things weren't going well. I felt disconnected from everyone, and even from my own life. Leaving the hospital with no baby was really hard, and so was returning to work the following Monday. But I used these experiences to create a new plan for my next pregnancy, and the two that followed. I learned to speak up about how I was feeling, to plan for hospital visits and other unexpected scenarios, and to express what I needed and wanted.

As my communication skills grew, I saw greater results in my relationships – even my relationship with myself. I would ask myself how I felt about things and what I wanted, and those internal conversations seemed to help my confidence and my ability to follow through.

Still, I was shocked when, a few years later, I took an Inner Strengths test online and discovered my top strength was — communication? How could that be, when I still felt that I had so much work to do to build confidence in my voice?

I remembered all those years, as a child and a teen, excitedly talking about my plans to have a big family. Now, four daughters later, I have learned how to bridge the gap between sharing good news and oversharing. I've learned how to talk about the bad stuff, too, the uncomfortable stuff. I taught myself how to use my voice, and to communicate effectively – in fact, I teach others how to do that, too.

It was a painful lesson with my first baby at such a young age, to make plans but also contingencies and to open up when things aren't going well. That Inner Strengths test says that I'm a master communicator, and today I'll proudly own that title. And I want you to own it, too. It starts with opening your mind to the natural strengths you already have. The Accountability Code requires honest communication with yourself, especially during the first step, Reflection.

First, I want to caution you not to dive too deep with this lesson. It has the potential to overwhelm you. There are many sources you can seek, instances to document, and ways to work on your goal. Keep it simple and intuitive, for now. Don't try to force some magical grand plan.

(SIDE NOTE – I have three online quizzes at my website for Movement, Mindset, and Nutrition. Pick one and take the quiz. You'll receive your results along with a 3-step action plan. When in doubt, start with my Mindset Quiz. Here is the link: https://www.funandsustainable.com/mindset-quiz)

My Mindset Quiz will help you uncover your main strength when it comes to pairing your mind and your body. Once completed, write down your results and carefully read through them. How true are each of the statements? What gets you through the tough times? How have you grown as a result of developing that strength?

Taking the Mindset challenge will provide an outside perspective of how your brain functions. This gives you a starting point to grow your strengths and make them work to your benefit. Documenting how this happens will then give you a sense of pride and accomplishment, knowing that you have been blessed with this attribute all along.

How does that tie in with the strengths you were born with?

They have only grown stronger, and more capable of producing results, and I'm here to help you apply them so you can master The Accountability Code.

What is your biggest strength? Mine is that I'm a realist. I don't leave things undone, and I'm not afraid of criticism. This skill has helped me stay focused without becoming a perfectionist. I also know that nothing happens until someone takes action, and I happen to be fantastic at taking action!

Once you've identified your strengths and cited examples of how they have helped improve your life already, it's time to further develop those skills during good times and bad.

As a realist, I know that I am capable of making fast decisions. During the good times, my quick decision-making skills allow the results to happen without delay. During challenging times, that ability demonstrates to others the power of acknowledging and moving on. But it might result in steamrolling over others in the process. I have to remember to be sensitive to others' needs, to take a step back even if I know what to do, so that I give them time to adapt and prepare.

My experience with Leah in the hospital after her birth forced me to implement a strict policy for my next three deliveries. I needed to communicate that I was not comfortable having visitors see my babies before I was able to do so. But I needed to do so in a way that still showed how important my visitors were, and to provide a plan for when they would be able to see the new babies.

You should acknowledge your strengths and write down how they serve you. Focus on the positive impact that you already have, and those strengths will magnify. The people in your life need those strengths, and you'll only help yourself and others more by improving upon them.

The fun comes when you create a plan to enhance those skills. Your strengths will be enhanced, and your weaknesses will be minimized. To create the plan, write down your three greatest strengths on three 3"x5" note cards. Write it on each in really big writing and leave room for a sentence below it. Then, on each card, write down one thing that you are going to do to make that strength more impactful.

On my "REALIST" cards, I wrote:

- Be sensitive to the feelings of others.
- Slow down and look for flexible solutions.
- Others are allowed to be successful, too.

Then place those three cards somewhere where you'll see them often. Read the sentences out loud, and let those words chip away at anything that brings your performance down.

You're an amazing person, and the world needs to know your strengths. The world, in fact, will be a better place as those strengths grow stronger!

As you reflect on who you are, what strengths you have to offer, don't forget to insert them right into The Accountability Code.

Meditation Practice

Here's a quick 5-minute meditation. It's brief but very impactful, and something you'll enjoy using many times. It is a fantastic way to reflect and start using The Accountability Code effectively right away.

First, find a comfortable place where you can relax and clearly visualize the words you are reading or listening to.

Imagine walking in your front door and through your house, all the way into your bedroom, and then to your closet. Inside the closet, you'll find every piece of clothing you own. You'll find favorite clothing, treasured hand-me-downs, and outerwear you hardly ever think about when it isn't snowing. Each article also represents an emotion.

The first thing to do is select an item that screams "NO!" to you. Let's say, a pair of pants or bottoms. They're in the closet, but you never wear them. You certainly don't love them, but you've kept them, for some reason.

The bottoms I would choose are a pair of blue metallic leggings. I was really excited when I bought those leggings, because each of my trainers had matching pairs, and we used them to film some videos while teaching. They were super cute, but not high-rise, which meant I had to be very careful doing squats, if you know what I mean! I also noticed that every time I washed my blue leggings, they lost some of their metallic shine.

To preserve their luster and reduce washes, I decided to wear panties with them. The next time I went to the gym wearing my blue metallic leggings was a day focused on arms, so I wouldn't have to worry about squats and potentially flashing anyone. I was really progressing on arm work and pull-ups, so I asked my trainer to film me doing the exercise.

When I watched the video later, I was horrified! My leggings were so tight on my panties that my butt looked like a package of hot dogs. Wearing panties with those particular leggings to the gym was a big mistake! I decided I would never wear those leggings again and stuck them in my closet, where they remain a big reminder of a bad decision.

Return to your focused breathing and realize this is what *"NO!"* feels like: It feels like embarrassment, ignorance, and failure. Take a moment to define why the piece of clothing you picked is a *"NO!"*

So put those back and, instead, reach into your closet and grab a top. Pick the one that is the most comfortable. It could be a nice dress shirt or an old, worn hoodie. Hold it in your arms, touch it. It feels good, soft, well-loved. If you could, you would wear this top every single day. You never have to worry about your appearance when wearing this particular top and, if you lost it today, finding a replacement would be a major priority.

My favorite top is a grey sweatshirt with pink and white chevron stripes. I bought it for $10 at the mall years ago, and it's still as soft as ever. I can wear it while working out, or even for casual dress-up. I always get compliments when I have it on, and people ask where I bought it. I instantly feel relaxed when I put this top on. It's a big *"YES!"* for me.

This is what *"YES!"* feels like. It feels accepting, like it belongs to you.

Now, even though you didn't literally touch these two items of clothing while we were doing this meditation, you still experienced tangible emotions when thinking about them. You know what *"NO!"* feels like and what *"YES!"* feels like.

I'm going to break down the steps of this meditation so that you can apply them when tapping back into your emotions to effectively reflect and customize The Accountability Code, as needed. This process will help you experience a deeper level of these *"YES!"* and *"NO!"* emotions. It's a powerful process that will align you more with how you feel and how you act based on those feelings.

Okay, now imagine yourself back in your closet, pairing certain clothes you own to specific emotions. Your emotions are already here — let's just bring them to the surface.

We're constantly experiencing different emotions, but we don't often pay attention to how they impact our decision making. When you get dressed in the morning, you have to stop and think about what to wear and perhaps why, but you don't necessarily think about how each item of clothing makes you feel. So the first step in this process is to slow down, close your eyes, and say out loud, "I can experience a wide range of emotions."

Next, picture the layout of your closet. There are clothes in front that you wear often, and clothes stuffed in the back that either aren't right for this season, or you just don't love much.

Emotions are like those clothes. Some you experience frequently and are right on the surface. Others are hidden away, unwanted or inappropriate.

To represent ANGER, I would choose an expensive dress I bought with a zipper that began detaching from the bottom the first time I wore it, inappropriately exposing too much of the back of my legs. What is your ANGER item? Pull it out, touch it, and tap into what that feels like for you.

Then choose a LOVE item. I would pick my solid black leggings, which always make me feel fit, comfortable, and ready for anything. I feel loved when I look good and am ready for action. Choose your LOVE item and ask yourself why you love it, why it makes you feel loved, and why it's important to feel this way often.

The lesson is that tangible items can help you instantly tap into your emotions.

In this next step, I want you to select three solid *"YES!"* items from your wardrobe.

What if I tell you that this meditation teaches you that unconditional love can have a new meaning? When you identify love in a tangible way, you begin to create more loving situations, reactions, and applications. Imagine giving a beloved scarf to someone you care about, or passing on a stunning suit that helped you nail your last job interview, to someone transitioning out of homelessness. See your item, picture the person receiving this item with love, and feel the energy you receive in return.

Alternately, when you find yourself in a tense situation, imagine putting on one of your LOVE items before you respond. You'll not only feel more relaxed, but you'll react from a place of love that will help to diffuse that tense situation.

You know the old adage of picturing everyone naked when you're nervous about a public speaking engagement? This works similarly to that notion in that it will reduce anxiety. Picture the people around you who make you feel nervous as all wearing your LOVE items. It will help you remember that everyone deserves love and is doing their best. Apply these feelings to the small decisions you make each day, and you'll notice that you respond more lovingly and patiently, but you also help those you are in contact with become more patient and loving, as well.

The amazing thing is that your ability to produce love is as abundant as all the clothing on this planet.

Each day, just as you decide what clothing to wear, you're also going to choose the best emotions to put forth. Get up in the morning, imagine your **"YES!"** clothing, and, as you put each item on, say, "This is my **'YES!'** item." Allow yourself to be clothed in love and extend that love to others. Throughout the day, look at the clothing worn by those around you. Tell yourself that each person you encounter has chosen to wear their **"YES!"** clothing and say to yourself, "I see love."

When you constantly tell yourself that you see and feel love, you'll find ways to show more love. You may smile more, be more affectionate, or go out of your way to help those in need.

This meditation is designed to move your body through more tender and loving experiences. I hope you'll use this exercise to see, create, and give love more often.

Remember that you have the power to make your Reflection positive and useful. Creating your first version of The Accountability Code will be easier when it's all-around focused on creating positivity.

Creating a Vision

Creating a vision board centered around your goals is a great physical representation of what you'd like to bring to pass. Not only will it help with your Reflection, but it also puts into perspective tangible action steps to plug into The Accountability Code.

A vision board is a collage of images and words representing a person's wishes or goals, intended to serve as inspiration or motivation.

My first experience with vision boards was years ago at a conference. The speaker told us about how he pinned an advertisement of an expensive digital camera he really wanted on his board and how one day, months later, somebody sent him that same camera in the mail! It was in lieu of monies owed, but the sender had no idea that they were giving this man exactly what he coveted.

The speaker continued, bragging about things he wanted and placed on his vision board and eventually received. Every item he mentioned was more expensive than the last, and everyone in the room cheered each time, except me. I wasn't sold on the idea that, "If you build it, they will come," but I couldn't deny that his message was validating to many others.

But a few years later, I created my own vision board at a New Year's event some friends were throwing. I actually had a hard time figuring out, initially, what to put on it! The one item I knew I wanted was a pair of nice headphones. I printed a photo of Beats by Dre headphones and pinned them to my board.

They were expensive, but not ridiculously pricey, so I felt justified in adding them as my first item. I thought I would feel better about spending the money to buy those headphones someday if I knew I really wanted them and worked hard to get them. Then I added a few other images, such as an athlete deadlifting 135 pounds, a writer holding a book they had written, and images of earning $10k in one day.

Once I had a few items on my board, I shared it with my sister. She pointed to the headphones and said, "Hey, my husband has a brand new pair of Beats he wants to get rid of. He got them at a work Christmas party, and he'll sell them to you super cheap."

My instinct was to say no. I thought I had to work for what I really wanted. How would it feel if I just bought them, even at a discount, right now? That night, I talked to my husband. "How crazy is it that— just like that guy with the digital camera and all those other luxury items he just magically got after pinning them on his vision board — something like that could happen to me, too?"

Aubrey asked what my brother-in-law wanted for the headphones, and when I told him, he said, "Yeah, buy them. That's a no-brainer."

So, is that how a vision board works? You decide what you want, focus on it, share your goals with others, and allow that thing to make its way to you? Yeah! That is exactly how to gain what you want. It's called "a tangible belief practice," and this process will pave the way for you to get everything in life that you want, including a healthy body. I wanted those headphones because they would make my workouts more enjoyable. I wanted something that would cover my ears and let me listen to my music LOUD.

"Tell me what you want, what you really, really want!" — Spice girls. It sounds silly, but I promise that a little reflection and action will go a long way. Let words, images, and feelings motivate you. Tell yourself what you want, what you really, really want!

It's okay to want things. Let's normalize receiving what you want and create goals to help you get them. I want you to write down everything you can think of that you want. There are no right or wrong answers, just your desires. My list includes taking a cruise, horseback riding with my daughters, owning a vacation home, full-time cleaning help, and for my life to be filled with amazing music.

Once you have your list, put a visual on them. Find a picture of that item or an illustration of that activity, and stick all those images on a board where you can see them often. I put mine in my office. You can place yours anywhere that you'll see it every day. You can buy an inexpensive cork board at your local dollar store.

Seeing your desires on a daily basis entices action to help you achieve your dreams. Whatever you're dreaming of is possible.

Every time I worked out before getting my Beats, I thought about how nice it would be to go on runs and have my favorite music right in my ears. And once I had my dream headphones (and at a great price), then I set my next goal: A car with captain's chairs!

At the time, I was driving a Jeep Commander with a bench second row seat. But I have four daughters, and they often have friends with them for me to carpool. It was so annoying having to flip over the second seat so that kids could climb in the far back, and then flip it back and fill up the second row. Flip, flip, flip, all day long!

So I did some research and found another SUV that would better suit my family needs. I printed a picture of the newest Subaru Ascent and pinned that to my vision board. Every day I looked at that Subaru and imagined the ease of driving a car full of laughing girls around town in it. But I didn't just stare at the picture and dream — I made a plan.

I opened a savings account at my bank and literally named it "Subaru!" I put money in that account as often as possible, knowing I would probably need around $30k to purchase it. And each time I climbed in my flippin' Jeep, I was reminded of a better option. Of course, it's important to count your blessings. My Jeep was a great vehicle and, although I wanted something different, I still felt grateful to have a safe and reliable car to get me and my kids around.

But all these behaviors — the hoping, the planning, the saving, the gratitude — were each preparing me for that Subaru to eventually be mine.

It's also important to share your goals. Imagine what might happen if you told your spouse, "I want more alone time with you," or you told yourself, "I'm taking you on a walk today!" When you open the doors of communication, you invite opportunity in. You send a message to the universe that you've got your eyes on the prize, and it starts paying attention.

I'm a windows-down kind of girl, and before I got that new car, I promised my daughters we would celebrate with a summer ride through the canyon in our bikinis, music blasting. They got so excited, and that made it easier over the next few months to get them to do the little things I asked of them. Think of everyone who will share your happiness when you get what you want. Some goals may feel too personal to put on blast, but share what you can. I bet you'll find a lot of supporters and opportunities, too.

After I shared my vision board on social media, my wealth coach DM'd me to let me know about a tax incentive that allows you to buy a car tax free when you purchase it through your business. Working together, we created a strategy to get that car sooner. You never know who your allies will be, and who might be encouraged by your dreams to create their own.

Whatever it is you want right now, there's someone out there who has already achieved it. When you put out an earnest message of desire, the universe begins conspiring with you. **Energy flows where intention goes.** Each step brings you closer to fulfillment, even a simple post saying, "I can't wait until I can take my girls on a summer drive in our new car!"

And I got that new car! After further investigation, I picked out a similar vehicle to the Subaru but one that fit the tax code I needed, and I have LOVED it! It was all thanks to creating a vision board and pairing it with The Accountability Code: Reflection, Humility, Planning, Implementing, Commitment, and Feedback:

Reflection — created my board

Humility — got clear on why these were worthy goals to have

Planning — set up bank account

Implementing — added money to account regularly

Commitment — acted as if there was no way to fail

Feedback — got input and help from others, and made a sound decision

Thanks to money I earned and saved, sound advice I implemented, and including others in my vision, I get to enjoy that car every day. That car didn't just show up in the mail one day, I promise. In fact, I've worked hard for everything I achieved that began with an image on my vision board. I couldn't deadlift 135 pounds without developing strength or buy a car without the means to pay for it. But with hard work and focus, action steps will appear for you to follow.

Every step I took toward my goals brought me closer to success and made me feel good in the process. I was earning my dreams, and I knew those dreams would be worth it!

What are your goals and dreams, and what actions are you taking toward making them a reality? Create a plan, share it with others, move along your path, and then allow that thing to make its way to you. My best advice is to get out of your own way. If all it took was working hard, we'd each be millionaires. There are other factors that we sometimes cannot visualize, and every once in a while, something will just show up for you before you expect it.

I told you that one of my goals was to deadlift 135 pounds and, through hard work and the help of a trainer, I accomplished that. Want to know when I deadlifted 145 pounds? The same day I deadlifted the 135! I had no idea I was making that much progress. I met my goal, and then I surpassed it. What is happening in your life right now that's preparing you for so much more? Is there a dream available right now that you just need to grab? Remember, too, that once you acquire what you want, you're in a better position to help others.

Vision boards can create success. I not only got my headphones and my car, but I also found much success during my time on the reality show, too. Vision boards work because they allow us to connect our desires, the reasons for them, and the emotions attached to the hope of achieving them. And the bonus is that when you get what you want, you create more of that emotion for yourself and for others, too.

Abuse Cycle

At the very beginning of my coaching journey, before I learned to set boundaries, I had a very needy client sign up for one of my free challenges. We'll call her Tawny. Every day, Tawny had new questions for me. She needed to know everything right away! She peppered me with so many questions about the process that I actually began to suspect she wanted to rip off my program!

After the challenge was over, Tawny posted her results online. She was raving about how she finally lost her stubborn weight and found the strength to keep going. She was especially proud that she finally got control over her eating habits. Then she sent me a message, asking me to call her on the phone. I felt apprehensive and thought, "Oh, what now? I have given her so much time already. She's getting the results she wanted. What more can I do for her?"

Looking back, I realize that I was very prideful about the situation. I was focused on how exhausted I felt, giving to this needy client and so many others. Tawny was the squeaky wheel at that moment, and I felt I had no more grease to give.

Reluctantly, I went to the phone and called her. "Hey!" I said, in my most upbeat voice. "What's up?" Tawny thanked me for my time, and then began to cry. She said that in all of her years of counseling and fitness training, none of her prior therapists and coaches had ever helped her deal with her eating issues. She told me that all they ever wanted to talk about was her past, insisting that something traumatic in her childhood was causing her to hold onto weight and develop disordered eating. "Never once," she told me, between tears, "did anyone take the time to educate me on what was in my food or how to listen to my own body, until you."

She explained that she now understood that she had treated her body horribly for years, neglecting her ability to get well and eating her emotions. She was using food all those years to numb the cues her body was sending her to deal with her issues. She cried, as she expressed gratitude for her new life, and I began to cry with Tawny.

All we had done together, really, was take the approach of food to help her get in tune with the rest of her health, including her mindset and emotions. Once Tawny understood the value of her food and the nutrients it could provide or deprive, she could make conscious choices while working on other areas of her wellbeing.

Getting healthy isn't about being perfect or stripping away your identity. It's about creating awareness of how you treat yourself and how to sustainably shift habits to become more of who you want to be.

Tawny had experienced years of damaging experiences at the hands of trusted professionals and, in response, she learned to suppress and abuse her body to make the bad feelings temporarily go away. She was able to break that cycle and eventually arrive at a place of self-love and respect. There are four steps to this cycle and, as you read through them, I want you to identify which one you're ready to change first.

This will be a deep exercise in Reflection so I ask that you give it the time and attention it deserves.

First, are you abusing your body? By abuse, I mean that if you are not actively caring for your physical and emotional well-being, you are misusing it. Let's dive into those four steps to see which one you need to tackle first.

Tension Builds

As life happens, we experience emotions that we don't know how to properly feel or use. Unless we deliberately learn healthy habits to utilize these emotions, our brain will go into stress mode over time. Stress mode means conserving energy, attempting to feel safe, and reaching for instant pleasure. In Tawny's example, she had few modes of emotional expression. Her husband had passed away and her only joy was her grandchildren.

It's important to understand that stress and tension happen to all of us, and that they should not be regular phases of life. They manifest in physical ways: tight muscles, racing heart, aches and pains, exhaustion, and insomnia. Experiencing these on a regular basis is cause for concern and should be addressed immediately. But when we accept tension as a regular part of our life, we begin to anticipate stress and those symptoms. Tawny welcomed tension as a way to feel her emotions, which she then unconsciously enjoyed suppressing with food.

Tension Happens

Tension is actually necessary to grow. It gives us the opportunity to adapt and become stronger towards that which challenges us. Tension in our body also serves a purpose. Within the muscles, tension pushes us to stretch. Tension in our relationships encourages us to better communicate with others due to an event.

Pinpoint what tension in your life is good and which tension can be damaging if left untreated. You can actually reduce the intensity and frequency of these symptoms by taking appropriate action. Or you can let the tension build. Tawny recognized after our work together that her tension was due to masking her emotions with food.

Do you relate to this struggle? If so, I recommend meditation, asking for help, separating yourself from the unhealthy environment, and adapting with care. Give yourself a break. Tension points out what you think you should be or could achieve. Relaxation allows you to find out the truth.

Your body communicates with your brain. Tawny's body was grabbing unhealthy foods, thinking it would provide her survival fix and, instead, fueled her with calorie-dense and nutrient-empty foods. She failed to understand that there were nonfood methods to satisfy that need to release stress. If she had continued on that course, something bad was going to happen and her health would have declined even more.

An incident triggered by tension can take many forms. It could be the inability to get out of bed, snapping when someone makes an offhand comment, or as big as bad news at the doctor's office. But when negative things happen, they can be an opportunity to change. An incident is simply feedback on how to proceed.

Remember that Feedback is the last step of The Accountability Code and naturally leads into repeating the process again with Reflection. Tawny faced an incident nearly every day, as she looked at her late husband's clothes hanging in the closet and realized she had no valuable way to spend her days without him.

The cycle of self-abuse can be addressed after an incident occurs. Tawny responded to her emotional disordered eating by withdrawing, hoping tomorrow would be a new day.

Reconciliation

Reconciliation occurs when the victim understands what has happened and wants to change. They recognize that their response didn't make the tension go away and that real damage has been done as a result of their actions. Without shaming, I tried to bring her to a place within herself where she felt calm and accepted, her questions were answered, and solutions were offered in an instructive way.

The body has the amazing ability to store things it thinks it will need later. Even excess weight provides protection, in some form. Your extra pounds might hide you from truly showing up. It can help you feel more comfortable around others, or even pacify your current progress in goal setting. What habits protect you from returning to healthy behavior?

One of the brain's functions is avoiding pain. During reconciliation, your brain is going to want to avoid the pain of seeing the habits and triggers that caused your behaviors. Pain avoidance will work short-term as an effort to survive, but won't support your long-term goals. We all numb ourselves to avoid pain or discomfort.

Give yourself credit throughout the reconciliation process. Your body wants to find peace again. But aim for happiness and progression, not perfection! Use this cycle to make improvements in your life. Tell yourself, "I am amazing! I am working to improve every day. My body provides powerful protection to me! I can use my past to create an amazing future!"

Calm

Calm is when we slip back into the life we remember after reconciliation. It may last several weeks or a few moments before the tension starts to build again. Tawny learned, during our work together, that this was the phase she most needed to work on. She began to find peace and clarity when she could make effective personal changes. I firmly believe that making change in the phase of least personal resistance is where we find the most success. It's when we are actively working to change that damming roadblocks are minimized. We train ourselves to see hiccups as stepping stones.

You've heard the phrase, "the calm before the storm," of course. It's that feeling that no matter how peaceful we feel now, something worse is coming. This is actually the most important part of the cycle, in my opinion. It's the moment when we recognize danger and can take steps to protect ourselves. It was during one of those moments that Tawny first reached out to me. She followed me online for a while and decided to take action when things were going good for a while. She was ready to take the next step. What are the best decisions you have made when anticipating danger during a calm?

When I work with clients, it's my responsibility to get them into consistent moments of calm and clarity. In this state, they can be realistic and truthful about their actions. It offers hope to change and addresses tension, incidents, and reconciliation. When we consider the cycle as a whole, we are empowered to conquer each step toward the next. Can you recall times in your life when your choices helped reduce the impact of the negative cycle? Understanding the Abuse Cycle will help you not only improve your health habits, but also find calm and equilibrium more often. Tawny achieved this by walking every day, giving her control to step away from her temptations and lessening her feelings of loneliness. She found purpose in creating a healthy lifestyle free from unhelpful rules and restrictions. As she reduced her tension, increased her nutrition knowledge, received accountability through my program and coaching, she noticed less incidents of secretive emotional eating.

As you work through improving your health, take courage knowing that you love yourself enough to break the cycle. You are not what happened to you. You are what you choose to become.

This is some of the most powerful Reflection you can do as you learn to use The Accountability Code. You will become more familiar with how you may be misusing your body and it's capabilities. I promise that you have so much goodness in you, and when we understand how our abusive habits manifest themselves, we can change them.

Look Inward First

Taking control of my own thoughts was difficult for me, as a newlywed and young mom. Aubrey and I were married only four months when I got pregnant with my first child, and I didn't always feel like myself. Doctors told me that feeling that way was due to pregnancy hormones, but I didn't care for feeling out of control.

I struggled the most after my third baby, Liz, was born. I know now that I was experiencing postpartum depression, but I didn't know it at the time. I often dropped her off with my mom during the summer so I could play with my older girls, Leila and Lexi. One day at my parents' home, my dad looked at me and said, "If you ever think about hurting yourself, come talk to me first."

That was a bold statement, and I asked him what he meant by that. That's when he told me about his family history. Nearly all of his siblings have been treated for mental illness, depression, or anxiety. I remembered that one of my uncles was super crazy, but that day I also learned that my grandmother lost her mind before she died, and my great grandmother died in a mental hospital.

This information scared me. I didn't want to end up like my family. At the time, I not only had three small children, but I had just finished student teaching, ate out for lunch nearly every day, had a scary experience with Liz's birth, and my life was missing both social interaction and consistent workouts. No wonder I didn't feel like myself!

I wanted to gain back the most enjoyable parts of me, and I knew it had to start with gaining control over my thoughts. I was happy to be done with school, but I'm not the kind of person to sit around and do nothing. I thought the best way to get back in touch with my thoughts was to get moving again.

At this time, I received an FB message from a woman in my neighborhood. We hadn't met, but we had friends in common. She told me she owned a dance studio and wanted to know if I was interested in subleasing the space to teach fitness classes.

The space was only two blocks from my house, I had a gym full of equipment already and knew several people who would enroll as students. I told Aubrey that we were going to start moving my equipment to this new place. He asked, "You're opening a studio?" and I told him, "Either I start going there every day, or to the mental hospital. Take your pick!"

It turned out to be a great experience, and it gave Aubrey and me a reason to connect in new ways. Many of my family and neighbors became students, and I wound up teaching three classes a week. It was the perfect amount of activity, at the time. I was able to move my body consistently enough to clear my head.

It took a while to figure out that balance, but it started with my dad asking how I was doing that day. I'm sure my family had great intentions to help me, but nobody had taught me before to look inward, pay attention to how I feel, gather data, and then act accordingly. I recognized that in my family, nobody really prevented depression. They just dealt with it as it happened. I wanted to choose differently for myself.

I also understood that just doing physical things doesn't keep depression away. But connecting my thoughts and my body does help me recognize when things aren't quite right. That ability is priceless and requires some self-control. As you develop it, you get more in tune with your mind and body. Here are some of the questions you can ask yourself, to help develop that control:

Is there something you need to make right?

Think carefully about the things you think, but don't feel comfortable saying. Where do you not feel supported, and how can you communicate those needs clearly to yourself and others?

Is there something that feels off?

Anytime you go through major life changes, it takes time to adjust. If you have recently dealt with a death, birth, illness, or other trauma, remind yourself that it's okay to slow down and consider the unseen stresses put on your mind and body. List some of the biggest events that have occurred in recent years and examine which of them feels unresolved.

What parts of you haven't been addressed in a while?

Have the big shifts in life recently diverted your attention outside of yourself? It's the small things in life that create the lifestyle that keeps you thriving. What basic habits have you been neglecting: sleep, self-care, water intake, movement? If you've been caring for others, it may be time to put yourself on the front burner again.

Where do you need support?

We often let ourselves believe that we can do everything. We take to heart the idea that we won't be tested above what we can handle. However, that never means you have to go it alone. It's good to ask for support or for help with the big things demanding your attention. Allow yourself to ask for and to receive the support you need to adjust to life's changes.

What boundaries are you violating?

If you feel that you're not in alignment with your values and goals, you probably aren't, and it's probably because you are avoiding or damaging yourself rather than supporting yourself. I wasn't honoring my body during those months that I felt depressed. I needed to move regularly, and for my sanity, I needed time away from the home to tune into Marci.

Remember that you don't need a clinical diagnosis of depression to experience depressions. I learned that, when my lifestyle was sedentary, my depression got worse. What triggers your depression, and how might increasing your physical activity might help you take control of your happiness?

That doesn't mean you have to become a fitness instructor to lead a healthier lifestyle. That was just my choice to work with what I had! You have to find your most optimum self, your greatest passions and purpose, and feed those every day. Focusing on your passion is a choice you can make to create and find more happiness.

Who are you, and how are you neglecting yourself?

During college, I went from teaching fitness classes and learning how to teach sports, to full-on student teaching, all while being pregnant three times. It was a busy time in my life, but instead of asking for the right support, I powered through it and paid the price.

I wasn't eating well, my equilibrium was off balance, and I was away from home too much. I was neglecting who I really wanted to be. I learned a lot from the experience, enough to recognize that neglecting actions towards what made me ultimately happy brought me further into depression.

Being aware of what brings you down brings to light what lifts you up. Declare to yourself your best intentions in order to realign what you want for your future. I live by what I teach others, and part of my contract includes daily actions to focus on the basics of health:

sleep

self-care

water intake

movement

If I focus on those things each day, I'm on the right track, and I tell my clients the same.

Don't underestimate the power of the basics! I promise that these four foundations of health will bring about greater success and happiness, and diminish your chances of depression.

Sleep

The general recommendation for sleep is at least seven hours per night. Choose quality over quantity, and get into a regular sleep pattern. The best way to do that is to get rid of the distractions at night and wake at the same time every day.

When your body develops a pattern, it will trust its ability to relax and move into deeper sleep. When you're habitually getting quality sleep, I recommend increasing the time to eight hours.

Self-Care

You need to develop a regular habit of relaxation and reflection. It's key to helping you identify and work toward your goals. Self-care is about development, not distraction.

Shoot for around ten minutes OF RELAXED REFLECTION each day, reviewing your progress and accomplishments, and listening carefully to the messages your body is sending you. The more you develop this habit, the better your body will be at communicating what you need. You'll also become more comfortable in taking as much time as you need.

Water intake

Water is necessary for full and proper physical functioning. The general recommendation is to drink at least 64 ounces per day or half your body weight in ounces (if you're 150 pounds, that's 75 ounces). Water helps digestion, improves nutritious eating choices, and aids in the elimination process. Dehydration leads to poor choices, mental fog, and decreased mood and energy.

Movement

Exertion is a great way to condition the body. It elevates the heart rate, tests the muscles, and strengthens your joints. You can activate your fight-or-flight stress response in a controlled environment and prepare your body for life-threatening and stress-inducing situations.

Remember that you get to choose how you live your life. When you have a firm foundation of health, you'll be blessed with greater happiness and consistency. As you work on each piece of The Accountability Code, you'll come to truly know that you cannot fail! It's all a process and it's meant to adapt as you and your life develop into what and who you are meant to be!

Must Be Trained

To develop our ability to reflect effectively, we need to recognize feelings and where they come from. Take a second to think about a pet peeve you have. Picture something you can't stand and say out loud, "I hate it."

Then picture something you really enjoy and say, "I love it!" Just by saying those words and creating the images of the items you love or hate, you get more in tune with your emotions and how your body responds to each.

When I said "I hate it," I pictured gum. Call me weird, but I cannot stand the thought, sight, or nasty smell of bubble gum. I stepped on gum too many times as a child and, as a result, I associate gum with uncomfortable feelings.

When I say, "I love it," I think of donuts. They are my treat of choice, and I will never cut them out of my eating style. I eat them when I want to, they make me feel good, and it's the perfect amount of sweetness at the end of a long day or first thing in the morning, depending on the day.

The ability to recall things we love and hate and to instantly feel the accompanying emotions is a skill that will help you develop your intuition. What exactly is intuition? It is your ability to understand something immediately, without the need for conscious reasoning. How cool is that?

Take the body, for example, and let's talk specifically about working on our glutes, our booty. Do we automatically know how to sit and stand? Sure, because we do those things every single day of our lives. But do we instantly know how to work out our glutes by using a Smith Machine in the gym? Not unless you have been taught, right? It's an advanced understanding because it does not happen naturally.

Some of you might be familiar with a Smith Machine and the many movements you can do with it, but if your glute workouts have previously been limited to sitting, standing, or walking upstairs, the Smith Machine might overwhelm you. And if you jump into major movements without proper training, you can be injured. The same is true of our intuition: We have some basic abilities to know the difference between good and bad, because we make those types of decisions every day. But sometimes our ability to execute based on that knowledge gets blurry.

Now, just because we know something is bad doesn't mean we're great at avoiding it. And just because something is good does not make it an active priority for us. Our intuition can help solidify our ability to choose wisely when it's most important. Wouldn't you love the ability to follow through on more good things and less of the bad ones?

Practicing physical exercise helps you prevent injury, increase lean muscle mass, and enables you to see progress much faster. Developing your intuition through Reflection and meditation every day does exactly the same thing. Habitual practice will help you reduce stress, increase the amount of good choices you follow through with, and enable you to grow faster, with fewer distractions.

With a quick body weight/booty workout, I'm going to show you how to develop your intuition workout style.

Before you start this meditation, grab a paper and pencil and the stopwatch timer on your phone. Think of this as gathering your workout equipment. Then think of four different things you love. Picture each item or activity clearly, and then say out loud, "I love that."

"I love that." Playing a game with my girls at the table.

"I love that." I imagine walking from my garage into a clean kitchen.

"I love that." I see Aubrey and me, waking at the same time.

"I love that." I picture baking on a Sunday and smelling the goodness coming from the oven.

Think of *your* four love items and write them down.

Then, to deepen the love you feel for them, take a deep breath and say, "I am training my intuition, and it's getting stronger!" This creates a pattern of deliberate intention. Because you are 'working out' your intuition, you should create an environment that supports your intention.

Find a space that is comfortably lit, and temperature controlled, and, most importantly, free from distraction. You can have some soft music if it isn't too disruptive and helps your emotional well-being. To prevent falling asleep, sit in a chair, or sit on the floor, with feet crossed and a straight spine. Sit in a space that magnifies love and feel the emotions associated with each of your four items. The emotions that came up with my love images were happiness, support, and celebration.

With your list of love items before you, set the stopwatch and be prepared to focus. Prepare to hear exactly what your intuition has to say. Intuition is a feeling, and you're going to use all of your senses to bring in supporting information. Make sure that you're in a place where you can feel, see, hear, smell, and potentially taste.

It's one thing to have a workout to follow. It's another to actually demonstrate it. Now that you are in your space, start your stopwatch and focus on your first love item. Mine was playing a table game with my daughters. Take a nice, deep breath and let your first image settle in your mind. Imagine you were a friend, looking on. Now, you're going to go through your senses.

Sight

With closed eyes, what do you see in this image? I see my daughters smiling and the expression on their faces as they decide what to do with each turn. Take a deep breath and say, "This is love."

Hear

What do you hear in this image? I hear laughing, innocent banter, and cheers around the table as the game progresses. Take a deep breath and say, "This is love."

Taste

What do you taste in this image? Is it sweet, salty, savory? I taste salty tortilla chips and mild chunky salsa with plenty of cheese melted into it. Take a deep breath and say, "This is love."

Smell

Touch the tip of your nose. What do you smell in this image? I smell freshness in the absence of mess around the kitchen table. Take a deep breath and say, "This is love."

Feel

Clasp your hands together. What do you feel in this image? I feel the cards in my hand and the wooden chair beneath me. Take a deep breath and say, "This is love."

Once you have gone through each of the five senses, open your eyes and stop your stopwatch. Record the time and take note of how long you spent feeling love. If your time was less than five minutes, continue on with the next love image. I recommend following this process for a meditation workout that lasts fifteen to thirty minutes. Just like working out, it's okay to ease into it. Adjust your equipment (your love images) by pulling items from your vision board or picturing the big goals you have coming up.

By practicing getting into a state of love, your body and your intuition will more easily notice when it is out of balance. Just like moving your body, your intuition can get out of shape and suffer the consequences. But training your intuition is also like fitness training in that consistency is more important than intensity.

When implementing The Accountability Code your intuition will serve as one of the most powerful tools for pointing you in the right direction. It all starts with Reflection, and training your intuition will always be worth the exertion. If you need help tuning in with yourself, I recommend you take my free Mindset Quiz on my website. It will help you connect your mind and body.

Getting Help

I am not a pet person, but my husband is, and we have this cute little Shih Tzu named Mia. Aubrey got her as a puppy and spent time training her properly. She is well-behaved, she doesn't bark a lot, and she'll even wake up from a dead sleep to play fetch, especially if you squeeze her squeaky donut toy.

As a result of Aubrey's training, I feel Mia is very smart for her breed. Aubrey has set up various 'traps' for her to get to her toys. He'll put them in a bin or between couch cushions, so that Mia has to figure out how to get to them. It's really entertaining to watch.

One night, I came upstairs to hear Aubrey and all the girls laughing hysterically. They decided to put Mia's toy inside a used shipping box. Each of the flaps of the box overlapped to interlock, and Mia's toy was inside there.

Once she knew it was in there, Mia went crazy. What was making everyone laugh was that Mia got her head stuck in the box, and she was running around the room and running into things. You could tell by the squeak when she was trying to lock onto the toy inside the box, and you could tell when she was trying to remove her head from the box. It became easy to differentiate her intentions and movements.

I think she decided that getting her head out of the box was more important, because she started running backwards! She was trying to get away from the box, and this just made everyone laugh even more. We have seen her succeed many times in reacting to pranks, and we couldn't wait to see how she'd pull this one off. We kept encouraging her to grab her beloved donut toy.

As she ran backwards, she was making her way all around the room, and she just happened to back up right between the two couches. The opening between them was large enough that her body could fit through, but the box couldn't, and it finally came off her head, releasing her.

Watching Mia's antics taught me an important lesson. How often do we get so consumed with chasing something that we become blinded by the obstacles that keep us stuck? How long should we allow ourselves to run around with no release or direction? How silly is it that sometimes we even start to move backwards? And when we finally find success, it's because we've been given support that would have been impossible to provide on our own.

Mia is a dog, so she can't take clear directions from humans. She wouldn't have understood Aubrey and the girls telling her to let go of the toy and release herself from her confinement, but she trusts Aubrey. Luckily, as humans we have the ability to communicate and listen to the messages from others, helping us better understand our predicaments. It starts with building a reliable support system that facilitates clear Reflection.

Here is the process for creating your support system: Start by defining your goal. What parts are you capable of completing, and which parts, at this current time, are unattainable for you?

The thing is, you cannot read the label if you're inside the bottle. This story seems silly when it's about a dog, but when it's about the truth of our own situation, it's not so funny. I think about times in my business when I was busy hustling, but not seeing major improvements in the bottom line. What experiences in your life taught you that getting outside help is necessary at times?

Success does not come just from asking for help. We have to be willing to do the work. As an example, if you want someone to hold a baby shower for you, then you need to be pregnant first, right? What proof can you provide that shows you have been working on your goal and could use some support?

When you have done your share of the legwork, you can be more specific about what you need. In this situation, you could write on your baby shower invitations, "Registered at Target." You just made giving specific help much easier for everyone involved. Imagine you're asking for help as if the help was on a registry. What items are on the list?

When we are in the midst of our problems, it can be difficult to see all the factors that aren't right in front of us. Trust others to read the label from the outside. When we trust others, we'll be given access to information we weren't yet aware of.

Experience provides expertise. I love when moms-to-be ask for advice at their baby showers. Each woman shares something from her own experience of raising kids. That is extremely helpful, especially to new moms. A baby shower just might have been the first mastermind meeting!

We often need the most help when we're right in the middle of a sticky situation. This can be a helpful time for a friend to come in, to validate our experience, and provide solutions. Who are the people in your life that have lovingly provided help because they can see the whole situation?

If someone drops their wallet and doesn't realize it, someone walking by can come to the rescue, saving the victim lots of stress and heartache. Take a deep breath and say, "I allow others to observe from the outside and to offer their help."

Many times, we get stuck inside our problems because we're so focused on getting out of one specific situation. Reaching out to others 'in the same boat' could allow us to gain support from those who understand our struggles. What resources are available to people in *your* situation?
As you work to reach your goals, it's important to put yourself in a position to learn and grow. You are always going to need some help. A baby shower for your first child isn't going to help you raise multiple children later on, or

even help deal with the teenage years. There will always be aspects of your journey you are trying to figure out. As you allow others to observe your progress and help you where needed, what areas of growth would be helpful for them to address?

When I had specific questions, I was able to get specific answers. I could also ask someone who I knew could help me instead of putting my problems 'out there' for everyone to see, and risk getting feedback from someone who doesn't know what it's like to be in my shoes. With your specific questions, pinpoint a few individuals with experience and perspective who can help you in your specific situation.

Now it's time to put your reflection into action! Start raising your baby, whatever that baby is!

Having a worthy goal, guidance on how to improve, and people who can help you shift toward success — all means you have no reason to fail. Continually evaluate yourself, and don't forget to celebrate your progress throughout Reflection.

Keep a journal of your experiences so that one day, you can look back, see how far you've come and how you got there, and help others achieve the same goals.

Chapter 2 - Humility

Humility – A modest view of one's importance

Any time I hear the word *humility*, I am instantly reminded of the time my dad compared me to Satan. A lot of my experiences of growth stem from my relationship with my dad, because as the years have gone by my view of what he taught me has changed. With him, I am constantly finding the need to get from point A to point B.

One day, I was visiting my parents on a Sunday afternoon. A common occurrence was unfolding. He was mad that my mom moved his things in an effort to clean up, and now he couldn't find what he was looking for. Everyone in the room offered to locate what he needed, yet he continued to yell at my mom for what she did. I let him know his behavior was unnecessary and that we could help him. That made him more mad because I was now "arguing." I reminded him he taught me to stand up for what's right and that I was doing that now.

Angrily, he told me that my job was to be obedient and not to argue. I know what you are thinking: I should have just left, but I continued to stay and defend myself. I tried to convince my dad that my ability to speak my mind had led to great things for me.

"Dad, you taught me to speak up, and because of that I have a great marriage, my kids are awesome, I show up and make a difference, and I think you should be really proud of what I have become." He quickly responded with, "So now you think you're better than everyone." It brings a chuckle to me as I recall how quickly that had escalated.

Finally, I returned home to my awesome life and continued on the journey to be the best I can be, but I was hurt. How can he justify being so bad to others? I put into action what he taught me, but now that it goes against him, it's so bad — and now he says I think I'm better than everyone else for just trying to be my best?

A couple weeks later, during a Father's Day visit, my dad asked me a question: "Marci, what single characteristic can Satan not have?" I answered, "Beauty. He doesn't have a body." I thought that was a pretty good answer, because being beautiful is not only a physical benefit but I feel beauty is defined by being unselfish, compassionate, brave, and honest, none of which Satan is capable of. Immediately, my dad said, "No. Humility." He got up and left, implying I was acting like Satan when I declared any ounce of confidence, as I did the last time I was visiting his house.

My reflections often include this conversation around humility. My dad taught me to be confident and to stand up for what I know is right. Why can't I have confidence and stand by my life choices, knowing they are good, especially because they are anchored in Christ? Why couldn't I use that skill to stop my dad from yelling at my mom and everyone else who was trying to help him? Can't I be humble and proud of what I have become, even if my dad is not? Am I guilty of not having humility? Being humble means understanding that we are not able to achieve everything on our own. It means improving the gaps where our human experience displays daily. Being humble means reviewing our actions and knowing we'll need help to improve them.

Without the belief that we can learn and improve, we won't take action. When we recognize our imperfections and have desires to improve, we are demonstrating humility. And we rely on the one and only person who has allowed us to be, Jesus Christ — or your choice of higher power.

Not only is the pursuit of humility beneficial, but people who are humble are happier and less stressed in life. In order to be accountable to yourself, it requires humility to the source that enables you to do all that you do in life.

Here is how to gain humility in an enjoyable way:

1. Pray.

Turn to your Creator or Source of ultimate strength. Having a habit of prayer makes it easier to open up when you have struggles. If you are religious, turn your efforts to improve what you are taught. Get back to the basics and deepen that relationship with God. To pray, address God, express gratitude to Him, ask for specific help, and close each prayer in sincerity, which can include the name of Jesus Christ, amen, or however you prefer to end.

When you pray, you are proving that you believe in a source stronger than yourself. You are acting with hope and faith that you can overcome all things with help. When you don't, you are choosing to lean only on what you are, which is an imperfect human being.

2. Recognize that you came to earth and will leave it the same way everyone else has.

You brought nothing to this life, and the only thing you can take are your experiences, knowledge, and light. You have the potential of becoming something great, just like everyone else, and you are the only person who can be just like you.

When I am open about what I am struggling with, I usually find others who feel like me. Sharing that my dad has become a toxic source in my life has allowed my clients to open about their own families and in turn get to that point B with supportive individuals.

When you recognize that everyone is fighting a worthy fight, your ability to overcome struggles with help increases. When you don't, you are choosing to believe that you and your hardships are unique and therefore are unsolvable or unworthy of connecting with helpful sources.

3. Embrace different stages of life.

Realize that you are not the person you used to be and that you will not remain the same person forever. Look over your past through pictures, video, text, or documents to verify a dramatic change in appearance or goals and patterns. I really like what I see in the mirror, but there are times when I have seen an old picture of myself and really cringed.

I have to remember that in that moment I thought I looked good, too, and that is why I shared it on social media. You may have the opposite experience, in which you look at a photo and wish to go back to what you looked like.

When you embrace different stages of life, you are practicing gratitude for what you had then and what you have now. When you don't, you are dwelling in a place of stunted growth and disappointment.

Take a few moments to see your progress. Focus on the good that has happened from then until now.

4. Count your blessings.

You did not create all that you have. Much of it was given to you; you were in the right place at the right time. Actually, none of us are incapable of creating all we want in life without help from others. We need not only a community to help us, but also a higher power to provide what we and our community can't.

When you count your blessings, you take advantage of all that you have been given and utilize it for creating more progress. When you don't, you find yourself focusing on what you don't have instead of what you do have.

Reasons for resistance to being Humble —

1. Fear of failure

Fear of failure is when not trying feels better than admitting you didn't live up to your goals. If you have to overcompensate by inflating your achievements to feel included in a group of people, chances are you are ashamed of your lack of progress.

During the first year of my business, a brother-in-law said to me, "It looks like you're doing pretty well in business." Curious, I asked him what gave him that impression and he said, "Your website looks pretty good." Knowing that a nice website doesn't translate to income, I felt pressured to pretend that I was doing better than I was, and therefore my fear of failure increased.

I had a choice — work smarter to be content with my progress, or put on a front and pretend that I was rolling in the dough.

In order to beat this resistance, know that you don't need to answer to anyone that doesn't share your values and that success or progress isn't always measured in money. Practicing the steps to humility will give you new insight on your own abilities, because you value how those around you have created what they have.

2. Negative sources

Oftentimes, we are conditioned to be a certain way based on who we are surrounded by. If we are never shown what true humility looks like, it can be challenging to model it. Think of someone you know who inspires you to be the best you can be. Chances are, they are continually working to become better. They listen to guidance, they are willing to learn, and they value people over their own assets or achievements.

In order to beat this resistance to practicing humility, only enlist sources that help you feel good about yourself. I think we can all relate to being triggered by someone on social media due to being compared to them. If a once good source becomes negative, cut it out and turn back to the sources that inspire you to keep going.

3. Wrong expectations

If you are constantly feeling that you can't get ahead, it's time to reevaluate what direction you are heading in. Our bodies have a way of creating resistance when we pursue areas that aren't right.

I once had a marketing manager who told me I needed to change everything in my business. We paid him to help us reorganize, but as a result we lost focus on growing, and it ground my business to a complete halt. Our judgment can get cloudy about who we should enlist to help, what sources we listen to, and the amount of energy and stress is increased when energy doesn't flow.

In order to beat this resistance, spend some time reflecting on the direction you are going and determine if it's in line with what your ultimate goal is.

As you work to develop true humility, you should realize that this world is constantly working against you. Continually working on The Accountability Code will put you in a position to stay close to your true purpose and follow through with what that means.

Shut down the negativity

When I was young, I found it easy to choose happiness even when things weren't going right. I just adopted a different attitude, even when I was struggling. I knew that if I wanted to be happy I could change my mood in a matter of minutes if I was the one to decide that.

That worked well until I got married. I was still very young — I graduated high school, turned 18, got married, and then got pregnant just four months later. And with all these exciting adult changes in my life, my ability to control my emotions evaporated.

Maybe it was the pregnancy hormones or the uncertainty of making decisions with a life partner, but I found myself unable to regulate how I felt about small disagreements.

One night, as my husband Aubrey and I were driving home after work, I mentioned that I wasn't able to eat lunch that day because, even though the break room fridge was stocked with deli items, there was no mayonnaise in the refrigerator, only Miracle Whip.

Aubrey asked why didn't I just use the Miracle Whip? When I said I don't like it, he suggested that I should eat Miracle Whip three times and that, by doing so, I would begin to like it.

Folks, please laugh with me here! I was not going to agree with my husband, and I'd like to believe most other people wouldn't, either. In his defense, nearly 15 years later he claims he didn't know they were so different.

When it was clear I was not going to consider eating Miracle Whip three times, Aubrey then called me stubborn and picky. He believed that anyone's taste could adapt if you wanted them to, but those words stung. This was my husband, the man I dearly loved, and I wasn't in high school anymore. I couldn't just choose to feel differently and walk away.

In fact, late that night, I found myself crying, thinking about his words to me. I realized it was seven hours after our conversation about Miracle Whip, and I was losing sleep to a silly disagreement. During those seven hours, I could have told Aubrey how hurt I was by his words or simply let it go. I could even have gone to the store and bought some new mayonnaise, instead of rehashing a hurtful exchange with someone I love.

Instead of ending the conversation when we stopped talking about mayo and Miracle Whip, I continued to carry it through the day and night. Instead of accepting that we have a difference in how we view our ability to change, I got mad and resentful and, worse, I isolated myself so that my husband wouldn't see me crying or even know how I felt. I didn't know how to handle my emotions, and I could not stop the cycle of negative thoughts.

There were many moments like this early in our marriage, as we learned to live together and make decisions together, and even fight and argue together. In time, I learned that it was acceptable for two people to lovingly disagree. It is okay for me to like mayo and for Aubrey to BELIEVE he can eat something three times and like it (even if that's still really weird to me).

It took years to learn how to choose a happier pattern for dealing with changes in my emotions. There were more days after the mayo argument where I chose offense, withdrawal, and tears. When things weren't good, I found a way to prolong it. But after I had my daughters, I made a conscious decision to take control of my emotions instead of letting my emotions control me. I had an army of four girls following my footsteps and I didn't want that for them.

I'm a work in progress, but when I think about how far I've come, I realize that even little bits of effort make a big difference in the long run.

One benefit of my wholly healthy lifestyle was learning how to reclaim emotions in the midst of conflict. I am excited to give you the steps to reclaiming your emotions and choosing happiness more often. There is a critical reason why humility is included in The Accountability Code.

Humility is understanding that we aren't "all that." We're flawed human beings who are here to learn. You must become comfortable with facing your flaws in order to master accountability.

48

Ask yourself, how much time does an unpleasant topic get to consume you? Is it ten minutes, two days, an entire week? When you let the negative emotions from a heated conversation linger, you don't allow room or space for happiness. Do you lock yourself away and review a play-by-play of each argument, instead of owning your feelings and finding solutions? Are you choosing where your energy is well spent?

Obviously, disagreements will pop up in marriages and partnerships. Nobody is perfect. Life isn't blissful. Understanding this helps lessen our negative reactions when they occur. The next time you find yourself getting flustered during a debate or conversation, take a deep breath and turn your awareness to whatever emotion you may be feeling.

Then recognize that you have a choice to continue the conversation. If you are talking about a difference of opinion, you might say, "I am willing to entertain this discussion." That's an appropriate response when arguing with someone you care about. You don't want to disregard them or their feelings, but it sends a signal that we can choose how we spend our time and energy.

If, during the course of a heated exchange, you begin feeling a flux of negative emotions (such as when discussing the latest hot topic from social media), I recommend a statement that releases you from continuing, such as, "I need a break to think about this topic more on my own." This allows you to let go of the overwhelming negative feelings and to schedule a continuation of the conversation in a state of peace and clarity. The sooner you release negativity, the faster you create space for what you want and need.

Accepting that disagreements are a part of life does not mean that we allow name-calling or permit unmet expectations to trigger more stress or negativity. The longer we allow negative (or nasty) discussions to go on, the greater the impact of the emotion will be. When we learn, instead, to navigate and control our own reactions, the responses of others will often improve.

Disagreements are a fact of life, but living in them doesn't have to be. When dealing with someone that you aren't close to, it's still important to be kind about how you entertain or exit disagreements. If you must engage, protect your energy at all costs and, if possible, exit the conversation as soon as it becomes unpleasant. Say, "Thank you for including me in this conversation. I must go now," and walk out of the room.

It's in those pauses where you can collect your thoughts and determine how you really feel before you do or say anything you'll regret. Just remember that when you are serious about your intentions, it's much easier to be accountable to following through.

If the other person doesn't respect your statement or prevents you from walking away, you may feel the need to defend your energy, verbally and physically. They might yell, "Where are you going?!" or "We're not done!" In response, you should say, "I will return when I have enough energy to be productive." Get your message across and leave the space safely.

It takes practice, but I guarantee that when your actions are consistent with how you feel, you'll keep away from the most negative situations. Anytime you're pressured to engage before you feel ready, use the statement, "I have given this more thought and have decided I will not spend more energy on it."

It's called setting boundaries, and it's the best way to provide protection from negative, consuming, unproductive emotions. Our response to any situation indicates where we spend our energy. You can determine when a conversation ends and how to proceed once it is over. For Aubrey and me, our mayonnaise versus Miracle Whip conversation could have ended the second we got out of the car that day. I'm sure it was, for him. For me, it was just the beginning, like a hot coal being passed to me, and I chose to keep carrying it when I could have set it down anytime.

As you practice leaving unhealthy conversations and situations, initially you'll find that you're not ready to let go of the words spoken or the emotions felt. You'll want to process what happened, wishing that you'd said something different or continuing to defend your opinion in the privacy of your own thoughts. But the best way to preserve your mental energy is to bring your focus back to a place of productivity. Humility is not about bowing down, it's about really deciding what you're going to stand for and where your strength comes from.

Demonstrating humility takes patience, thought, and clarity.

If you find yourself often hastily leaving conversations with topics that you actually care about, then you may need help processing how you feel before articulating it to others. Can you talk with a trusted friend, or seek guidance in formulating your position? Aubrey and I have many heated exchanges about parenting, and to help me understand my feelings about raising our daughters, I've read several parenting books for advice.

If you find yourself in a conversation about a topic you don't particularly care about, make it known by your actions. Leave those unpleasant Facebook groups that conflict with your beliefs, lessen your interactions with negative people, and be deliberate about where you want to spend your precious energy. You have the power to obliterate negative thoughts by owning them, understanding them, and releasing them, or you can hang onto them, which only enhances their power over you.

As we continue to learn about humility and how it works in The Accountability Code, be sure to practice slowing down and monitoring how you handle conflict and differing emotions. It would be helpful to document the ways you have been able to shut down and stunt negativity.

Your journaling will come in handy as we plug your goals into The Accountability Code. I invite you to take my Mindset Quiz to determine your inner strength.

Knowing this information will help you develop humility in a way that works in harmony with your values.

Judgment

"Don't expect things to happen. It's better to be surprised than disappointed." You may have heard this expression before and thought it might be true. Well, I'm here to tell you that nobody will be surprised by sudden great health. Nor will you suddenly wake up to a happy marriage, a college degree, or the loss of excess fat.

Be sure to remember that you are the only one who sets the right expectations for yourself, and you need sound judgment to do that. But we are all too often surrounded by the judgments of others, and it can be hard to separate ourselves from what they think about our choices.

Let's talk about how our judgments and the judgments of others can help us pursue the right path for us, when paired with humility. Remember that having humility means having a modest view of one's own importance. If we lack the understanding of our importance, any and all judgments can become pretty damaging.

People I loved told me to have more kids. To have kids faster. To put more space between the birth of each of my children. They told me not to pursue college, or to wait for college until after the kids were older. They told me to put others first, no matter what, and when it comes to my health goals — oh boy! — did they have judgments!

As a personal trainer, I got in the habit of staying in my workout clothes because I was either:

- going to work out
- working out
- or just finished working out

So people looked at me constantly in my workout clothes, and they made certain assumptions and judgments based solely on appearance, not on fact.

Recognize judgments —

Do you judge others based on their appearance? Do you assume that someone who is skinny must work out all the time, and eat very little? Did you make these judgments without knowing anything about what was happening in their life?

We all do it, but then we don't want to be unfairly judged ourselves. It's time to level up and create our own expectations without worrying too much about what others think of us. Notice how I said THINK and not KNOW? This process is going to take a bit of humility because it's not about who is right or wrong — it's all about how we choose to show up, and for what purpose.

Personal judgments —

What are your personal expectations of yourself, and what are the judgments you make based on how you measure up to those expectations? You have to weigh them, and sit with and ponder them for a while. Sometimes it takes a few moments, and sometimes that process takes years. I wasn't capable of making a clear decision about how many children I would have, and when I would have them, when I was an eighteen-year-old new bride. I had to revisit that issue many times over the years.

Think about when others share their expectations of you. Do you agree with them? Do you judge them? Who are you putting your trust in? Do you feel that they even know you? Do you let their advice go in one ear, and out the other? Do you take it to heart and commit to making it happen?

None of these are wrong answers, but it does depend on who is making those expectations for us. More importantly, it depends on how much we trust our own judgment. The deeper we know ourselves, the better we are able to funnel through the expectations of others and decide where they belong. Some will become a priority, and others are properly put in the trash. Only *you* get to decide.

I ultimately chose to listen to the advice of others, but then make decisions with my husband based on our expectations formed together. I chose to have kids and go to school at the same time. I chose to put others first only when I was healthy and able. I chose to have kids fast and exactly the number that Aubrey and I felt was best. I learned to judge my own situation and needs, helping me implement the correct expectations for my life. When you have the correct expectations for your life, you'll be surprised at how often you will feel that you're on the right path for *you*.

The first step in using good judgment to set correct expectations, is getting clear with who gets to be involved with the process. Hint: It's just you, God, and maybe your spouse or partner. But not your parents (if you're an adult), kids, or even close friends. Most of those demanding expectations I listed above came from some of my closest friends.

Who is most important in your life? If your goal is to get a promotion at work, then you might have peers or a supervisor who can be involved in that goal. Write down a list of candidates, focusing on those you know who have your best interests at heart and are in a position to offer well-intended support, advice, and guidance.

Then decide HOW you want them to be involved. The actual act of getting a promotion falls upon your shoulders, but if you have listed others as allies, you know it's because they can assist you in reaching your goals and setting proper expectations. I hope you pick only people who are firmly on your side.

What expectations do you think are reasonable to apply to yourself? How about being honest and open, and taking care of yourself in order to reach your health goals. Remember again, that nobody accidentally gets into great shape. They set clear expectations for themselves (including healthy meals, daily exercise, and deliberate self-care), and they don't give in to the unrealistic judgments of others.

Expectations are actually great ways to challenge ourselves. What do you expect of yourself, and what are you willing to do to achieve those goals? If the goal is to get that promotion at work, do you need to take on a bigger workload, maintain longer hours, or enhance your people skills? Some expectations might include better communication (like timely email responses) or a happier attitude. Clear that inbox every day, and smile at each person you encounter. Write down what you expect of yourself. But put reasoning behind those expectations: With those improved communication skills and a happier attitude, what else are you achieving other than the chance of a better job?

Focus, at first, on simple goals — know what they are, and why they're important to you. Then, as you fulfill each expectation, you'll be blessed with confidence and higher levels of success.

This is your template for what takes priority in your life. Trust your ability to judge the information that comes in. Others will still offer their advice and judgments. If you feel their words fit into your personal plan, great! Adapt that value so that it works with what you are capable of now. And if that feedback doesn't feel right for you, just say thank you and move on. After all, nobody knows *you* better than *you*!

From time to time, evaluate how you're doing. Share the results with the people you trust. If you are meeting most of your own expectations, maybe this is a good time to set some new ones. If you are struggling with your goals, ask for help.

Remember that you always get a say in your journey, including who gets to walk beside you and offer their advice. There'll be times when people provide you with unsound feedback and unhelpful information. Keep stock of who is on your most trusted list. Stay in tune with your body; it will let you know if what you are hearing is right for you. Use your personal judgment to block out the noise.

Who's the Boss? *You're* the Boss!

You are also an intuitive being. Going through this process will help you tune in to your needs and judgments more often. Anytime you are struggling to move forward, repeat this process and build upon the accomplishments you have worked for. And trust your mind and your body. As they connect, your ability to judge will get clearer.

Remember that so many people are ready and happy to help you, especially when you are clear in what you want, why it's important, and proving that you are already working on that path.

I'd like to demonstrate the importance of documenting your process whether privately or on a platform you feel safe to share. I wrote this post a while back and it has served as a vital reminder to live my best life and release the constant judgment from others.

Fixing Mistakes

This is usually the part that no one wants to talk about: How we've failed. Even though we make mistakes every day, it's not always easy to own up to. It's not a good feeling to know that we have failed or hurt other people. But the moment you stepped into this journey of accepting accountability, you knew it wouldn't all be all sunshine and rainbows. "True happiness comes only when we learn to control our bodies, training them to be governed by the laws of God." That means we also have to face our own demons.

In this step of The Accountability Code, it's not easy, but I can promise that when you change the things you know you need to change, it's much easier than for someone to tell you what you are doing wrong. Take this step seriously.

In recent years, I have been dealing with a contentious relationship with my father. We share many of the same strengths: leading, teaching, speaking, and taking authority. I also inherited his dancing skills, humor, and his ability to speak the truth even when it makes others uncomfortable. Dad taught me to be a hard worker and not to be afraid to speak up and demand the room when I had something to say.

I have emulated my father in several important ways, and I have really valued all he has taught me. After the death of his father and the family fight over his dead father's assets, his demeanor and temperament changed. Rarely was there a visit that didn't end in his disgust of people disrespecting him. This family conflict changed his view, and the demand for his kids to be obedient increased dramatically.

During disagreements, I noticed that we were trying to use the same superpowers on each other. Each of us was convinced we were right in the situation, but each of us also had different hopes.

I hoped he'd address the sadness, depression, and trauma in his life and become more loving and supportive. Dad hoped that I'd remain a strictly obedient child and respect his truth enough to do whatever he said, right when he said it. In his eyes, my arguing with his statements, ideas, and attitudes showed the ultimate act of dishonoring him.

Eventually, I had to stop talking and start acting. I had to transform my communication from emotion and verbal, to mental and physical. During one argument with my father, I stood up and announced to my children that it was time to leave. Days later, I journaled my thoughts to get clarity, and then called my father to discuss them. After that, I decided it was in my best interest not to visit him in his home, but rather to send love and support in the form of encouraging letters.

The best apology is changed behavior. If I wanted my father to change, I also had to be willing to do so myself. If I was like him, as I knew I was, I might need to own some of the same behaviors. He couldn't apologize, and I knew I needed to. I had to start by figuring out which parts of my actions and words I should apologize for. There are many parts of myself that I love, but there are also parts that I'm trying to change. There are things I have done that I am not proud of.

A few years ago, I made a grave mistake that hurt my brother badly. My brother is an accomplished DJ, and he entered a contest which, if he won, would provide him with a rental space to host events. He asked all his friends and family to vote for him in the contest, and what did I do?

I entered the same contest, in competition with my own brother.

It hurts to admit that I did this, but it's because of the work I've done since then that has allowed me to face my failings and own them publicly.

I entered the contest because I also wanted a big space for my fitness event. I believed that I could win the contest because I had a bigger social media following than my brother. I didn't consider how my actions would make my brother feel, but deep down I knew I had done something wrong because I felt guilt. But I still wanted to win, even promoting the contest on social media.

My husband asked me what I was trying to do. I remember the disappointed look on his face, and yet I tried to justify my actions by telling him that if I won, I would share the space with my brother. Then, sensing that I was making the wrong choice, I just pushed the matter out of my mind. I stopped posting about the contest, but didn't withdraw my name. Instead, I ignored the contest and kept my feelings to myself. I withdrew socially, out of pride, a sure physical sign of my mistake. Pride is the root cause of many of my misjudgments.

I might have continued living in this shame were it not for the fact that my brother contacted me. He had every right to yell at me, to call me out, but he didn't do that. Instead, he had the courage to tell me how he felt about my actions. He didn't make accusations. He articulated his hurt and told me he would have liked my support, not my competition.

I didn't truly understand the magnitude of my actions until he lovingly called that day, and I was humbled. I don't remember my exact response, other than to apologize to my brother. I needed time to understand what I had done, what the impact would be, and what I could learn from the experience.

I didn't want to emulate my own father in this situation by digging in my heels. I had to be willing to own my mistakes. I decided that I wasn't going to keep creating negative energy in the world, and that I would not hide again or try to forget what I had done.

It was painful, but it resulted in my coming to a deeper awareness of who I was and who I was capable of becoming. Just recounting this mistake encourages me to never hurt anyone like that again. Unfortunately, not every mistake can be easily or successfully addressed through one conversation. Again, behavior change is the best apology.

What excuses or justifications have you used to make yourself feel better about your mistakes? What are the ways that you know you have to change? We are often harder on ourselves than anyone else will be, but it's important to own our failings and make conscious choices to do better without adding more shame.

The deeper you let yourself go without taking action to correct your mistakes, the harder it will be to dig yourself out. But when you are ready to change your ways, ask your Father in Heaven (or the higher power you believe in) for love and guidance. When our intention is to receive help, become more like Him, we will be supported.

Make a list of the people that you know you have impacted negatively. Can't think of anyone? Think again. Open the communication pathways between your old self and the person you are meant to become. Be loving but firm, and you'll discover those you need to make amends with. Then choose a way forward. Admitting you have erred is a strength that must be cultivated. Start small, and get used to saying, "I'm sorry."

Now, at times I would get so focused on work that I forgot to provide meals for my children. Again, pride told me to keep going on my professional tasks and that my girls would take care of their own dinners. There really is no excuse. My girls may be handy in the kitchen, but they can't drive to the store or order groceries online — they cannot manage a kitchen by themselves. I had to be better about providing nutritious meals for my kids even during busy, stressful times. I made the commitment to change and began ordering groceries online. I may not always cook a three-course meal, but I give my family the level of care I can. You're not a failure for doing what you can in the moment. Listen to your conscience, and choose one thing that you can do better.

During times when you made mistakes that affected others, you probably experienced emotions that indicated you were going down the wrong path. I could literally feel an uncomfortable feeling in my bones, when I was in competition with my brother and saw that we were neck-and-neck in votes. Yet I ignored that feeling and kept petitioning for more votes for myself.

Momentum is one of my better skills, but sometimes also my biggest failing. When I get going on something, I like to plow through and see results. During the contest, I ignored my awareness, my emotions, and my conscience, and I paid the price for it.

Emotions are gifts because they indicate what outcomes our actions are producing. In this step of humility, it's how we learn, as humans. When we take time to pay attention to our feelings, we'll receive a sign of how we are doing. It gives us pause, and time to reflect on possible consequences of our actions. How can you stop your mistakes before they become big blunders? It starts with communication and humility: checking in with yourself, your emotions, and even your body. You were born to make mistakes, but you were also born with a system to check your progress, to improve and grow.

Don't forget to acknowledge those who helped you improve your behavior. You might resent those who point out your mistakes, but, in the end, they're valuable members of your accountability team. They help you find the truth and take control.

I encourage you to share your shortcomings with someone you trust. Letting mistakes eat away at you can stunt all other steps of The Accountability Code. Please don't let yourself go down a path of negativity due to pride and a lack of humility. And I can help you with that.

Standing up

I come from a large, kind of crazy family. I was raised in Utah, one of eight kids. My mom started having babies at 18 and finished at 30. We gained a reputation as one of the largest families around, even by Utah standards!

My upbringing was based on the teachings and activities of The Church of Jesus Christ of Latter-Day Saints, and I loved everything about it. I loved being in a big family. I loved going to church, and I loved visiting my grandparents and many cousins each Sunday.

I valiantly followed the teachings of the gospel and found happiness in marrying young and having children quickly, just as my parents had. I was engaged in high school, married at 18, and had four children by the age of 24. I never drank alcohol or smoked or did bad things with boys.

Everything was going perfect — until my siblings and I grew up, and the family drama began. As each of us became adults, we chose our own paths. We found careers, married, and started families of our own. New families meant merging our lives with those of our spouses, as well as with each of our in-laws.

My father took this especially hard. In his mind, his children began placing a higher value on their new families and were disrespecting his wishes to keep family traditions in place. For years, we all bickered over where we would spend holidays, who was going to attend, forcing us to make tough decisions that often resulted in drawing a line in the sand. When anyone suggested adjusting the calendar to accommodate everyone's needs, we were met with accusations of selfishness, greed, and pride.

It went on for years. As we kids were growing up, my dad constantly preached to us about accountability, integrity, honesty, and transparency. But he failed to deliver on the same when it came to his treatment of his own family. He still believes that we should each be obedient to him and that, if we aren't, it's because Satan is working in us and because we refuse to be humble.

Trust me when I say I have studied humility in excess while working through many issues with my dad. Managing so many direct family relationships successfully requires it, too.

Things came to a head after an incident where my father made a very clear mistake at a family function and would not apologize, let alone address his actions. I was so fed up with his abuse and his hypocrisy, and I decided to speak my truth. It was time to set some boundaries and make them public. In the past, I would address my concerns with him in a personal discussion at his house. Attempting to have a heart-to-heart with him has always resulted in him trying to teach me the truth and him reminding me who's the patriarch and that I am supposed to be obedient and not argue with him.

I knew in order for me to stand up for what I knew was right, I had to take a different approach this time. For years, I just wanted my dad to value his family. With each and every interaction, he was pushing his entire family away.

I aired my grievances in a video, which I then uploaded directly to our family's private Facebook group. In the video, I called my dad out for his childish and outright abusive behavior. I let him know exactly how I felt, and I shared my perceptions of how my siblings also felt, based on our efforts to support each other through raising our own individual families. I explained that we were being treated badly just for becoming adults and choosing to live our lives according to our own conscience, which is something our parents taught us.

I let it all out on the video, hit SEND, and then waited to see what would happen. For the next two hours, I went into a tailspin. I actually feared for my life, imagining my dad coming to my door with a shotgun and shooting me on sight (I know he wouldn't actually have done this; this was just my panic run amuck). I chastised myself, saying that I should have talked to him privately (I had tried for years, though) and that maybe this time he would listen to me (he hadn't before, which is why it got to this point). But I still hoped that the video would have an impact, that maybe he would finally listen to what I had been feeling for years.

I was used to being called disobedient for standing my ground. I was sick of leaving my parents' house in tears, crying to my husband on the phone after yet another argument with my dad. I was sick of this pattern and ready for it to stop. I was trying so hard to be a good person, but how can I when I am breaking the commandments and rejecting the truth my dad continues to teach? I've had a lot to work through.

After two hours of sweating out the possible repercussions of the video, my phone started to blow up with text messages from each of my siblings. They were thanking me for being brave enough to stand up, and it was about time someone did. Their words lifted my spirits and confirmed my decision to take action. I could not let this man continue to treat his family this way.

I wish I could say that everything got better after sending the video, that he was stunned into awareness and took accountability for his actions and realized the severity of his behavior, especially since his father passed away. Instead, he only felt hurt by my video. And I realized that I would be hurt, too, if someone did that to me. It would give me a serious pause to adjust my words and actions. The days and weeks that followed the video were hard, scary, and downright life-changing.

Still, his actions haven't changed, and neither have his words. We know he has some serious mental issues and, until he admits he needs help, we need to protect ourselves against harmful interactions with him.

There is no perfect way to deal with family conflict. But I know it has to start from a place of compassion, self-respect, and humility. The way you treat others speaks volumes about where you are in life. For many people, demanding accountability from others or from ourselves starts with a breaking point. This was mine. I could no longer leave the conflict with my dad behind closed doors. I could no longer remain trapped in an abusive cycle.

My father grew up in hardship, and his own personal traumas remain unresolved. Yet I knew that I couldn't feel compassion for him by acting like everything was okay. I couldn't properly love him without letting go of my anger at the way he treats my mother, my siblings, and me.

You can only love others as much as you love yourself. And you can have compassion for those who have harmed you when you demand respect and accountability. When they refuse to own their wrongs, you must release yourself from their actions. I was ready to stop being merely the obedient child. Of course, I will always be his child, but I am not a child anymore, and he should treat me like an adult.

It didn't matter that I could adjust to his demands. My in-laws were more flexible with holiday celebration scheduling, and I technically could help my dad stack wood or pass out brochures for his next election, but the moment I realized that I could love and honor my dad without being his constant servant, I found compassion for myself and the courage to speak my truth.

How have you changed in your family relationships? How do you need to shift in order to grow, and how have you met resistance from those you love?

Many of my clients struggle with 'Empty Nest Syndrome' and with setting new boundaries for teens that are hesitant to move into adulthood. Change is hard. Ask yourself, what can you do to make their transition easier? It helps to talk with someone who has been where you are. It's imperative to talk with your loved ones, to find out how they are doing, and to offer your help.

The video I made reflected an inner turmoil I had been holding in for years and couldn't tolerate anymore. Even though my words were blunt, my emotions were clear. Talking to my siblings in the days after helped me navigate my next steps.

Children grow up — it's a simple fact of life. We cannot control them as adults, and we must let them live their lives without holding them back. I now see that, during my childhood, while I liked to push people's buttons, I really was programmed to follow
the rules.

Why was that not okay once I became an adult? Because the obligation to obey as a dependent child was gone. Instead, the only obligation I had was to God, myself, and the family my husband and I created together. I changed because I wanted to change, not because someone forced me to. But that change meant that I outgrew my old behaviors, and even some of my old relationships.

I used to listen to my dad talk about his painful childhood, and I thought that the best way I could support him was to do whatever he asked of me. But as I grew up and changed, I realized that what I needed to do instead was to express my love for him while protecting my own values and needs because we are on different paths with different goals.

The only way to gain clarity was to give myself a way to update my views and behaviors. I'd done everything my dad ever asked of me, and when I put my foot down out of necessity, I was met with abuse and scorn. Once I released the video, there was no doubt what I meant when I said I would not be coming to visit, and why. I gave solid reasons for my choices and, honestly, after a while felt joyful as a result. It lifted a burden from my shoulders and allowed me to find the respect and compassion for my parents that I needed in order to be happy.

I want to have a good relationship with them, and currently we are working towards that. I know that I can control only my own attitude, behaviors, and actions, and not that of others. I also know that I'm responsible for how I allow others to treat me. There are still topics we cannot discuss, and when they surface, I change the conversation or leave. Actions speak louder than words. Putting physical distance between my dad and myself sends a message that I am of value and will not tolerate mistreatment.

That video became a catalyst for change in my life and that of my crazy family. I spoke to my dad before I wrote about all this in this book, and I reminded him that I love him and want my kids to have a relationship with their grandpa. But I also reminded him that I need to keep my distance, and I won't pretend that things are fine when they are not. I urge him to get help and to take action on all that he preaches.

What makes you feel unsafe in your current relationships, and what can you do to control the situation to protect yourself? It's okay not to have it all figured out right now. What can you do today toward preventing regret in your life? Are there relationships that require action? What must you step away from, and who do you need to speak the truth to?

I'm not perfect, and you're not perfect. So let's respect that and be imperfect together!

Throughout my journey of sharing my struggles in this situation, I know that I am not alone. If you are struggling with setting boundaries, staying safe, and maintaining healthy relationships, I invite you to join my Mental Strength Challenge. You can access it by visiting my site www.funandsustainable. com/360

That challenge was born out of my commitment to staying mentally healthy while enduring this relationship with my dad. I know that each and every person deserves to be who they want and to be free from the expectations of your past.

The Mental Strength Challenge comes with a workbook that will help you take these concerns deeper and provide you with a path to active healthy change.

Shared Control

Learning to co-parent with my husband has been one of the greatest joys of my life, but also one of the biggest challenges. Yes, we live together and are happily married, but I use the term co-parent because it means sharing the duties of raising children. Just because children belong to a happily married couple doesn't mean they'll be parented successfully.

Aubrey and I were each raised by folks with very different parenting styles. I was one of eight kids. Aubrey had just one older brother and grew up feeling like an only child. I didn't grow up with pets (my parents thought siblings were all we needed to play with), while Aubrey always had a loyal dog by his side. I had to pay for everything I wanted, including finding a job to earn money for a car as a teen. At 16, Aubrey was given a car by his parents so he could go get a job to earn money. They then encouraged him to put his paychecks in the bank while they paid for his needs and wants.

I knew I wanted my daughters to have more than I'd had growing up, but I did value the independence I gained by virtue of my upbringing. I also loved having a bunch of siblings, and then I went and had girl after girl after girl after girl – haha! Did you catch that? I have four daughters. There happens to be a run of four girls in my parents family, as well.

I will admit to being pretty bull-headed, and I started to realize just how much, as Aubrey and I began to differ in our parenting skills. I found myself claiming to be the authority on how our girls should be raised because the situation Aubrey and I created was similar to my upbringing. I wasn't interested in giving them the lifestyle Aubrey got as basically an only child. I didn't think it was realistic to lavish as much as Aubrey's parents had on him, and I worried that our girls wouldn't develop confidence or independence without the structure I had.

When we married, I naively thought that Aubrey and I would easily merge our parenting styles. I fell in love with him and married him because I knew he would be a great dad and yet, by the time we had four kids, I had adopted an extreme and inflexible parenting style that was having a negative effect on my relationship with my husband. Thankfully, my amazing husband helped me understand that his childhood, while different than mine, also prepared him well for the responsibilities of marriage and parenthood. There are pros and cons to every family or living situation. I had allowed my pride to get in the way of creating balance between what is right and what isn't right for our individual family.

In life, we all need trusted individuals who can pull us back when we're getting a little crazy. There were actually good things that came once I tried to adopt some of my in-laws' parenting styles and, of course, the most valuable lesson was learning to share. In the end, it felt good to let go of the mental and emotional burden I was carrying about how I alone really understood how our daughters should be raised in their growing up.

Whether you are a parent or not, there will also be instances in your life when you need to turn over the reins of leadership to someone else, to admit that you don't have all the answers, and to acknowledge when you are struggling. Let's get deep and real about what you are struggling with and how you can turn that into a message that honestly expresses your need for help. Can you tell why this story is under the step of Humility in The Accountability Code? It's not easy to admit when you are wrong and that you must release control for the greater good, not just what you want right now.

What is your greatest challenge right now? At the time, my greatest challenge was worrying that Aubrey's mom would be too generous with my children, they would become spoiled, and that I wouldn't be able to provide for my four children the way that his parents did for him. In essence, I was struggling with my ego and learning to compromise for the better. I didn't understand how to accept his parents' abundance, and I felt uncomfortable depending on it.

When life gets blurry, adjust your focus. Let it all out and take the time to journal it. Don't hold back on exactly what you are thinking and feeling. I find it helpful to write it down. This is a message just for you, to help you acknowledge what you are struggling with. It will help you adjust what is, in the moment.

My inability to peacefully co-parent with my husband led to a lot of anger for me. Anger is a response to perceived threats, and the threat in question was an unfair judgment of the way my husband was raised. How about the way I was raised, too? I was not given extra opportunities and was often expected to provide my own necessities. What are you comparing your struggle to? What outcome have you let yourself believe needs to come to pass, and how are you willing to loosen up to let that happen?

Sometimes struggles are triggered by a belief that we aren't on the right path. What caused me to suddenly doubt my husband's ability to care for our kids, after marrying him specifically because I KNEW he'd be a great dad? Something caused me to discard that idea and instead become obsessed with my own upbringing. Yet I knew that the ways in which I was raised weren't better. But they had made me who I was, and I'd reached a point in my life when I could acknowledge that and find the positive value in it.

Shared communication equals shared control. After all, how long do we really get to control our kids? Maybe to age eleven? 16? 18? We don't know how everything will work out, and we have to know we won't always get our way. What would the end results look like if you got everything you wanted, and your partner got none? What would the opposite look like? What would an even distribution look like, and what would it look like if you switched back and forth in sharing power?

Can you see how your struggle is impacting others? Look carefully at the messages they are sending, both non-verbal and explicit. I encourage you to approach your kids and ask how they are feeling. Don't interrupt or correct their answer. Simply listen and let them know you are there for them. I consistently let my daughters know that I am trying to improve and that I have never raised 4 daughters before, so I'm not sure how it's supposed to go, just yet. I have found it helpful to journal how you are feeling so you can gain some clarity and use it for reference later.

I hope you can see that there is value in taking a step back and collecting your thoughts. You aren't always going to be right, and that's okay, but you do need to be okay with accepting suggestions from others on how to proceed. There is a way to withstand every struggle you are up against, and there is light at the end of the tunnel. You just have to be willing to work through this with a level head. Stop right now and say to yourself, "Everything will work out. I am becoming aware. I am grateful for my life and all the challenges it comes with." As you let loving sources in, you'll see that you are not doing this alone — a controversial thought, but maybe you don't have to hoard all of the control.

How does hoarding control diminish your self-control? Have you been too busy to pay attention to your lifestyle and emotions? You aren't in this life alone, so stop acting like it.

The people that you are in conflict with are also part of the solution. They are the people you love and care about, and they are integral pieces of this messy puzzle, whether you like it or not. Write down everyone who is involved with your particular problem. That list is also your support system.

Small problems tend to trigger big struggles — getting behind on laundry or dishes, missing out on sleep, comparing ourselves to others, missed date nights, low sexual energy, and stress — all have a way of building up. That tension leads to heated exchanges with others, but it all stems from the failure to check in with ourselves. We must be willing to work on the parts of ourselves that aren't helping. I've applied this exercise so many times that I find my common problem is usually the same every time. What do you think is the real reason for your ongoing problems?

Once you identify the root cause of your struggle, this is exactly where your energy needs to go right now. I'm proud of you for taking the time to identify your troubles and find solutions that consider the needs of others. You have a responsibility to take care of yourself first and allow others to do the same. We are all in this together. Write down how giving yourself adequate care will enable you to share control and solve your problems together — because when you try to control everything, I promise, you enjoy nothing.

If you need help or accountability to the basics of health, let's talk about the best starting point for you.

Adversary

Don't be surprised when opposition comes your way. Every day of our lives we come in contact with others who may support us or may disrupt the path we are on. We cannot survive without human interaction, and we are at risk of allowing impulsive actions with others to take precedence over our values.

We use our intuition to discern between good and bad situations. At times, it feels as if everything in the universe is working against you. There certainly will be people who try to pull you down into old habits and patterns. No matter how positive you try to be, and how firm in your resolve, the devil will show up to test you. Keep in mind that you are worth the work it takes to defeat the devil. Practicing humility with The Accountability Code turns your mind and soul to God or your higher power.

I love the point made in this old Chinese fable:

"A man traveling through the country came to a large city, very rich and splendid; he looked at it and said to his guide, 'This must be a very righteous people, for I can only see but one little devil in this great city.'"

"The guide replied, 'You do not understand, sir. This city is so perfectly given up to wickedness... that it requires but one devil to keep them all in subjection.'"

"Traveling on a little farther, he came to a rugged path and saw an old man trying to get up the hillside, surrounded by seven great big, coarse-looking devils."

"'Why,' says the traveler, 'this must be a tremendously wicked old man! See how many devils there are around him!'"

"'This,' replied the guide, 'is the only righteous man in the country; and there are seven of the biggest devils trying to turn him out of his path, and they all cannot do it.'"

I related this fable because there once was a time in my own life when I was being dragged down by the challenge on the hills I was trying to climb. I could feel pressure to remain the same, revel in comfort, and justify my reasons to stagnate. I found every reason to find offense if I wasn't experiencing what I wanted. I was winning the blame game.

I felt down for days and told myself that pausing for now would be better. But what was I pausing in the first place? I realized I had to make some changes because I did nothing productive while waiting for everything to come together. I had to pause my unrealistic expectations of immediate success. I had to recognize the darkness and find a way to stay out of it and that was by turning to God and taking action on what was next.

We won't experience hardships just with extreme situations — you'll also find them in the monotonous tasks of life. Each of us has experiences that make us wish we could separate the good from the bad. The truth is, we can.

My client, Amy, was ready to get out of this pattern. She realized it was a time for change when she found constant irritation in her young children. She would turn to food because it seemed as though her life revolved around finding the next snack for her demanding children. She began to wish for a break, some adult interaction, and a way to forget this stage of life she was in.

She came across a post of mine that talked about putting yourself first even when you are the main caretaker for others. My having four young children helped her realize I knew the position she was in. She reached out, and she admitted that she knew her mindset was poor.

She desired to get back to her old self. She wanted to be that mom who took time to work out, loved playing with her kids, and had a few friends to meet up with. In those moments where she reflected on her goals, she realized the only way to really see change is by starting with herself.

We started her on my Mental Strength Challenge. It has 14 mini lessons given over a period of two weeks where I teach how to recognize why you do and don't do certain things related to your health. The mini lessons are all under 15 minutes long, and they are accompanied by a workbook that helps you formulate what your next plan of action is. Not only do we focus on updating your mindset in a healthy way, but we also include accountability to the basics of health, too: sleep, self-care, water intake, and movement.

I have had hundreds of clients participate in the challenge and it's proven to show that when you work on your mindset, your physical actions to improve your health are much more effective because you are clear on what the best actions for you are. The Mental Strength Challenge is my mindset intro program and can be accessed by going to www.funandsustainable.com/360

After the first few days, I was wondering how Amy was doing with the Challenge. I hadn't seen her accountability tracking come through yet, so I reached out. Nothing. A few days later, still nothing. I sent her messages to let her know I was thinking about her and that we could hop on the phone to discuss if she needed to.

At the end of the two-week Challenge, I was surprised when I got a fantastic message from her. Amy told me that although she wasn't great with tracking or checking in, she faithfully completed the Challenge and the workbook that goes with it. The very first lesson in the challenge is called Insanity Stopper, and it's about discontinuing a habit that you know leads you down a negative path.

She instantly knew that checking her phone in the morning was that very thing, so she resolved to start with prayer, instead. She apologized for not responding to my messages but she was determined to talk to God first each and every day. Her changing just this one thing led her out of the darkness on a consistent basis. What a wonderful realization and solid practice in humility! She didn't say much about specifics, but she made it clear that her head was now in the right space and that she experienced happiness in a way she hadn't in a long time.

Amy's is a perfect example of how the adversary gets in and tempts us to go the wrong way. We have our agency, and it's up to us to improve the life we have or to numb ourselves with unhealthy habits. I know exactly how Amy feels because I have gone through it multiple times.

I had to challenge my ideas of things that I was taught because I realized they didn't support the direction I was moving in. But instead of being met with support and understanding, I was accused of being prideful and lacking humility, sometimes by others and sometimes in my own head, sadly.

How do you feel when the people in your life hold you back and say damaging things to you? There will always be someone in your life who triggers the most negative emotions. The trick is to make sure it isn't you. Once you recognize your triggers, you can mentally and emotionally prepare before interacting with them.

The truth is that the human experience requires us to be tested. What grade are you trying to earn?

There are three things you can do to instantly change the process, like Amy did —

1. Admit your unhappiness and that you are contributing to it.
2. Reach out to a trusted source for help.
3. Commit to including God in your struggles.

Practicing humility is not about being perfect — it's about recognizing where your strength comes from and knowing that you have unlimited resources to tap into. What does your intuition tell you about what needs to change? I learned that I need to stay out of some environments, such as heated political debates on FB, my parent's house (because of constant contention), and phone conversations that are overly negative with gossip or complaining (I can feel them drain my energy), for the sake of my well-being.

It's a form of self-respect to listen to your intuition and the messages it is sending you. It is there to keep you safe. It is there to warn you when you are not safe.

When you look back at your most negative interactions with others, whether it be kids or yourself, do you see a track record? How will you refrain from jumping into the same ruts again?

Some mistakes or misalignments make themselves known quickly. After I was a first responder to a group of teens that crashed their car into a house, I immediately made a mental note to be more aware of my own driving habits and conditions.

But when you experience a never-ending chain of struggle, it's harder to receive those messages and get clear about resetting the circumstances. How did you get out of alignment? It could be from not taking care of your health, a lack of planning, or failure to ask for help. It's a chain reaction, but it starts with one small problem. Where do you think your chain of struggles began?

Draw a line in the sand. Prepare in the best possible ways and set a good example of self-care and self-respect to those you love. How can you use your experiences to support others in their growth?

At the end of the day, Humility is about turning to God for help. We all engage in actions, attitudes, and behaviors that don't match up with what we really want, and there is help. I urge you to use The Accountability Code to nip your poor behaviors in the bud. I promise it's possible, and you'll experience a greater sense of happiness right away.

Humble Help

Throughout this book you will come to realize that The Accountability Code has the power to help you develop a great sense of empathy for others. By working to master yourself, you'll see just how powerful other people are in your transformation. Knowing this will help you develop the humility to show up in life exactly how Heavenly Father, God, or your higher power hopes for you to.

When my first baby was born and taken straight to the NICU, my postpartum plans went out the window, and I had to create a new plan. Luckily, Leila's condition was not life threatening, but I had no idea how to handle leaving the hospital with an empty car seat. I was just eighteen years old.

When my baby Leila and I met with the doctor days later, I happened to be wearing a t-shirt with the name of my high school alma mater and graduating year. He mentioned that his son had just graduated from the same school and, in shock, the doctor said to me, "I can't believe *one of my son's friends* is already having a baby!"

I immediately thought, 'Friends?' I sure wished I had a friend to talk to at that moment. None of my high school friends could relate to what I was going through. I didn't even tell anyone outside of my family when my baby was in the NICU. I felt alone in my struggles, trying to focus on learning how to pump the milk from my breasts instead of nursing.

Seven days later, my newborn and I were able to go home together. Once we were home, I started to feel more normal. I began to merge back into life slowly, and I tucked this experience into the back of my mind. I still wasn't sure how to express the massive amount of sadness and loneliness I had just experienced.

Years later, a neighbor had a preemie baby, and as soon as I heard "NICU," my memories flooded back to those days right after Leila was born, when I felt so alone and unable to express my feelings and fears. I decided that I would reach out to this mom and just let her know that I, too, had a NICU baby, and I could relate to what she was going through. Due to the extensive danger of her experience, she had many people who rallied around her to make sure her family was taken care of, and she got the support she needed until her baby came home.

Instead of feeling jealousy for the support she was receiving, I was incredibly happy that she wasn't alone. I was glad that I could show up for her in ways that I wished I had received. From that moment on, I stopped the pity parties that encouraged me to feel bad about my situation. I needed to practice expressing my feelings and needs in order to be of support to others. As a result, I have found deeper happiness in the act of serving those in need.

As you embark on your healthy journey, I encourage you to be that support you wish to have. I promise that you'll be much happier, and you'll be more in tune with your body and emotions by learning to express them transparently.

Here is a solid way to connect with those feelings:

Recall a time in your life when you wished you had some support. Think about the strong emotions you felt at that time, and how you can channel that energy to take action. Hearing the word NICU brought back feelings of sadness and loneliness to me. But because I took action with my neighbor, now the word NICU is associated with getting out of my comfort zone, service, and tenderness. Having gone through the experience of leaving the hospital without my baby, I can now share vital information with other parents that may prevent them from feeling the same way. What experience can you recall that comes with strong emotions?

You may find that recalling certain experiences will bring up unpleasant emotions at first. But you deserve to be happy and to conquer your goals, and you have the power to prevent others from suffering in the ways that you did. Without going too deep into bad memories, think about a recent situation that really sucked, and how it made you feel. Something like that happened to me a few years back.

One winter day, I left the gym after teaching class to find that my tire was completely flat. I called my dad, who lived about a mile away, and he came to my rescue. We took off the flat tire, and when we reached for the spare, we discovered that it, too, was flat! My dad took both tires and we drove to his house, where he showed me how to patch them. Believe it or not, a couple years later I was able to fix a friend's spare tire because I knew exactly what to do from that experience with my dad. I love being able to serve in this way, knowing what it felt like to be stuck on the road, unaware and unsure what to do.

How can you be the answer for someone because of what you have been through? Even more, how can you communicate to the universe that you are ready to help others who are in situations familiar to you?

As you look for opportunities to serve, you'll find that more and more of your life experiences will be tied to good emotions instead of bad. You have the ability to continuously create goodness from misfortune. Take a second to brainstorm what situations you can associate good emotions with, in preparation to share and serve. I regularly ask in my prayers for opportunities to serve, because I don't want to become numb to the suffering or needs of others.

Don't assume that opportunities to serve have to be grand. I have a friend who walks to church each weekend with a plastic bag so she can pick up the trash she sees along the way. In her small but significant way, she does what others are unwilling to do. And she becomes more aware of small changes she can make to improve herself and the world around her better, as a result.

A person's most useful asset is not a head full of knowledge, but a heart full of love, an ear ready to listen, and a hand willing to help others.

What emotions do you create by helping others? When you are clear on your ability to serve, that ability will become an unstoppable talent.

Being ready to help is a blessing, as well as a skill. If you feel obligated to help others, you won't receive the same benefits as doing it because you genuinely want to. I understand not wanting to help. Look, we all get tired, caught up in our own lives, and frankly need a respite from the demands of work and life. But when you understand the positive emotions that are created by your generosity, it's easier to go out and do it. With the examples we have talked about here, what good things have come from your most painful experiences?

Sometimes it seems like the best thing we can do is hide in our own little bubble, especially when we are stressed. But when you help others, your needs are met, too. When you continue to engage in the habits that bring positivity, they will snowball, and soon you'll have a community where you are giving and receiving appropriately and automatically. Take a deep breath and say, "I am that person that helps others. I value the cycle of giving and receiving."

Make it a habit to practice helping and serving others, where possible, and you will associate each experience with positivity and generate fuel for energy to continue to serve and do good.

Count your blessings, but don't forget to also spread those blessings around to others. Be humble about all that you have received, and use it to magnify the amazing person you are aspiring to be. You are a good person, so go out and prove it to yourself.

Chapter 3 - Planning

Planning — Making a detailed proposal for achieving success

If you look at the world around you, you'll see that the car you drive, the store you shop at, and the food you eat all came to pass because someone created an effective plan. From ideas to consumption, every purposeful product or service has a good plan behind it. As you follow The Accountability Code, you must know the outcome you are trying to deliver.

When I started my reality TV show experience, I was most excited about going through an "Uncovery." The purpose of this was to get clear on which direction we were going. It included getting to the core of who we are, what we do, and what change we desire to make in the world.

Knowing that my purpose, without a doubt, is to help people connect their minds and bodies through self-mastery habits, my mentor and I began to work backwards. How will I get my message out? How will I convince people of the happiness that lies in a healthy body and a sure mind?

We mapped out a plan of how I'd share content, how much info I would give at each level, and how to naturally lead people to want more in their lives. Each person must be empowered to decide when they are ready to move forward. Anything forced on them is neither right nor natural for real progression.

My plan enabled me to help others at their own level and allowed me to stay in alignment with who I am and who I want to become. Having that plan laid out essentially helps me focus on the bigger picture. The times during the TV reality show — when I had to deviate from the plan to work with the show — is when I struggled the most. Outside forces are powerful, and that is exactly why a plan is crucial in applying The Accountability Code.

Here is how you begin creating a plan to be accountable to:

1. Start with the end in mind.

> You cannot get where you want to go if you don't really know just where you want to go!

> Keep in mind that your plan doesn't have to be grandiose. The entire goal here is to follow through with smaller steps to get to progressively bigger steps until you get to the big one at the end. Based on your reflection and humility steps, you

need to define what it is you want to be accountable for.

When I make a plan and follow it, I am so much more productive because I know what needs to happen and what the result will be. My days that lack a plan are filled with household chores because that always needs to be done, yet it doesn't fulfill my ultimate goals.

When you start with the end clearly in mind, it's easy to see what actions your day should be planned with. Then you won't feel like you're wasting your time doing monotonous tasks that steal the zest from your life.

2. Ask lots of questions.

Your plan won't be perfect the first time you put it together. Oh, man! When I agreed to be on the reality TV show, I should have asked sooooo many more questions, because I am a planner. Had I known what was really going to happen, my actions and my plans would have been much different.

As you start your plan, you'll see how it needs to be tweaked and adjusted, but in the beginning use these questions as you plan:

- What did I learn from my last plan that will make this one better?
- Who do I know that is great about putting together effective plans?
- What threats will entice me to abandon my plan?
- What inspiration am I using to put this plan together?
- What is the number 1 goal of my plan?
- How will I know if I have accomplished my plan?

When you plan, your intentions are clear and you have ammo to back up your actions. When you don't plan, you are vulnerable to any outside influence, regardless of its drawbacks or benefits.

3. Gather needed items/expertise.

In order to see results you haven't seen yet, you need to do things you haven't done yet.

I don't care how many times people say, "I know what I need to do, I just need to do it," because there are, without a doubt, good reasons why they haven't actually done it yet. For instance, there are still things I would like to accomplish, such as having 4 rental properties to let each of my children use as starter homes, or make over 1 million dollars in 1 year in my business. And those goals are not completed yet because I have failed to gather the needed items, and so I am still working on the business expertise in order to be able to accomplish them.

Your list of necessary items will be different than anyone else's. Depending on your goals, you might need a new coach, new resources that excite you, or new equipment to get started.

When you gather needed items and expertise, you are proving that your outcome is worth the proper preparation. When you don't, you're sure to have another random experience that is hard to measure and difficult to fit into gaining success in
your plan.

4. Write it all out, and share it with someone.

When it comes to writing out your plan, it's imperative that you fully understand the mapping or outline. This is where you take what's in your head and put it on paper in a way that others can understand it. Sharing it with someone is a great way to increase your abilities with the first 3 steps of reflection, humility, and planning.

Don't underestimate the power of a good friend and a clearly laid out plan. Taking the planning stage seriously will do wonders for your ability to be accountable. Write your plan in a journal, on a white board, in an excel spreadsheet, or on a calendar. Put it somewhere you can see it often. And be sure to provide lots of space to add notes when you get into the next chapter on implementing.

When you write it all out and share it with someone, you are taking the first step of executing and setting yourself up for success. When you don't, your desires stay a mere wish, never to be realized.

Reasons for resistance to Planning –

1. Overwhelm

Finally, putting your plan on paper can seem daunting, because it becomes something real. Many people argue that you should never tell others your plan, because if it doesn't happen, then there are no social repercussions for failure. That is the exact opposite of accountability, which means taking responsibility for both success and for failure.

In order to beat this resistance, give yourself permission to start small. Plan out a small goal, such as what you wish to accomplish during the first three hours of the day.

2. Lack of understanding of purpose

If you aren't sure of yourself, then you can't be sure of your plan. Not being sure, right now, is common, especially if you've been feeling out of alignment. Allow yourself to feel deeper into your reflection. During my uncovery process for the TV reality show, I learned that my business model was holding me back from sharing my deeper message. I forgot the ultimate message behind sharing workouts, meal plans, and developing self-accountability.

So now I provide coaching and programs that directly impact my exact purpose. Are there messages you have been ignoring or that you feel too scared to embrace?

In order to beat this resistance, have someone look over your plan and see if it is clear with what you really want. Allow a trusted source to tighten up loose ends and validate your plan.

3. Embracing spontaneity

Valuing being able to do whatever you want in the moment is a blessing, but that can work against you. Being spontaneous can be impulsive if not backed by a plan.

You do not need to create a plan that includes tedious steps, but you do need to know exactly where you're going and just how you are going to get there. When you create a plan customized just to you, you can plan on being spontaneous because you know that aspect will help you achieve your outcome.

In order to beat this resistance, plan to include fun aspects that allow you to be yourself. You are the one responsible for your plan, so it needs to be something you are fully comfortable with.

Planning can seem overwhelming before it's done.

However, in order to develop accountability, the plan is "the what." WHAT are you trying to be accountable to, and about what? Your plan is essential to counting success and seeing continuous progress.

After you have the plan laid out, it's time to get to work. Not only will it require sacrifice and letting go of poor habits, but your plan also requires that you put it fully into action. Implementing is where massive growth and results happen. Let's go there next.

Your Path Is Correct – for *You*

"Marci, you are one of the only people I know who say they're going to do something really big — and then actually do it!"

A friend told me this after I explained that I had moved my family out of our 4,000 square foot home, turned it into a rental property, and was living with my husband, four kids, and a dog in a neighbor's basement apartment with one bathroom – in the middle of the pandemic!

When I mentioned these facts to friends and family, I usually got rather dreary comments and responses. But this particular friend complimented me on my current crazy path toward happiness.

I've also been sharing some of these big life changes on social media. It's a great outlet for me to talk about my life and all that I'm pursuing. As an extrovert, it feels natural to let the world see what I'm doing and why I'm doing it. For the record, we were downsizing so that we can pursue international travel with our daughters, so that my husband and I, who both work online, might explore other lands for possible travel and investment purposes.

While some people respond with compliments or curiosity, others respond with judgment. They tell me I'm crazy for doing what I'm doing, and some even told me that it was too dangerous to take my kids out of the United States. A lot of people have said that our plans are unrealistic. One person even had the nerve to call the city and try to get my short term rental shut down!

The reality is that no matter what path you choose in life, someone you know isn't going to understand. I see my goals clearly, but from your perspective, you may not see them. Rather than letting the doubts and judgments of others affect you, you have to choose your own path, knowing it's the only one for you. It may seem crazy to others, but that's because it isn't their path.

You have to connect your choices with your passion, you have to adapt when the path gets rocky, and you absolutely have to love the journey!

Can you define your current path right now?

What led you to those specific choices?

What is the next step in your journey?

Reflecting on Your Path

Imagine that you ran into a friend you hadn't seen in ten years. How would you describe your life to them? What are your biggest accomplishments? What has been the most consistent thing in your life? What are the wildest events you have experienced?

For instance, my own answers to those questions are:

> I have been married fourteen years and have four daughters. I got a degree in physical education and health, and I started a business six years ago. I love my siblings and am rebuilding a rocky relationship with my parents.

> My family and I rented out our home and are living in a tiny basement apartment, so that we can travel to three different countries this year. Oh, and I'm currently on a reality tv show!

Seeking Humility in Your Path

You shouldn't have to defend or explain your life choices. But the truth is that people will ask, people will challenge you, and you'll feel the need to explain yourself. Keep in mind that you don't have to answer to anyone but God and those you care about.

Understand that where you are today is only possible through the grace of God. Your strength and possibilities come from Him, and you should never have to apologize for what your path includes if it's centered around that.

If you haven't really created an intentional plan for your life, well – join the club! When I got engaged to Aubrey, my dad encouraged us to talk about where we wanted to be as a couple in five years, ten years, and beyond. ,

I didn't think that was helpful because I was convinced we were just going to live happily ever after! I was only 18 years old at the time, so my fuzzy idealism is to be expected. But in time I learned that success means thinking in specifics about what you really want and creating a plan to achieve it.

Once you have a plan, you can take steps to make it happen. I encourage my clients to write their plans out and place them somewhere they'll see them daily. And put them in your phone reminders or calendar, so that you can revisit those plans in three months.

Pray over your plans. Seek help from God to know which direction is best, as you move forward. From experience, I know now that writing your goals down gives you short and long-term direction that not only motivates you, but makes you happier with your choices.

Examining and Planning Your Path

You should understand exactly why you are making the choices you are, so that you can increase your odds of success — and plan for it!
Above, I talked about imagining a conversation with a friend you hadn't seen

in many years and telling them about your current life choices. Can you see your path from their perspective? Ask yourself questions as though you were that friend, and explore their natural curiosity about what you're doing and why. Are you missing any blindspots that need to be accounted for?

Ask yourself these difficult questions:

> Why are you doing this?

> What do you hope to gain?

> Is this a realistic plan?

> How are you going to pay for this?

By asking these questions, then aspects that you hadn't thought about before should come to light. Your answers will help you examine where your plans may need to shift. If you're really motivated, you'll make sure your dreams become a reality, but you may need to rethink just exactly how you will do that.

If you fail to make plans, your grand ideas are just a waste of time. Save yourself the wasted energy and the heartache of failure by creating the right path for your plans.

Implementing Your Path

Now that you know exactly what you want and why, it's time to break down your path into actionable steps. Regardless of how specific or broad your plan might be, you'll always be able to find sections that need their own special attention.

Implementing cannot happen unless you know what the specific outcome will be. For example, Aubrey and I cannot travel if we don't have money. It would also be difficult to manage four children if there is no plan for them. In order to implement my plan, I must break it up into manageable chunks, such as,

> Finances

> Time frame

> Proof of success

We will know we are implementing our plan by increasing our savings, having set dates to travel and reservations for our stays, and we'll stay on top of how each family member feels about our progress toward our goals.

Committing to Your Path

I will admit that I've made some crazy choices in life, and I've been reminded plenty by others that my choices aren't for everyone. I can even see their perspective, but I know that I get to decide what steps I take and why. Of course, most of my decisions are made as a family, including the decision to participate in a business reality show, and the choice to travel with our kids.

But our choices require us to adapt. We do that by constantly revisiting our plans and dreams, but with a solid background of understanding why we're doing what we are doing and what our goals are. This allows us to move forward intentionally in alignment with our happiness.

To ensure commitment to your path you must understand that problems will arise. Outside forces will demand your attention, you'll be tempted to take the quicker route, and oftentimes life can shift with one major life occurrence.

When these things happen, just knowing they will, prepares your mind to adapt to change. Before I was selected to be a contestant on a reality tv show, I mentioned my family planned to travel. Once I decided to pursue this opportunity, our travel plans were halted due to monthly filming here in Utah.

Travel was still on the calendar, but it was only for me. I found myself flying multiple times a month, out of the country without my family for 5 weeks, and focused on strict business growth.

The effort to keep my commitment had to be updated to following through on creating the lifestyle Aubrey and I want for our family. Keeping your commitment can be as easy as 1, 2, 3:

1. I created affirmation statements that reinforced my ability to stick to my goals, even when it became hard to adjust, such as:

    Aubrey and I are awesome parents who are living and prepping for an amazing lifestyle. We want to give our kids a life we didn't have.

    I am doing the best I can and I am extremely grateful God allows me to live this life I lead.

2. I learned to successfully habit link, so that my time was productive. Habit linking can be easier than you think. It's when you add a desired habit onto something that is already happening in your life. To sustain commitment to

my family, I worked on habit linking my positive emotional connection with meal time.

I worked on meal prep, including more than just myself.

I connected with my family over dinner time, even if I had a big workload.

3. Lastly, I always took a break on Sundays to observe the Sabbath day to relax, recharge, and refocus.

   I was able to commit again on Monday, because I had given my brain and any negative emotions a period to process and reset on Sunday.

   I focused on only spiritual matters to ensure I was making the best choices that I could.

Regardless of how crazy life gets or how crazy your path seems, your commitment has the power to keep you going, no matter what!

Improving Your Path

Never apologize for creating a life that you desire. And it helps to surround yourself with people who support your goals. It's even more important to find others who can help you reach your goals.

Who do you know who has already achieved what you want in life? Those trendsetters might encourage you, or help you repair the holes in your plans based on their experiences. Social media groups are great places to engage with others sharing your goals. There are also coaches (like me) who specialize in helping you set and achieve your dreams.

Once you find your supporters, share your plans with them. Listen to their guidance and suggestions. You don't have to follow all their advice, but some of it will help you reach your goals faster. And don't forget the power of feedback and feed forward!

You also have to make yourself accountable by following TAC one step at a time: Reflection, Humility, Planning, Implementing, Commitment, and Feedback. It is a powerful process that will keep you on the right path.

Your life has to feel that it's yours, and you need a solid process to grow and execute the plan that aims for your happiness. Don't just hope for good things to happen — really think about what you want, and make it happen by creating a solid plan.

If planning seems overwhelming, please let me help you. I am always happy to get on the phone and discuss what you want in your path.

Our Own Story

Each of us has the power to make the best choices for ourselves, but we are not separated from our environments and influences. There will always be other people in your life projecting their ideas onto you.

Chances are one of the reasons you were drawn to The Accountability Code is because you feel you haven't lived up to what you expected. Accountability literally means "to fulfill expectations." Throughout this book, I am going to help you define what exactly you should be accountable to.

The Accountability Code has 6 steps to it: Reflection, Humility, Planning, Implementing, Commitment, and Feedback. I will show you how to apply The Accountability Code to your life, no matter what you are going through or what your goals are. But first we must get clear with what you expect of yourself. So — what is your plan?

My whole life, I aimed to be just like my mom. I was going to get married young and have a big family. I got engaged at seventeen, married at eighteen, and got pregnant just a few months later. Then, true to course, I had four children, each less than two years apart. I checked all the boxes. I met mine and everyone else's expectations. I never questioned how extreme that path was or how that would determine the rest of my entire life.

Getting married and having kids so young in life has been a huge lesson. I've learned that marriage isn't a guarantee of a happy connection, and that my husband and I together had to build a foundation of trust, respect, and love. I learned that being a mom doesn't automatically give me patience, nor does it automatically give my children compassion and cooperation. All of these things must be learned and defined, individually.

As I watched my daughters grow, I began to question the rush I had taken to get there. Did my desire to marry and to have kids so young come from within me, or from the divine path set for me, or was it purely an expectation that came from others? Did I want this same path for my own daughters?

It took me a long time in life, despite starting so young, to realize that I had a choice in selecting whose footsteps I was going to follow, and whose values I would adopt. There was no going back, and I have a potentially long future ahead of me.

Along with these realizations, anger sometimes welled up in me. I sometimes felt that I wasn't fully supported in who I was. I was only conditioned to get married and have children. At times, I was rebellious against this plan and committed to guide my daughters toward anything but early marriage and babies. It took a lot of work building up my value system, to come to a place of peace and acceptance.

My values are based on a solid foundation of belief in Jesus Christ. When I'm true to my personal path, and aligned with my Christian values, I fully utilize the true and divine power I've been given. It took full awareness of my personal values versus those that had been ingrained in me by others, for me to find peace. It took trust in my values to know that I was finally making the right choices for me, and that I wasn't somehow trying to recreate someone else's path.

Fully defining your values starts with questioning what you believe. Questioning isn't bad — it's necessary to our growth and to overcoming feelings of regret and shame. When you solidly know your values, you'll know when you need to shift or adapt, or when you need to tune back into the source of your strength. I came to a point in my life when I finally knew myself better than anyone else did, and you can do the same, too.

Journaling is an excellent way to help you fully discover your values, by understanding who you are, how you got here, and what you're going to do next. Nothing helps me more than knowing who I am and what my purpose is. It definitely isn't by trying to accomplish just what other people want for me. You are the most qualified person to define your life and your purpose. Other people — even those you love — may not always have your best interests at heart. You'll know who those people are because they're the people who expect a lot, but aren't willing to support you in fulfilling those expectations.

So write down all your values. List as many as come to mind.

It's the first step at living a life based on your values and avoiding the risk of going astray. Some of your values were formed at a very young age and were influenced by the people you were closest to. Most adults, frankly, do their best to teach their children good values, yet many times they fail to continue teaching themselves those values. Therefore, there are a lot of 'do as I say, not as I do' scenarios witnessed by their children.

Who did you learn values from? Did they live by those values? And just how were those values taught to you?

Many of our values develop as we grow older. The greatest indicator of progress is our level of happiness. Good value choices bring us happiness, and bad value choices bring us unhappiness. As you began to live your values, what indicators proved they were right for you? How did you know that what you valued led to correct choices?

Today, your values define your life. Are you someone who follows through on what you really want, or are you still bending over backwards to meet the expectations of others? I want to let you in on a secret:

You are not required to set yourself on fire to keep others warm.

For years, growing up, my siblings and I helped our parents keep our home warm by chopping, stacking, and moving wood for our wood-burning stove. As a kid, I enjoyed this activity. But once I grew up, moved out, and was married, my dad continued to ask me to come over and help him with this task.

I found myself making excuses in my head for why I should continue to help him. He was my dad, after all, and they still needed to keep warm with that old wood-burning stove. But I had other priorities, responsibilities, and values by that point. I didn't want to spend Saturdays chopping wood and moving piles of collected junk that seemed to grow every time we went to help.

I wanted to be with my own little family, or even just to relax after a busy week. Piling wood was part of my life as a child, living in my parents' home. It no longer was an important part of my life, as a young mom with four little children. I needed to focus on caring for my own home and to establish independent values from those instilled in me as a child.

Here's another secret: *Walls keep everyone out*.

Boundaries teach people *where the door is*.

Boundaries are also the *highest form of self-respect*.

A deeper sense of self-respect will emerge when you live your life by your own definition and following through on what you say and believe is important — to *you*. Start setting boundaries that prevent unwelcomed requests and unsolicited advice. Get clear on who you are and what you want from your life so that it's clear to others where the boundaries are. Decline anything that isn't in alignment with your values or your true path.

After you write down your list of values and how you have incorporated them into your life, you should take a deep breath and tell yourself, "I'm doing a pretty great job!" Accept ownership of your life, including the good, the not-so-good, and the bad.

As you trust more in your own values, you'll also clearly recognize the people who want you to return to behaviors of the past. It will be evident that most of those people were benefiting off your time, money, or energy. Again, choosing to forge ahead on your personal path sets a boundary that others must respect. When you step back into old patterns (even with the best of intentions), it can pull you away from your updated personal values.

Write down some of the people and possible situations that may tempt you to slip backwards.

Now it's time to hold firm to your new values and growth. Remember what a disconnect feels like between what you know is true and what others expect of you.

If I choose to go back to acting like a child who lives in my parents' home and obeys each command my dad gives me, I will be disconnected from the life I have created for myself as an adult. Allow that awareness of disconnect and the emotions associated with it to motivate you to stay true to your path, based on your values.

Declare your values in writing and aloud. Your ability to keep your most important values at the forefront of your mind will guide your body to be in the right place and time. And as you focus your energy on your personal values, your happiness will be evident. As you hold yourself to maintaining and growing those values and personal expectations, your happiness will increase.

If you need help defining what you still want to become in life and how to set boundaries with damaging people or environments, I invite you to start my Mental Strength Challenge (my two-week program with 14 mini lessons and an accompanying workbook. It helps you learn why you do and don't do certain things related to your health, allowing us to create the best plan of action for change, beginning with your mindset). I'll guide you through the work it takes to love where you have been to get where you are going.

You can join the Mental Strength Challenge by following this QR code.

Foolproof plan

By failing to prepare, you are preparing to fail – and without a foolproof plan, you prove you're a fool!

At fifteen, I had the opportunity to travel to Brazil to play soccer. I was excited, because the trip would include soccer camp, a tournament, plus service and sight-seeing. But I knew it would be expensive, and my family could never pay for it.

Still, I begged mom and dad to join me for the meeting to discuss the upcoming trip, where the price would be revealed. It was $3000, definitely more than they could afford. But I wasn't deterred. The trip was nearly a year away, and if I got creative and worked hard, I thought I might be able to raise enough money myself.

Since I was not of working age yet, I couldn't just get a fast-food job. But, thankfully, my mother is an excellent writer, and my father knows a lot of people. I asked my mom to help me write a letter asking for odd jobs within our community, so I could earn money. Those letters proved successful: I cleaned my aunt's blinds for $50, baked treats for my neighbor for $10, mowed a bunch of lawns for $15 apiece, and my orthodontist generously donated $75 to my cause.

I needed to earn around $300 a month to be successful. So, I hustled, was helped, adapted, and learned to get out of my comfort zone and ask for what I wanted. That meant showing up on time, sometimes negotiating prices, and carefully arranging my schedule. It also meant following through on commitments, even when I didn't feel like it.

There was no wiggle room when it came to the cost of the trip, and I was warned in advance that there were no refunds. Every month, I had to hand $300 to my coach and come up with another foolproof plan to earn more.

Before I turned that money over each month, I first committed to paying tithing (donation of 10% of my income) to my church. I asked my Heavenly Father for help, and I read and reread and reread the scripture, "Ask in faith, believing that ye shall receive in the name of Christ" (Enos 1:15). That's what I did: I asked, I prayed, I worked hard, and I left the rest in His hands. I paid $30 monthly to my church first, so I actually needed to earn $330 each month in order to set aside the money to give my coach for the trip. I believed that if I gave generously according to His guidance, I would receive the help I needed.

But in order to receive, you have to have goals and a foolproof plan. Our goals help us become who we are supposed to be. We cannot guarantee outcomes, but with a plan, we can do all that is in our power.

Four months into working and saving for my soccer trip, I got an unexpected phone call from my coach. He had broken his back, and the trip was off. Despite the earlier warning, we actually would get our money refunded.

Let me tell you about God's tender mercies: Receiving that money back, the money I had worked so hard to earn, didn't get me to Brazil – but it did help me buy my first car at age sixteen. And wouldn't you know it, the week we were supposed to be in Brazil, that country had a massive earthquake! It's like God was saying, 'You weren't supposed to be there, Marci. Thank you for your hard work, and I'm proud that you created a plan for yourself and carried it out, but I've got a bigger and better plan in mind for you.'

Here's why plans are so important – if you don't plan for what you want, you won't follow through when situations get hard. We cannot coast our way into achieving our goals with no plan for achieving them.

Make a list of some of your toughest experiences to date. Write down your past goals that required the most work to achieve. It's good to be reminded of your capabilities and determination. Having proof that you have succeeded in the past is a great motivator to set and achieve new goals.

I've remodeled a bathroom all by myself, purchased a car with cash, and participated in a reality tv show. None of these were easy, but I'm still standing and still thriving.

In addition to recognizing your own accomplishments, it's also important to acknowledge your helpers. I am thankful that my parents – though they couldn't pay for my Brazil trip – helped me through my mom's writing abilities and my dad's many connections. All of my life's experiences have been aided by others: my parents and siblings, my husband and in-laws, my wealth coach, the YouTube community, loving friends, church members, and many mentors.

There is so much power in recognizing your past accomplishments, and it's a practice I invite you to participate in. When writing down your list of accomplishments, include the names of those who contributed to your success.

And remember to acknowledge your own worth! It helps you build confidence to move forward.

What goals are you still hoping to accomplish, and how will they challenge you? If you can anticipate specific potential pitfalls, you can plan around them. When those difficulties pop up (and they will), you'll have a solution process that will keep you going. Trust that along with the plans you are making, you are also part of a bigger plan. $330 a month was really hard to keep up those months when I was saving for soccer camp, but I trusted in the Lord and His principle of tithing.

What's the main reason you don't reach your goals? If you want to lose fifteen pounds, what prevents that from happening? Do you quit easily, not understand how to follow through, self-sabotage, or overstress? Maybe you experience all of the above, and at the same time!

Other people have succeeded at losing that amount of weight. What makes them different from you? Remember that there isn't one plan that is best for everyone looking to lose weight. And there isn't just one reason why many people don't succeed.
I asked my Facebook group to share their answers to this question:

"Will you please tell me one reason why you haven't lost the weight you want to yet?"

Here are a few of their responses:

> I like food too much.

> I give up easily.

> Nobody in my family wants to get healthy.

> I can't afford it.

> I'm too lazy.

If you know your pitfalls, you can create a plan to prevent failure. If you don't plan, you'll just be one of the many who wants to lose weight, but simply doesn't work through a process to do it.

If you think you can't succeed because you love food too much, create a plan based on portion control.

If you claim you can't lose weight because you lack will power, ask a friend to be your accountability coach, or hire me to help you succeed this time.

If you are sure that your family doesn't support your healthy eating, then plan separate meals to hit your goals.

And if you cannot afford to eat clean and organic, you have many other options for improving your health and losing weight, including exercise, hydration, meditation, and getting enough sleep to recharge your strength every night. Every one of those ideas is free, and each is beneficial.

If you think you're too lazy, correct yourself right now! I would not call reading a self-development book lazy. Deep down, you really care, and you just need to demonstrate it in many small ways.

So what are your three biggest goals right now, and what do you need to do to take action? Need to drink more water? Buy the most beautiful water bottle you can find. When you choose to prepare and plan for your goals, you understand what will make or break that plan.

When I was trying to earn $330 each month, I would sometimes think about other ways I wanted to spend that money. But my plan was to put $30 into tithing and turn the other $300 over to my coach. So, knowing that I was being tempted, I would say to myself when dreaming of other things that I might buy, "Do I really *NEED* that?"

Does your short-term impulse support your long-term need to succeed?

Momentum demands movement. For your plan to work, you have to follow through. Create your three action steps that move you in the right direction and enlist the allies and coaches that will help you see it through. You're the boss, though. Listen to their advice, be open-minded, but keep moving forward toward your goal. If weight loss is one of those goals, then stick with simple advice that works best: Eat foods that fuel you, eat only until satisfied, drink plenty of water, and walk every day.

The last step in any plan is to start again. Habits don't get set in stone on the first day, and you aren't perfect. Plan for setbacks, and use each new day as another opportunity. You will see changes as you not only hit your stride, but as you have to double-back. A foolproof plan proves you're no fool. You have been successful in other areas of your life, and success simply means to keep going.

The Accountability Code is absolutely needed in order for you to see success. Take this very simple approach and apply it to your weight loss goal. Answer these simple questions and journal prompts and see how your planning is already setting you up for success:

Reflection – What factors determine your need to lose weight?

Humility – Do you believe God can help you achieve this goal? Why?

Planning – Meet with a coach who has a track record of helping people in your situation.

Implementing – Take it one day at a time. Trust your coach, trust yourself, and trust the process.

Commitment – Obliterate setbacks and remove all reasons you failed in the past. Include affirmations.

Feedback – Celebrate your successes every single day, and keep going.

I know this whole process is easier said than done, and that is exactly why I have made this process easy and painless. I promise it's doable and it's easier than you think. I am here for you. Let's get on the phone and create a custom plan for you *right now!*

Broken Record

Nothing will drain your energy more than simply repeating your patterns, even though you're not getting the results you were expecting. Without a plan, your actions will be impulsive, draining, and negatively repetitive.

Like every married couple, my husband, Aubrey, and I have had some challenging times. A few years into our marriage, there were a couple areas where I felt he was disappointing me.

Let's talk about Date Night, or the lack thereof. I can't tell you how many times I've told my husband that we need to go on regularly scheduled dates. I pictured him making plans, hiring a sitter, showering, and taking me out on a date where I'd feel like a queen. But it never happened. I would whine about it, and complain to friends and even Aubrey's parents, but it still didn't happen.

Comparing notes with girlfriends only left me feeling more disappointed. Everyone had the same complaint. Their husbands never asked them out — they'd rather play video games, or watch tv at home, or go out with friends. Some of my older clients would tell me, "Oh honey, my husband hasn't taken me out in decades!" This scared me. I didn't want to be one of those wives perpetually complaining about their husband, but I kept whining at home about our lack of romantic outings.

On top of this, I was irritated with Aubrey for other reasons. I felt that we were just on different paths (maybe because I kicked him out of my business), and we weren't clicking like we once had. I felt dissatisfied with his efforts and became withdrawn as a result. But I didn't like that feeling. I had no interest in just having a roommate. I wanted to share my heart with someone who was just as ambitious about creating an amazing life as I was.

I'd yell and I'd cry, and I'd complain, and nothing changed. I felt like a broken record. Then I realized, if I wanted something different, I had to be willing to do something different. And I did.

I'm going to walk you through the exact process I took to obtain the results that I desired. My hope is that by going through this process, you'll learn how to behave so that you get what you want, too. It requires planning! I already knew what I wanted, but the way I was going about it was poor and useless.

The first thing I realized was that my behavior had to change. His behavior would also have to change, but I couldn't do anything about that. I had to work on myself. So I cracked open some books and learned ways that I could communicate better.

What I realized was that I wasn't communicating what I REALLY wanted. Sure, date nights sound fun and romantic, but they represented something more to me. My words to Aubrey were, "I want to go out," but my true desire was actually to feel deeply connected to my husband.

I wanted to feel connected, and I thought that meant going out on intimate dates together, but my behavior was communicating something else entirely. Why would he want to go out with someone who's always complaining and trying to convince him to do something? I was literally acting like one of my daughters — each of whom is under thirteen, and so, yeah, I wasn't even behaving like a teenager.

I asked him to take me out on a date and, instead, I acted like a kid who wasn't responsible for her own actions. I acted like he had to initiate our date nights and make all the decisions. Does that sound sexy or romantic?

Problem solving is most effective when you begin with the end in mind. And having a plan requires knowing where you want to go. What do you really want? I wanted to have fun with my husband and reconnect emotionally. I wanted to have something penciled in on my calendar that the two of us could do together. I missed spending time together, with just the two of us alone.

Write down what you really want. You'll find that each of your desires comes with a certain expectation. I wanted intimacy and connection with my husband, I wanted to feel loved, and I expected that love and connection to look a certain way: like a romantic Date Night. But that isn't how my husband expresses his love for me. Putting your efforts into a written plan will help you recognize this.

When I expressed what I really wanted — that I missed our time alone together and wanted to reconnect — Aubrey understood completely and expressed that he felt the same way. But he still wasn't responsible for making all the arrangements. We put all our cards on the table and discovered that our lack of connection was directly related to miscommunication. We needed to express to each other what end results we were hoping for and skip the expectations.

I now understand that when I need to spend time with Aubrey, to reconnect again as a couple and I start picturing a date night — then I need to plan that date, *not him!* And here's a fascinating idea — connection can happen right here in our home. You don't have to leave your house or spend lots of money to connect with your loved ones. 2020 was good for something! My actions needed to change so that I got the desired results.

When you discover what you really want, you can consider what unfair expectations you've been placing on those desires, and how you may have failed to communicate your needs. When I was unhappy and complaining to Aubrey how we never go out, he responded exactly as he should have: with avoidance. I don't believe my husband went out of his way to ignore my requests, but I do know that I created a situation of fear that whatever he planned wouldn't be good enough. I made it clear that I wasn't satisfied, and I placed unfair expectations on the man that I love.

Now, communication works for those who work at it.

And planning works for those who put their wishes down on paper with the intention to implement it.

If your messages aren't being received by the intended recipient, there's got to be a reason why. I give you permission to halt the energy you are wasting this way. Instead, shift your energy and expectations, get out the paper and pencil, and you'll get better results.

One of the best books I've read about relationships is *The Dance of Anger: A Woman's Guide to Changing the Pattern of Intimate Relationships* (2014) by Harriet Lerner. She has a great way of helping me remember why I love Aubrey and why I picked him over a decade ago. He shows his love in quiet ways, he's funny, he's kind, and he's incredibly smart. Ultimately, he has always taken care of me, and he knows what I need without me saying it. During the years where I found myself dissatisfied with his behavior, I was only making it harder for him to follow through on what I needed.

If you are experiencing dissatisfaction in your marital relationship, ask yourself why you picked your spouse in the first place. The way they express their love will become clear. Then be willing to walk a mile in their shoes. You have to get their perspective on how things are going. Ask questions of your spouse or partner that aren't intrusive or combative.

When it comes to plugging this all into a plan, please don't think I mean a plan with a detailed calendar. Your plan can be as easy as holding hands when you talk, sending fun texts, or reminding yourself to count your blessings when things get tough.

I began my plan by asking Aubrey questions like, "How is work going?" and "What do you like about your new game?" The trick to gaining real insight from another person is to ask without the intention of adding new information or even responding. This exercise is designed to get you into the habit of asking questions with the intention of only listening. Ask your person at least three questions with intent to listen. Give them your undivided attention, and respond only with short responses like, "Okay."

Take a moment to pause and write down what your three questions will be. Get creative.

The more questions you ask, the more information you'll gather about what they're thinking or how they're feeling. By not responding with your own information, you focus on gaining a comprehensive idea of how they are doing. Don't fool yourself: You aren't doing this with a complete stranger. You know them well, but putting yourself in their shoes reminds you that they aren't your possession. What did they answer that you agreed with? How were you reminded of your love for them?

Keeping together, as a couple, is a process. When I would whine and complain, I only drove a deeper wedge between Aubrey and myself, created more negative feelings, a bad example for my daughters and, you guessed it, no Date Nights. When I gained insight on how my husband was actually doing, I could gauge how he was feeling and be more patient with him. Little did I know that changing my plan was actually changing my behavior and the time that we did spend together!

Communication makes a strong team, but it starts and ends with you.

Over time, asking my husband questions and listening intently to his answers, I realized how involved he is with our kids. He found time for each of them, even though he was stressed at work and often wanted to come home to play games as a means of relaxing. He wasn't checked out; he knew exactly what was happening around the house, but he needed to relax without his wife demanding those Date Nights. I know now that, when I'm stressed, my standards get raised disproportionately. But when I reconnect with myself and ask for help when needed, Aubrey shows up for me.

What events in your life have been stressful enough for your behavior to change? How can you relax your standards or expectations in order to feel more aligned and focused? What are the most important areas that really need your attention?

Write them down in your personal plan for change.

Do Aubrey and I now go out on date nights every week? No, we don't, and we don't need to! Our ability to connect no matter what's going on is strong. We go out when we're both seeking fun together. And if one person initiates it, they make the plans, and it happens. There's no passive-aggressive beating-around-the-bush with feelings or getting mad when Date Night doesn't happen. And best of all, I know that when I want different results in any area of my life, I know exactly how to behave to make it happen.

I'd like to show you how my personal behavior changed by taking accountability with my actions. I will plug this scenario into The Accountability Code. Please know that your answers will be different, but the process is foolproof (if you need help plugging your answers in, please, let's connect and chat about your situation):

Reflection — When I think about what I am missing, I realize I have unrealistic expectations. Aubrey and I have always connected in personal ways and intimate ways. Why was I expecting that Date Nights would magically change my life forever? I just want to be intimate and obsessed with my husband again.

Humility – I am not making it easy for him. Planning dates is hard work! That is exactly why I don't do it consistently. I should cut him some slack, because I wouldn't want to go on a date with me, either, right now (chuckle).

Planning – I will change the way I interact with Aubrey. I will connect with him now instead of demanding it be on a date. My plan is to practice listening, showing interest, and increasing my physical touch with him.

Implementing – Go into a conversation with the goal to succeed with my plan. Talk for the sake of talking. Engage for the sake of being a good companion.

Commitment – I picked up and reviewed one of my favorite books on relationships. Not only was I engaging in self-improvement, but it allowed me to change with a clear perspective. I valued connection with my husband more than fulfilling unrealistic expectations.

Feedback – Happiness! You know how nice it is not to be annoyed by your husband every time you look at him? Did he change dramatically? No. Did I? Yes! It's just a matter of repeating the process to stay self-aware and growing.

The only way I want you to become a broken record is by repeating the process of The Accountability Code. I promise that using this system will help you find the gaps in your good habits. I am here for you!

From Pain to Plan

Life is full of warning signs. We only see them, however, if we slow down and look for them.

During my honeymoon at Seal Beach in Southern California, my husband and I were excited to swim in the ocean for the first time. We were especially looking forward to seeing the sunsets, which are supposed to be beautiful there. So we headed to the beach just before the sun was due to set so we could swim a little before watching the sky glow.

I knew the ocean could be dangerous, especially if you swim out too far, and I found a depth that felt comfortable for me. The salt water was a new experience, but I wanted to avoid getting it in my eyes and mouth, so I decided to enjoy my time in the ocean with my head above water, jumping up and down with the waves.

Suddenly, I felt a stabbing pain on the side of my foot, and I thought I had been pinched by a massive crab. I yelled out to Aubrey, already feeling my body go into shock, and he carried me out of the water and onto the beach. I looked down and saw blood pouring out of my foot.

I was panicked, Aubrey was panicked, and we didn't know what to do. I know what you're thinking — have him pee on it! Luckily, neither of us had heard that jellyfish stings can be minimized by peeing on them, because I would have been traumatized, getting peed on by my husband of only three days on a beach full of other people! Plus this wasn't a jellyfish wound.

Aubrey had the sense to call out for help and soon, a crowd surrounded us. One man suggested putting alcohol on my foot and asked me what kind of booze I preferred. A woman accused me of being dramatic in hopes of getting a hot lifeguard to take care of me. But she's also the one who suggested it was probably a stingray wound. I was confused. If I hadn't seen what did this to me, how could anyone else know?

Turns out, stingrays are extremely common at Seal Beach, and the locals are used to that familiar screech when someone gets stung. Just that moment, a lifeguard was making their last round of checks before sunset and found us. I was transported by truck to the nearby medical station. While Aubrey filled out paperwork, the lifeguard put me in a chair near a waterspout and placed a bucket beside me. He started putting warm water in the bucket, then my foot, and then incrementally adding hotter and hotter water to increase the temperature.

The lifeguard told me to breathe and ordered me to stay in the chair. Then he walked across the room and grabbed a small bottle and brought it over to show me. It was a specimen bottle with a stingray barb inside. The barb was three inches long and looked like a knife with very sharp teeth on both sides. When a stingray barb punctures the skin, the teeth break off and release venom.

The treatment to dissolve venom, the lifeguard told me, is hot water up to 115 degrees or as hot as the person can handle. I felt that I was dying! He kept pouring more hot water in to draw out the venom, which looked like clear jelly in the water. He told me, "Tell me if it gets too hot," and I immediately shot back, "IT'S TOO HOT!" and he patiently told me that it needed to be hot to stop the infection from going up my leg.

I said, "Well, quit asking me if it's too hot, then!"

The lifeguard then told me about something called the stingray shuffle. Stingrays aren't aggressive by nature, but when they are stepped on, they will attack. I caused this attack, apparently by jumping up and down in the waves and on top of a stingray. I grew up in Utah. We don't have stingrays or oceans in Utah, since it's landlocked, so the stingray shuffle was not a concept I was familiar with. I thought the danger was drowning or getting salt water in my eyes. I had no idea the real threat lay under the surface of the water.

This brings me to the step in The Accountability Code of Planning. We must understand that we don't know what we don't know.

We are often worried about the obvious threats in life – the ones that are right in front of our faces. We don't realize that what can hurt us the most are often the issues and problems we don't see.
Once the lifeguard had sufficiently drawn enough venom out through the hot water bucket process, I was able to leave. But now, I had a burned foot and was unable to walk. Aubrey and I soon departed to the next leg of our trip, with me hopping on one leg the whole time.

When I returned home, the medical staff in Utah had no idea how to treat stingray wounds. Again, we don't have stingrays in Utah! I was a newlywed with no health insurance, trying to care for a wounded foot, and frankly treated rather dismissively by the staff at the care center.

But after slowly recovering from my wound, I remembered something: There had been a warning sign, on the beach, about stingrays. I barely paid attention to that sign because I didn't think it applied to me. Surely that happens to other people. I had a sunset to catch on my honeymoon. Instead, I got a painful lesson in paying attention.

We can't take everything at face value. There are warning signs, some of which we need to pay heed to. The best way to do that is to give ourselves adequate time to observe, check in with trusted sources, and listen carefully to our intuition. After gathering necessary data, we can make an adequate plan. Something in me that day told me to be careful in the ocean. I was just worried about the wrong things.

I still have tenderness on the foot that was stung. The right side is still tender, and I don't take the use of it for granted. I protect my feet at all costs. I buy shoes that support them, and I look around carefully anytime I'm in the water. I have even found myself using the stingray shuffle just in case.

Look back closely at your past regrets and negative experiences. Were there warning signs that you missed or ignored? Did you even have a plan in place? In the moment, we are too filled with emotion, but after things have calmed down, we can usually remember something that told us to be cautious, to be aware. Looking at it from another perspective, I also see that Aubrey and I were so focused on getting to the beach in time to watch the sunset that we missed what we needed to see.

But would I change the experience altogether? Would I miss out on my honeymoon, that sunset, this crazy story I can tell for the rest of my life, just to skip jumping on a stingray? Probably not.

What are you willing to do even if it risks injury or hardship? We can be cautious in life, but we cannot keep ourselves and those we love 100% safe.

Every challenge presents a blessing. What are some of the worst decisions you have made that led to surprisingly positive outcomes? How can you open your awareness to learn from your mistakes and become accountable to finding the good in even the worst experiences? How might you better protect yourself, knowing what the full risks might be?

Much of life is about making mistakes and learning from them, and then avoiding the mistakes the next time. The better lesson is to slow down and look for the warning signs ALL the time. They are there if we know to look for them, to spot them, and to pay attention to them.

Today, when I go to ocean beaches with my daughters or others, I always tell them about my foot and the stingray shuffle. I use that painful experience as a warning sign to others. I can't force them to pay attention, but at least I can try.

I remember being really agitated, that night at Seal Beach, by the woman who accused me of trying to attract a hot lifeguard. I mean, I was a *newlywed* — I only had eyes for my husband! But she was also the person who helped me understand what had happened to me. Helpers are everywhere, and they don't always look or seem the way you might expect. Meanwhile, the doctor in Utah who prescribed my treatment didn't take my injury seriously, and it took much longer to heal as a result.

I left the doctor's office feeling frustrated by the level of care I had received, but I was determined to find a healing process that would work for me. Thankfully, I no longer had venom in my foot, and I knew I could recover from the burn. But it took time to gain full use of my foot again. Aubrey was by my side, praying for me and helping me. I followed the process and left the rest in God's hands.

How is your healing process supported by others? How will your planning prevent massive pain in your learning?

I'm grateful that I had the experience of being stung by a stingray. I recovered, gained new insight, and had a cool story to tell others. I can be a witness to the power of healing and share that wisdom with others.

You are not defined by what happens to you, but you do have a message to share with others about your journey. Can you turn your trauma into a success story? Maybe your experience will help someone else be stronger or wiser. Perhaps you can be a warning sign for others. Either way, having a plan to use it for the better is crucial to becoming accountable to growth.

Choose Your Struggles

What if you could choose your struggles before they choose you? What if you could plan what your struggles would be, or even plan to avoid them altogether?

Humans are no strangers to opposition and hardship. Working to pair your mind and body can be challenging and learning to master self-accountability takes a lot of work.

We are each born with both our own individual light, and the darkness and deliberate opposition that is part of human nature. Unfortunately, we aren't just battling the unseen forces of evil that are a natural part of life. We are also battling ourselves, the human part of ourselves, including our bodies.

What you may not realize is that the choices you make determine what sort of opposition you are going to face.

I chose to get married young, at 18, so I'm going to have a lot of marital conflicts. That means that I don't have the same issues as someone who is single or who is older.

I choose to go to the gym, to use equipment to improve my fitness. Someone who doesn't go to the gym has to decide, instead, how they will move their body to get similar results.

I chose to start my own business. I will spend a lot of time determining my plans and goals. I will have different struggles professionally than someone who clocks into a 9-to-5 job. I have faced different challenges, working from sunup to sundown, trying to understand new concepts about business that I would need to embrace.

I also chose to participate in Ace in the Hole, a reality tv show. With that, I have different struggles than someone who doesn't put themselves out there in tv land.

No matter what you choose to do in life, the challenge is to put yourself in a position to make more beneficial decisions and to reap better consequences and greater rewards.

Here is another example: I live in a house with a husband and four kids. Chores have to get done. I can either choose to do them all, or I can empower and teach my family to help. If I choose to have everyone participate, then I must decide whether to force them to take certain tasks, or will I reward them for volunteering? Either way, the chores have to get done, and I have to spend a certain amount of energy deciding which path I'll choose.

If I'm working on having a better relationship with my husband, I can decide where we go on Date Nights and make the plans rather than having another wasted conversation about how he never takes me out. Focus on the kind of problems you want to have.

You can choose your struggles. Don't let your struggles choose you.
A couple years ago, I got concerned about money because I worried that our

existing retirement plan was insufficient. As small business owners, we've struggled with getting adequate health care, and this led me to make some changes to where our money was being spent. So instead of waiting for money problems to find me, I decided that a more worthwhile struggle was taking the time to learn how to budget and invest wisely, in order to grow my retirement savings. It took a lot of time, and lots of discussions with Aubrey, but it ultimately led us to focus more on the money we had rather than what we had not yet earned.

When you approach the important decisions in life from a place of peace instead of stress or despair, you'll find your struggles aren't as big as you thought they were.

Here is how you can choose your struggles before they choose you. Get out a paper and pencil because it's time to plan!

What blessings are you most grateful for at this time in your life? Do you have your health and a bit of spare time to play? Does your family live nearby, or do they support you from a phone call away? Count those as blessings, and then **consider how you might improve your situation before your situation doesn't exist anymore**.

Great relationships are not guaranteed. Retirement isn't a sure thing. If there is something good in your life that needs to be reinforced, this is a great time to do that.

During college, I took a class called Fit for Life, and my professor constantly emphasized the idea of creating a healthy lifestyle regardless of our current health condition. One thing he recommended to stay fit was to always park at the back of the parking lot, no matter where you're going. He reminded us that some people don't have the luxury of walking that extra distance and that we could practice gratitude for our blessings while getting extra exercise. It's a great example of pairing our blessings with healthy habits.

Good family relationships are great starting points for making healthy decisions. If you and a loved one have similar goals to get fit, plan gatherings together that include healthy meals, walks together, or sharing resources that help you improve your perspective. How can you strengthen your relationships and health at the same time?

Remember that the basics of health are always free: sleep, self-care, water intake, and movement. Don't take any of them for granted! Evaluate how you can level up on these basics to improve your overall life. And don't just count your blessings — be a blessing to others.

Define one healthy habit you'd like to master. What choices would you make after that habit is firmly in place? Do you have the power to make those choices right now?

When your health is on autopilot, you will be free to do what you really want. When we treat our bodies well, we find joy in other areas of our lives. Our bodies are tangible evidence of our plans and of our successful execution of those plans.

If your health is good, take advantage and pursue progress in other areas of your life. I am a firm believer in working hard when things are good so that you can take a break when you need to.

If your health is currently in tip-top shape, what choices would you make right now? What is stopping you from taking action on that now, even if your health isn't perfect?

Many of my clients want to get in shape so they can keep up with their children and grandchildren. The best part of this goal is that the desire is there, fed by the desire to spend even more time with their loved ones. Could you make this choice now?

This shouldn't be stressful. Examine the choices you are making now, and implement a plan to minimize your problems before they begin. Making choices ahead of time is exactly what planning is, and it can reduce a lot of misery. After hundreds of nights hearing my kids ask, "What's for dinner?" I decided to hand that question back over to them once a week when we prep for the week. I let each of the kids choose a meal option, and I just order the groceries from my phone.

Talk about a stress reducer! The kids were sick of asking me that question, and I was sick of answering it, so I found another solution and planned ahead. What process can you clean up so that you reduce the choices that take up too much of your time
and energy?

Once the dinner problem was solved, I then moved on to dealing with the morning routine. It takes four girls a lot of time to get up and get ready for school. There were too many options, for instance, of what to wear. I made a life-changing decision. I chose to not care what my kids wore to school. Mismatched socks — who cares? A hoodie over a dress with boots — so what?! It really doesn't matter. What have you been wasting time over lately, and what can you let go? Yes, I literally planned not to care about
such things.

My best advice to you in choosing your struggles before they choose you is to plan for what you want and make a plan to avoid what you don't want. Too many problems arise from far too many choices.

You will continue to face opposition and hardship even as you pair your mind and body, but you can 100 percent use The Accountability Code to help choose your struggles and to create new habits.

Plan for Growth

As a child I found joy in making a name for myself. My dad was a people person, and my mother was a service-oriented planner. With these major strengths in our household our family was extremely outgoing and dynamic.

The Accountability Code has the versatility to help you plan and design your life based on your strengths, desires, and goals. Keep in mind that all you are right now is an accumulation of what you've been taught, what you've been through, and how you are currently showing up.

Using your natural strengths from how you were raised will give you a strategic advantage during the planning step of The Accountability Code. Let me tell you about how my childhood helped me determine the perfect plan for me.

As one of eight children, my siblings and I were often split up into two groups: the big kids and the little kids. As the sixth child, I was in the second group but often took on leadership roles among my siblings. This is partially because my sweet sister who is just 15 months older than me (and technically the older of the last four) is very quiet and relaxed and I'm — well, I'm *not*!

My next sister (just two years younger than me) seemed to copy everything I did and, as a result, I was constantly on the lookout to be different or to move on to the next achievement while she may have been catching up. I moved out of the house at eighteen and was the second child (out of 8) to be married. I then supplied my parents with more than half of their grandkids in a few years.

My siblings went on to be amazing stewards of all we were given. They are entrepreneurial, and between all eight of us we've been involved in dozens of businesses. It was common for multiple kids in the household hustling to sell something. My ability to get out of my comfort zone was evident, but I wasn't so enthused about continuing my education, so I never considered college.

It was my mother-in-law who encouraged me to continue my education and get a degree, and it was my husband who inspired me to start my business. Yet even then, my ambition was small — I wanted to train clients and help them improve their health and contribute to the household. I had a small local fitness studio and was satisfied with the results.

It wasn't until 2015 when, after receiving additional credits to recertify for group fitness, that Aubrey said to me, "You need to provide personal training to people on the Internet." I was quick to tell him how stupid that idea was because that took the 'personal' out of 'personal training.' But Aubrey is persuasive, and he showed me examples of how I could use his tech skills and really thrive with a larger clientele. So I decided to give it a try. I created a class for people to lose baby weight (as I had), and Aubrey designed an online platform where I could hold my clients accountable, no matter how far away they lived. Within the first year, my challenges hit just about every state in the country, and my business was, indeed, growing.

As I donned the title of entrepreneur, I became even more grateful for the ways I was raised. There were certain strengths instilled in me, and my childhood gave me a lot of confidence to go out and make a difference in the world.

Just by recalling memorable parts of my childhood I can see that I grew in different areas; leadership, speaking up, taking charge, following through, being helpful, and putting myself out there. These qualities are going to be very useful as I move forward if I remember they are gifts that need to be used.

How did I get to a point of understanding who I am and what my purpose is? I recognize that I am the only person just like me. I have the power to take every experience and create my own version of it. I used this understanding in conjunction with the process of The Accountability Code to get clear on what I really wanted in life, and you can do the same thing.

My hope is that through this process you'll be able to appreciate what you have been given, use what you have, and dig deep into what that means for your purpose and
your life.

Here is an exercise that will help you take a trip down memory lane to remind yourself of the talents you were born with, the skills you've developed, and how to keep running forward with fire. This is strategic planning in action.

I learned as a child to invite people in and treat them like family. Now, as an adult, I go out of my comfort zone to make sure people feel included because I was shown how to do that as a child.

What skills and positive traits have you had since you were a child? How have those attributes from your early experiences carried into your adult life?

If you are not sure what your natural strengths are, ask your family or close friends. They will have answers for you that will remind you of your gifts. Take a moment to list them now.

When I was younger, my sister Karlee and I ran the town! We were really good at including others in our activities. Now that we are older, we still have a talent for inviting people in and creating a fun environment for them. How have your gifts developed as you've gotten older?

Using your gifts will keep you in alignment as you deal with struggles. My ability to reach out to others is the same skill that allows me to ask for help when needed. As I tuned in to my emotions during uncertain times, I was constantly nudged to include others in my growth. Describe on paper how you feel when you share your talents
and gifts.

When I got married, I was exposed to different definitions of success. How have you adapted in order to follow your own path while honoring where you came from? How have your gifts been revealed as you challenge yourself?

Looking back, I realize that not having goals beyond getting married and having kids gave me an open slate to do and become much more than that. Graduating college and starting a business were not only bonuses, but much more. My goals continue to shift as my children grow up and eventually leave home, my business expands, and Aubrey magnifies his passions, too. How have your gifts morphed into more than you thought they would?

I had no idea that pursuing a business would help me change as many lives as I have. Each time I get a "Thank You" card or message from a client, I am reminded of the importance of developing and using my strengths. What great things have come from you using your gifts and following your passion? What magnificent path is unfolding before you as you take each step forward? Write it all down.

In order to be reminded of the good things in life, I must utilize what I learned early on as well as the skills I've developed as an adult. Getting out and talking to friends or complete strangers keeps my natural outgoing abilities sharpened and enables me to feel like my most authentic self. What actions put you in a state of remembrance of who you are? How are you feeding your gifts in order to grow them? Write it down.

My ability to include and connect with others is possible only because I have trained myself to get out of my comfort zone, put on a smile, extend my hand, and say, "Hi, I'm Marci. Tell me your name." That physical action is something I had to practice as I developed my gift. I actively plan to be that way because I know it brings goodness. I also enjoy starting conversations and helping people relax.

How will you practice going through the physical actions that magnify *your* skills? How can planning to be that way enhance your accountability to be true to yourself?

Give yourself credit for growing. It's one thing to know what to do — it's another to put it into physical form. Remember that accountability means to execute an expected outcome. As you train yourself to act, remind yourself how good it feels to act in alignment with who you truly are. Affirm that living true to who you are creates happiness, and that the impact you have on others is a positive one.

I know you have been given great talents. Now I want you to prove it. Plug your strengths and passion into The Accountability Code and put extra emphasis on the Planning step. If you plan how you would like to act, then doing the action becomes that much easier.

Here is an example of using The Accountability Code to magnify my natural strengths and how putting an emphasis on the planning stage is beneficial for success:

Reflection — My strengths are evident through my extroverted tendencies. I grow closer to others when I reach out. I am happy when new connections are gained and existing connections are strengthened. I want more of that in my life and I see opportunities to connect every single day.

Humility — I have a purpose in reaching out and I am grateful to God for the desire to connect with others. I know that as I practice getting out of my comfort zone I will be blessed with deeper connections with family and friends. I must use my talents to honor God as best as I can.

Planning — In order for me to connect more often, more intentionally, and on a deeper level I must recognize how it's worked for me in the past and what opportunities I have to connect with others and create more growth within me.

accountability thus ensuring success in other parts of my life.

Feedback — Looking back on that experience and planning for growth inspires me to be open about what can happen if I listen. If it weren't for this exercise of using The Accountability Code and focusing on the planning step I might forget how beneficial my natural strengths are to becoming the next best version of me. I usually find that my efforts have a positive impact on others too.

Planned Productivity

My ability to take a goal and break it down into actionable steps has proven to be one of my greatest skills as a life and fitness expert. Without planned productivity, execution can be daunting and misguided. Breaking goals down helps clear the pathway. They become easier to implement, and you can succeed faster.

So let's talk about setting up a successful plan.

Imagine you are standing on the bank of a river. You need to get to the other side without falling in and going down the river with your pack full of precious cargo. You see a large amount of rock piled nearby that you can use, but you cannot hold all your stuff while preparing to cross. You have to set the pack down in order to begin your prep work.

You test the waters and see that they're not too deep. You check the rocks to find the ones that are smooth and flat without being slick with moss. You eyeball the river to see how far across it appears, and you pick up two of the rocks. You will need to put each of the rocks in place, while remaining steady on your feet.

You walk to the edge of the river and place the first rock in. Now you have to decide how far apart the next rock will be. Do you place them closely together, which will require more time but allow for a safer path, or do you place them at a wider distance, allowing you to complete the path quicker? You want to cross this river as quickly as possible, and you notice that the sun is beginning to set. Time is of the essence.

But you decide to place the rocks at your natural walking pace, knowing that it will provide the surest and safest passage across the river. You go back and grab two more rocks, and place them at a natural distance, and you go back and grab two more. You know that you will complete the path and make it across the river just in time before darkness comes. But what you carry in your pack is precious, and you don't want to risk losing it. You want to make it to your final destination safely even if you have to camp overnight before continuing your journey.

Finally, as you complete the pathway, you put your backpack on again and easily walk across each stone with ease. Not only were you able to pass successfully, but that path is now available to others, and you have the knowledge to cross the next river you come upon.

While it may not seem like it, this is the exact process of implementing a solid plan.

By taking a step back with intention, you have the ability to put the correct stepping stones in place so that your day goes more smoothly and according to your plan. The trick to putting a speed tip in place is incredibly easy. Let me teach you how:

- First, make a list of the three things you need to complete tomorrow. My daily list includes a workout, client check-ins, and time with Aubrey.

- Second, for each task, reinforce your desire to get it done. Acknowledge why it's important.
    * *Workout: I need to keep my body adaptable, and it's fun to move!*
    * *Client Check-ins: I need to deliver on my work.*
    * *Time with Aubrey: Grow together, give and receive support.*

- Take a deep breath and write your intention for each of your three goals.

    When you identify the intention, you increase your commitment to succeed.

- Fourth, decide in which order you will complete each of your three tasks.

    I do my client check-ins first thing in the morning, so they get the feedback needed to start their day. I spend time with Aubrey in the middle of the day because the kids are in school, and he is least busy then. And I do my workouts in the evening so I can attend scheduled classes.

    What order makes sense for your tasks?

Write down your plans! A goal not written is only a wish. Reviewing your plan gives you time to adjust anything you might need to modify.

My check-ins happen every day, I like to remind Aubrey that I would like to spend time with him, and I'll double-check what time my evening classes are. Familiarize yourself with your plans the night before. When you see each piece of the path, your speed can increase while maintaining accuracy.

It does not matter so much what you think about — what matters is what you do.

To fulfil your plans, you have to move your body through physical actions that bring your plans to pass. What does your physical body need to prepare so your intentions will be a success?

I set my exercise clothes out the night before, and I leave my client check-in page up on the monitor before putting my computer to sleep. Lastly, to spend intentional time with Aubrey, I remind myself to step away from the desk and get close to him. What physical actions do you need to complete to see success with your goals?

In your written plans, think about creating the environment that will make you successful in your actions. I can do my client check-ins seamlessly when I sit at my laptop instead of using my phone, I make sure I have a clean space to be with Aubrey so I'm not tempted to tidy up while talking to him, and I will wash a load of laundry if I want specific clothes for my workout the next day. I also set my alarm to make sure I leave the house on time for class. What physical actions can you take now to make tomorrow better?

You might be thinking, 'How am I supposed to prepare for tomorrow when I'm already busy with today?' There are times when a super busy day means cutting your losses for the next day. It's okay to give yourself time to regroup when you're overwhelmed. This is why weekends are so great! Take a deep breath and say, "I am free to start with a clean slate."

If you have tasks that hinder you from taking care of the most important things, put them on your To-Don't list. If someone asks you to do something you don't feel called to, or if it prevents you from your most important things, consider saying, 'That task will go on my To-Don't list.' The key to failure is trying to do it all to please everyone. Instead, take a deep breath and say, "I honor my time and priorities."

Review your productivity on the days when you tackle your written plans versus those days with no plan set up. No plan means no goal, no direction, misguided action, and certainly no accountability. And when I take the time to prepare my tasks ahead of time, I am practicing integrity of accountability.

You'll notice quite a few benefits from planning your day ahead of time. Acting in accordance with your values reiterates your ability to live your true purpose. Each day you work on this plan — whether it's writing your tasks down, preparing for them, or executing them — take a deep breath and say, "I am living in integrity to my Accountability Code." I doubt during your planning session, you'll write 'waste 2 hours scrolling through social media.'

You'll still have people demanding that you conform to them, and you might have obligations that pop up unexpectedly, but overall, your self-awareness and ability to accomplish your plan will increase by planning ahead. Take a moment to list the benefits of your new plan.

Focus on the physical actions that go with each of your tasks.

We can think about tomorrow all day, but we truly don't know what's going to happen. So each day, return to the intention of doing your best. You should never feel bad for doing your best and planning for success. Focus on the basics of sleep, self-care, water, and movement — they will always put you in the best position to be ready for whatever tomorrow brings.

Take a deep breath and say, 'I enjoy the basics because they keep me healthy.' They also keep you in the here and now, which is the secret of a fulfilled life and mastering The Accountability Code.

Chapter 4 - Implementing

Implementing — Putting into use your desired skills or values

Nothing gives me more excitement than taking action!

Someone once asked me, "When you aren't working or spending time with your family, what are you doing?" I instantly replied, "I am walking around my neighborhood, looking for opportunities to serve, and it's a bonus if someone is moving in or out so I get to lift heavy things." I have been blessed with a desire to exercise my body, and it has become the means of taking me to places that have helped me grow as a person. Sure, we can learn from sitting behind our computers and staying in our homes, but that doesn't change the fact that our bodies were made to benefit from action and movement.

The Accountability Code is all about taking the right actions that pair your mind and body. I wouldn't have been able to write a whole book about it unless I knew without a doubt that using your body to fulfill your deepest desires is what will bring us the most happiness in life.

Implementing means the act of putting into use your desired skills or values. Let me give you a simple example on how to use The Accountability Code, thus far.

I am a mom of four daughters, and any family knows just how important chores are. At our home, we call them contributions because every member of the family is taught, and is expected, to help out and contribute around the house. I am not a maid, and I refuse to teach my children that I am. As I apply The Accountability Code, I will show you the simple steps I took to prepare and implement my plan:

A. Reflection — Evidence in my home reflects that something needs to be done. Clothes get left on the floor, dishes on the table, and it seems no one can find what they are looking for in the morning.

The desire to spend time together or to make a meal in the kitchen goes away when it's a mess. So giving serious thought and consideration, reflection, on this fact helped me see that things needed to change. Hardly anyone is happy when the house gets too messy.

B. Humility — We are blessed to have an abundance of space if our home. Each of my girls have their own rooms, my husband and I have our own separate offices, and we don't feel cramped. We have an abundance of things, including dishes, shoes, clothing, technology, and supplies for hobbies.

God has given us so many things that bless our lives, but why? What good is all of this stuff if we allow it to become a source of contention in our lives? What happens when we fail to remember the purpose of each possession? We know that we can do better with what we have, and, to prove that we are grateful, we must treat our things and time differently, with respect.

C. Planning — The plan is to bring the problem to the family's attention and decide what to do about it.

Everyone agrees that mom isn't a maid, that it's not fair for one person to do it all, and that we'd rather not spend all our time looking for things or kicking them around. We decided which tasks were necessary for happiness, harmony, and productivity in the home, and so we rotate who takes care of each task.

We call this family plan of ours, 'Rotations.'

In addition to setting up fair expectations, we wrote out our plan on a white board in the family room where everyone can easily see it every day.

D. Implementing — For each day of every week, every rotation is written up on the board, along with each person's name. The chart on the board makes very clear what each person is responsible for, what to plan for, and how to make the tasks easier.

Each rotation is given a clear gem magnet to indicate who the rotation belongs to, and each time that person completes the rotation, a colored gem is there to indicate it is completed and passed to the next person.

Taking action is necessary and clear because our plan is clear, plain and out in the open.

Here's how to implement your plan effectively:

1. Make S.M.A.R.T. Goals.

'SMART' stands for Specific, Measureable, Attainable, Realistic, and Time bound. If you take your plan through each of these steps, you'll create an accurate goal that sets you up for success:

Specific — House needs to be kept up and cleaned every day.

Measurable — Things are in their assigned place and ready to serve their purpose.

Attainable — Rotations are split up into small enough chunks to make them quick to do.

Realistic — Some rotations are easier for the big kids, and that is why mom and dad are available to help any child who asks for help and is willing to clean together.

Time bound — When the time comes for a child to ask if they can do something fun with friends, my answer is the same as the answer to the question, "Are your rotations done?" Always be ready to answer, not only because it opens up opportunity, but because it makes us happy.

When you make SMART goals, the outcome is clear and your success increases. When you don't make SMART goals, you'll find multiple ways to fail and, sadly, you'll be working on the same goal for way too long, without real results.

2. Check your intentions.

Doing something for the right reason is better than forcing yourself to do it.

I have learned what it feels like to force my kids to do chores (contributions), and that is why we changed the intention to 'rotations,' focusing on everyone helping out.

Also, when we focus on being grateful for what we have instead of what we have to sacrifice, we are much happier. My main purpose for doing rotations is to teach my daughters responsibility and to protect my own energy. So check the intentions of your plan, and match up your action steps with what makes you feel good.

When you check on your intentions, it's easier to include others, and it improves your resolve to stay committed. When you don't, you'll find yourself getting irritated during the process and focused only on the outcome, instead of the benefits of the journey.

3. Required outcomes or proof of production.

The colored gems on our board make it easier to see which rotations have been completed, and they also serve as an indication of success, not only for the family, but for that individual person. When my child does a rotation, we have gotten in the habit of checking it off and clearly letting the next person know that it's their turn next.

When the outcome is clear and can be proven, it serves as valuable feedback for implementing the next time.

One time my mother-in-law came over and, displeased with the condition of our family room, asked me, "Marci, do you need help cleaning your house?" I happily and anxiously walked her over to our rotation board. I followed my finger across the family room row until the clear gem indicated the rotation belonged to Aubrey. With a smile on my face, I told her, "This rotation is currently Aubrey's responsibility. You can ask your son if he'd like your help cleaning the family room." It made me laugh when she responded, "Oh, you're rude!"

You can see my current rotation board here:

When you have required outcomes or proof of production, you can celebrate your success along the way and happily relieve yourself from expectations that aren't yours. When you don't, you'll find it difficult to stick to a plan that doesn't seem to be working.

Reasons for resistance to Implementing —

1. Time inconsistency

"Time inconsistency refers to the tendency of the human brain to value immediate rewards more highly than future rewards." – James Clear (bestselling author)

The disconnect with following through happens when you set a goal for your future self, and not for who you are right now. The brain is trained to make immediate decisions for ourselves right now while the happy-go-lucky self tends to plan for the future. When it comes to implementing a plan, find a reason that you would benefit from right now. It can be happiness, clarity, self-mastery, or learning discipline.

In order to beat this resistance, practice calling out your successes as often as possible. With rotations, I have taught my kids to look around a newly cleaned room, take a deep breath, and say, "I did a good job!" Sometimes they feel it's a little kooky, but having that quick reward helps you see the goal in the long term plan, too.

2. Fulfilling others' expectations

If your heart isn't in it for the right reason, your motivation to complete the task is lessened. If I only wanted to have my house clean to impress my mother-in-law, I'd constantly be awaiting a reward from someone who should not control my life. Get to the bottom of WHY this plan is important. WHY will it benefit you now and in the future. If you can't think of a deep enough reason to follow through, then chances are it's not in alignment with your real reason — or else you're out there to impress someone who really doesn't care.

In order to beat this resistance, take the first three steps of The Accountability Code seriously. Revisit Reflection, Humility, and Planning in order to implement actions that are more in line with who you are and what you want. If it was up to my mother-in-law, I would follow my husband and children around, cleaning up after them all day long.

3. You want the outcome more than the skill.

Many times in our execution of tasks, we fail to recognize that the journey is just as, if not more, important as the outcome. No outcome or another day on this earth is guaranteed, but today, right now, is. What skills are you developing in pursuit of your goal? I am practicing letting expectations go, teaching my children how to take care of their belongings, and ask for help when needed. We are learning to take care of our own dishes and clothing in an effort to maintain a clean space.

In order to beat this resistance, focus on what habits are actually going to bring you the outcome you desire. It will make implementing so much easier because the skill is obtainable now, while the outcome is an accumulation of skills.

Now that you have a deliberate plan in place and are working on putting it into action, it's time to commit, which includes your commitment to adjusting.

Freedom

Let me tell you right now — I am not willing to give up pizza!

There are a lot of nutrition trends in the fitness industry. Seems like new ones pop up every week. When I first embarked on my own fitness journey, I was confused. The one thing I knew was that I was opposed to 'diets.'

I grew up believing that I could eat anything I wanted, because I burned it off through exercise and activity. That's actually a poor mindset, because it takes much longer to burn off calorie-dense foods, yet for me it worked — until it didn't. That was after having kids. I realistically knew it took nine months each time to put on the baby weight, and it would take nine months to take it off. Those were exactly the results I got with my first pregnancy. I was teaching fitness classes while I was losing the weight and felt satisfied that I was on the right path.

Then, with my next baby, I magically lost all the baby weight in ten days! Come to find out, I had gallbladder problems and wound up in the hospital. The doctors helped me understand that you can't just put anything in your body and hope to work it off. I needed to learn how to eat nutritionally to fuel my body — no matter what!

I had to give up fatty foods, which was difficult. My favorites at the time were hot dogs, cheese, and milk. I succeeded in conquering my problematic eating habits. And then came my third baby. I was again very busy, student teaching, dining out all the time for lunch, and after I delivered, I found I just couldn't lose the weight, no matter how much I exercised!

So I enlisted the help of a trainer at the gym where I taught fitness classes and worked out, and she gave me several solid tips to help me start losing weight. I followed her advice for a few weeks — until she told me I had to become a vegan. She claimed that I couldn't get rid of the extra fat because I was eating animal products. I didn't believe her. I had lost baby weight before and didn't have to go vegan then. Heck, there are thousands of healthy, physically fit people out there who eat meat. I was determined to find a way that fit my needs and preferences to a "T."

I learned all about calories, macro- and micronutrients, and the importance of water intake and self-care. All of these practices enabled me to find what was best for me, but the most vital factor in my personal transformation was that I had the freedom to choose. I never followed a diet plan that told me exactly what to eat. I never forced myself to eat extra healthy. And never told myself that any item was off limits for the rest of my life.

Freedom in a nutrition program is so important, keeping you at the center of your own transformation. You are the expert on your body, and you have the right to choose how to move forward, or how to adjust when things feel off. Freedom is the oxygen of the soul! If you don't take the reins on how you want to live your life, you'll continue to feel stuck and confused.

By the time I got to my fourth baby, I knew exactly how to manage my weight in a safe and effective way. I don't restrict myself from the foods I love. And I never give myself unhealthy ultimatums in order to look a certain way. I'm going to show you exactly how I used freedom to improve the health habits that were holding me back.

Everyone knows what foods are not good for us and which ones are better. We just fail to make the good stuff the focus of our meals. Deep down, I knew that I couldn't out-exercise a bad diet, if I didn't improve my water, self-care, or lunch choices during my weight struggles. But freedom is born when you change the person who is shackled.

Do you ever recognize that sometimes you make choices just to rebel against others, or just to prove a point? It actually limits your freedoms. But what if you chose to put your health first? Take back your power and write down what freedoms you would enjoy more if you had ideal health.

Next, you have to prepare for and implement your list of freedoms. Freedom means taking ultimate responsibility for our choices. If I want to be free from stress, I must work to prevent it. If I want to be free of excess weight, then I must avoid habits that cause me to gain it.

Write down what you would like to be free of.

Now, imagine having the key to unlock the chains. If you suffer from low energy, your ideas might include daily exercise, power naps, more water, or consistent mealtimes. What good habits will loosen the stronghold of your bad habits and eventually set you free? (Because the only person keeping you trapped is you.)

Make a list of what you will and won't do. For example, I was prepared to get better rest and drink more water. I was even willing to not eat out so much. I was not going to give up pizza, however! When I made myself the boss of my own eating habits, I found a solid way to make improvements on my own terms.

Freedom isn't worth having if it doesn't include the freedom to make mistakes. Your actions are important, not because of what others think, but because you have to live with the consequences. Learn from your mistakes and use those lessons to make better choices.

Describe the version of yourself who lives in accordance with your healthiest choices. Does she go where she wants and eats what she desires? Does she wear her favorite clothes and hang out with her best friends?

Describe what your life of freedom really looks like! If you had a magic wand, what would you change? Think about the triggers, the setbacks, and the events that halt your progress. Decide how you're going to learn from them to create more freedom.

As we change and shift our habits, routines, and schedules, it's necessary to chip away at what holds us back and add more to what is already working well for us. Identify it, write it down, and be clear about it. Enjoying freedom is possible, and you're going to start experiencing it *now*.

But don't confuse freedom with a lack of self-control. Arrange a daily check-in or join one of my programs to practice personal accountability to see how well you did with following your own standards. Once I decided I was the boss of my health, I felt excited about setting my own goals and having fun with it. I felt empowered, knowing that I could and would do better.

Now that you know what you need more of, it's your responsibility to implement it into your life. If you need more family time, put it on the calendar. If you need to exercise consistently, hire a coach to encourage you to be successful. If you need more earnings, consider where you are wasting money and how you might work smarter and not harder. Get out your calendar, vision board, and journal — and get to work!

Here's your chance to wave that magic wand. If you need less stress in your life, choose calmer paths. Take side streets on your commute home, instead of the freeway, even if it adds an extra ten minutes. If you want less drama, ditch the heated Facebook groups. And if you — dare I say it — need less pizza, plan in advance how often it is reasonable to have pizza. Your magic wand has all the power it needs. Let it work its magic while you cut those restrictive chains and give yourself the freedom you deserve.

Lastly, give yourself time to adjust. Old patterns can be hard to break for good, and new habits take time to solidify. It's okay to make adjustments, and even mistakes, along the way. The last step to creating freedom is a simple affirmation:

"I choose to be free!"

Say it as often as you need to, because it is a truth that will manifest itself. You have the power to get out of any situation you desire, including the ones you created for yourself.

Think of choice this way:

Choose the person you really want to be, and then let the rest of your options flow from there.

If you need help with implementing a plan that is right for you no matter your fitness level, my Body Sculpting Challenge will be perfect for you. With over 100 exercise modifications, you are free to pick your intensity level. I have made implementing your workout plan super simple.

The challenge also includes weekly focuses that cover exercise form, protein consumption, nutrition, recovery, and regular reality checks. I would love for you to join our next challenge.

You can join the Body Sculpting Challenge by following this QR code.

Health Basics

Throughout this book, you'll hear me refer to "the basics" of health. I'll go into some depth about why I hold each of my coaching clients accountable to these principles and share how adjusting them in all environments is necessary and possible.

I had the wonderful privilege of working on this book in Guatemala, near beautiful Lake Atitlan. As I prepared to spend five weeks away from home and my family, I tried to anticipate the challenges I would face.

I let my Pole Fitness membership expire. I packed a resistance band, bought a water bottle with a filter, brought supplements, and some tuna packets and Wheat Thins for the flights. I came prepared, planning to use this experience to change and improve my own life while writing.

(Let's shift, now, to a new environment — 2,644 miles away in Guatemala!)

I have learned that I don't easily write when there is construction next door. I should have picked the bedroom closest to the Internet router and brought even more food. (Hangry [= bad tempered or irritable as a result of hunger] is not pretty or productive!)

But despite the challenges and missing my family, this has been an exercise in living the principles that I teach to others about following the basics of sleep, self-care, proper water intake, and movement. As I spend four to eight hours each day writing, I realize that these four basics are not only necessary to my survival, but they are also the most helpful tools in dealing with my current challenges, regardless of where or what they are.

I admit that I've been burned out twice while working on the reality tv show Ace in the Hole. It's a six-month competition for business owners to scale their business. Imagine fitting two to three years' worth of business growth into six months. It's been very challenging, to say the least!

Environment is extremely important, but our pace and daily intentions are even more critical. So in this situation, I'm doing everything I can to prevent further burnout by relying on those four basics. It is typical for all great health programs to include some version of these principles, because you can't cheat on true principles of healthy living. If you master these basics each day, your health challenges are easier to overcome, because they support every system in your body.

I recognize that my current faithful execution of these four basics also offers me an opportunity to improve myself, as well as my writing, during this challenging and invigorating experience:

SLEEP

In Guatemala, I have been blessed with a nice, king-sized bed. I have enough pillows, and the temperature is perfect in this place called "The Land of Eternal Spring." The breeze that blows through the balcony is soothing and yet, that breeze rattles the door and wakes me up periodically. I also happen to be in the room next to the washer and dryer, and during early mornings, the other guests come to wash their clothes, which wakes me.

My solution: I can't fix the door, and I can't quiet the washing machine, and I can't move to another room. But what I can do is get to sleep consistently at a good time (around 9:30 PM). If I sleep soundly enough by reducing distractions, I won't hear the door rattle, and I'll be up before laundry time begins.

I can also make sure to get proper movement and exercise, knowing that they help me sleep even in this strange environment. And I can share my concerns with the others in the house, letting them know that I'd like to be up before they begin using the laundry. When I politely made them known, my concerns were met with sympathy and support.

Consistency is key, and it's the only thing you can control. Get into a routine so that your brain and body recuperate and develop together. If you're not getting enough sleep, set a specific time to go to bed and turn off the lights, and schedule a time each day to wake. Sleep promotes stable moods, stable metabolic functions, and stable energy levels. I don't take sleep lightly – nor should you.

SELF-CARE

For the last few months, I have worked on meditating. This temporary home on Lake Atitlan is beautiful, and the weather is wonderfully mild and enjoyable, so I've been trying to take a one-hour break each day to unplug, enjoy the scenery and the environment, and count my blessings. I also find great stimulation in talking to the other writers during mealtimes.

My main intention is to make meditation deliberate, knowing "Quiet the mind, and the soul will speak," as Ma Jaya Sati Bhagavati (writer, painter, activist) once said. It's important to take a step away from your problems and give yourself time to breathe, to reflect, and to reduce tension in the body and spirit. I find that when I'm consistently meditating, I gain a clear perspective of my life. As I focus on reaching higher levels of relaxation, my brain improves its neural pathways, making me more responsive to feelings and more responsible for right actions.

I know that I make better choices when I practice self-care and meditation. I increase my clarity and tolerance, and my brain has a better chance of fighting off real and perceived threats. Science also shows that we develop a higher tolerance for pain and more easily protect ourselves when necessary, when we meditate regularly.

And it helps with self-esteem and self-awareness, too. My journey into the fitness industry began as an effort to deal with depression. Finding meditation within this journey allows me to care for myself at a deeper level.

WATER INTAKE

It's a good thing I brought that water bottle with the filter, because the water in Guatemala is not safe to drink! We have to get bottled or filtered water to drink. I'm happy that I was prepared. I still have to ensure that I get the proper quantity, I pay close attention to how I'm feeling physically, and I reach for electrolyte water packets to add extra hydration.

Pure water is the world's first and foremost medicine. It increases digestion, breaks food down so your body can absorb it better, and normalizes blood pressure. Hypertension is more common in people who are chronically dehydrated.

Water also protects your organs and tissues. Hydration lessens the burden on the kidneys and liver by flushing out waste from the body. It will increase your energy and prevent premature aging. Alternately, a lack of water intake produces headaches, poor concentration, and fatigue.

MOVEMENT

I thought this health basic element would be easiest for me to maintain, especially in such a beautiful, natural place in Guatemala. But my commitment to my writing has resulted in getting less than 2,000 steps per day. I'm eating less than normal, so it's good to balance that out with slightly less movement, but I'm concerned about losing muscle mass. I know I need to find reasons to move each day. That starts with choosing a consistent time during the day in which I have two major fasting windows that my body isn't used to.

But I discovered that there are 200 stairs from the road to the lake. I can commit to going down to the lake at least twice each day, not only to enjoy my current surroundings but to keep my body mobile.

Exercise is a celebration of what your body can do. It reduces stress and controls our fight-or-flight responses. Exercise helps with weight management and stress, anxiety, and depression. Exercise increases your body's endorphin production and prepares your body for higher levels of exertion.

I may be away from home, but I know that my body is really my home, and it's up to me to treat it with love and respect, no matter where I am.

As you start every day, take a moment and set your daily goals for maintaining the basics. Keep them simple and effective. Know that you won't be perfect right off the bat, but when you are committed to even simple health practices, your body and mind will benefit greatly.

You can join the Healthy Eating Challenge by following this QR code.

Positive Mindset Affirmations

I want to introduce you to new tools that will help you feel better and do better in your journey to health — they're called *Affirmations*.

Oh, wait! I'll bet you've heard this word before, and it immediately brings up a negative connotation, right? Before you start cringing, let me tell you that I felt the same way, once upon a time.

When I began my fitness and nutrition coaching business, I was also looking for solutions for my own health challenges. I read about an anti-inflammation cleanse and was curious. I knew that inflammation was the #1 cause of illness in the body, and I wouldn't be interested in a typical cleanse, but the inflammation angle gave this particular cleanse some credibility.

I purchased the introductory offer, a two-week guide, for $15. In it, the creator claimed she healed herself of several conditions through this cleanse. She explained the meal plans and provided a list of recommended affirmations throughout the program.

The meal plan looked great, but when it came to those affirmations, I felt uncertain. How would saying things to yourself in the mirror get you through a two-week cleanse? But I put my feelings aside, believing that I needed to commit fully to this program in order to see results. After all, it was just fourteen days. Certainly, I could say a few silly things out loud while trying to get healthier! I taped the affirmation cards to my bathroom mirror and said them to myself, as recommended.

Then, I hit the grocery store. There was a very detailed grocery list, and when I was ready to check out, I made a quick emergency call to my husband.

"Honey, I got all the food I need for that program I told you about. It's $400 – Is that okay?"

My husband asked if all this food was for our family of six, or just for me? When I arrived home, he just looked at me and patiently helped unload the nitrate free turkey, seven heads of celery, expensive nuts, and other anti-inflammatory foods.

Once I started the plan, I discovered that the food (expensive though it was) was the easy part. I could commit to this meal plan and make it part of my daily routine. I liked eating clean and appreciated the new recipes. I especially loved showing my husband that our money wasn't going to waste.

But every time I walked into the bathroom and looked at those affirmation cards, my stomach flip-flopped:

"My body is a vessel."

"I breathe in light."

"Only goodness is allowed to enter my body!"

Ugh. It just never felt natural for me to say those words, even in the privacy of my bathroom. They never felt like things I would actually say in order to encourage myself. Within days, I abandoned the affirmations. I kept with the meal plan, but figured I'd leave the crazy talk to the hippies.

Fast forward a few years to a difficult time in my life. I was dealing with depression and feelings of low self-worth. There was a persistent loop playing in my head of the negative words that others had repeatedly said to me. They kept playing over and over, even though I was no longer surrounded by the people in question. I wondered, 'How could their words have so much power over me? Why did I revisit those statements so often, when they made me feel terrible?'

Then I remembered an article I read in a parenting magazine about encouraging children to be polite. This article shared tips on how to get your kids to say "please" and "thank you" and to be more respectful. 'Surely,' I thought, 'if there was a system for teaching kids to be kind to others, there has to be a way for me to be kinder to myself.'

The article suggested repeating phrases to your kids to help them see the benefits of being well-mannered. I realized that these same practices can be applied to the ways we talk to ourselves. And it made me remember those silly affirmations, years ago, taped to my mirror. Maybe those words weren't right for me, but I was going to create my own statements that actually worked, that I could repeat over and over.

At that moment, I just knew that I needed to feel better about myself. I had to make the negative words go away by saying something positive. But what should I say? How do I train myself to speak kindly to myself, to say good things that matter? That idea eventually developed into my Positive Mindset Affirmations.

There are three approaches to developing meaningful affirmations:

1. *What do I really want?*

2. *What must I say to get that feeling?*

3. *What is the result of doing it?*

Again, this began with needing to talk myself down from feelings of depression and overriding the constant chatter of negative words with positive statements. I started with some simple but meaningful phrases:

"You go out of your way to help others."

"You are the best mom."

"You're awesome!"

Within days, I realized that I liked saying good things to myself, and they had a way of getting repeated in my mind. I felt happy when I looked in the mirror and spoke those words. Maybe that cleanse lady knew what she was talking about! In fact, I kept feeling good long after I walked out of the bathroom. Throughout the day, I would hear those words on a loop — slowly erasing the criticisms I used to play in my head — and every time I heard them, I felt instant joy and absolutely no weirdness!

Here's how you can start your own positive affirmations. Let's go back to those three approaches:

1. What do I really want?

The reason those affirmations from the cleanse felt awkward was because they weren't mine. They weren't created with me in mind, and they were off base for what I needed at that time. I needed to feel joy and a sense of self-worth. You have to decide what emotions you're lacking in your life. If you've been in a negative state of mind for a long time, trusted friends may help you pinpoint those emotions.

Saying affirmations to yourself may feel weird – at first. But I promise that as you practice talking to yourself, it gets easier. Let's be real — we talk to ourselves all day long, but now we're making it useful, intentional, and positive.
What is it that you really want to feel? Is it happiness or joy, fulfilment or fun? Write down a list of five different emotions that you want to experience on a regular basis. Mine would be fun, love, safety, growth, and confidence.

Now, ask yourself: What makes you feel those emotions? Describe why that experience makes you feel good. As an example, my daughter is a mini-scientist in training. She enjoys creating experiments, and I love seeing the look on her face with each result. It makes me happy to see my child develop her imagination and logic, while having fun. So if I'm ever feeling low in happiness, I ask my daughter about her recent science projects!

To turn these experiences into your own Positive Mindset Affirmations, you'll create statements that bring your mind back to the desired emotion. Knowing that watching my daughter don her white lab coat and practice science will make me happy, it gave me the language to express the feeling that *"I enjoy seeing growth."* I then turn that expression into a positive affirmation, telling myself that I enjoy and appreciate *my own growth*, knowing it is part of what makes me most happy. That particular affirmation is also an action statement, encouraging me to make improvements in my life, when needed.

You can create your own Positive Mindset Affirmations in the same way. Pinpoint an emotion, define what it means to you, describe the feeling, and put it into words. Giving it language brings the message from the inside to the outside of your body through your throat and mouth. You are manifesting that emotion in more ways than one, and that intensifies and magnifies it.

Let me show you how I do this exercise.

Think about the emotion you want to experience. Let's say fun. What statements evoke that emotion? It doesn't have to be deep — it just needs to make sense to you. If saying "pink fluffy unicorns" brings a smile to your face, then start with that! Affirmations are for helping you instantly change your demeanor and mindset. Do what feels right for you, and use it over and over.

2.   *What must I say to get that feeling?*

Write down your emotion and a few bullet points describing what it means to you. Example: Fun!

- Swimming
- Getting outside
- Playing Games

Why are these activities fun? For me, I have fun swimming because it makes me feel like a kid again. I like being outside because it gets me away from work (and screen time), and I love playing games because I'm competitive and even a trivial win lets me interact joyfully with others. Bringing the WHY to your awareness sparks motivation — it makes me want to run outside and jump in the pool right now!

Think about explaining your reason for fun to a friend. Would you say to them, "Come be a kid with me again" or "Let's spend time outdoors together"? Once you know how you might articulate these ideas to others, then you can create a statement to say to yourself —

"I can be a kid again."

"I thrive on quality time."

"I love activities with friends and family."

These are simple but meaningful statements that actually make sense to you and definitely won't feel weird! Next, you're going to make sure your affirmations produce the results you're looking for.

3. What are the results of these Positive Mindset Affirmations?

I guarantee that anytime you make a deliberate effort to improve, you'll be guided to make change in ways that have an impact. It took me a while to refine my initial statements of "I'm a great mom" and "I'm awesome" into more actionable ones, but with time I developed a system that instantly uplifts me when I feel like a failure.

When you know exactly what to say to yourself, you can instantly create a positive mindset.

To make your affirmations effective, however, they have to evoke action. You'll be able to pinpoint exactly when you need those positive words — it's usually when you fail to act on what makes you happy. When I'm not experiencing a lot of fun in my life, my mood drops. I'll tell myself — out loud — "I can be a kid again," and it's the first step to feeling that joy.

Affirmations that you create sound weird only if you say them, but don't do anything about them. If I'm in a bad mood and tell myself, "I can be a kid again," but I don't go out and have some fun, then the affirmation loses its meaning. We're not little kids who can just say "please" and "thank you" and it automatically sinks in. Our adult brains need to see the bridge between mind/body and the affirmation that becomes that bridge. To make it work, you have to say it with intention and back it up with action.

When I say, "I can be a kid again," my brain remembers the emotions that prompted those words. As you get results from your own affirmations, you'll develop more motivation to act on those affirmations and to create more joy, fun, and happiness in your life!

Positive Mindset Affirmations are one of the best ways to implement The Accountability Code. Talking is easy. Defining what you want is easy. Your self-talk will never stop, so let's make it useful and powerful.

Implementing is all about taking action. You have to say the words, and then shift what you're doing to carry it through. Can you take a break from what you're doing and go for a walk outside? Can you play a quick game with your kids, or schedule an outing to the pool?

By creating customized Positive Mindset Affirmations, you increase your ability to regularly create the emotions you want to experience, and therefore you create more accountability in your life.

Comparison Is Not a Thief of Joy

I always wanted to grow a vegetable garden, but being a busy wife, mom, and entrepreneur got in the way of growing veggies. But a few years ago, my neighborhood announced they would be hosting a Facebook live series about gardening tips, which made me realize that a lot of people in my neighborhood were really good at growing gardens.

Just over my kitchen window, my newest neighbors were hard at work laying out 2x4s to start a new box garden project. I realized, 'Wow! I have a lot of access to people who know what they're doing. If ever there was a time to start gardening for my family, this would be it. I know I won't be alone in this project!" Now was the perfect time to take action and implement some change.

So I made my way over to my neighbor's backyard and started asking questions. I told my neighbor I wanted to learn from him and asked for his help. He gave me some advice, told me to buy certain supplies, but also generously offered some of his leftover material for me to use. Then he took me to his cold storage room and showed me all of the little plants he had already started growing. When his boxes were built and the weather was right, he said he'd transplant his garden.

My heart kind of sunk when I saw all this prep work. I thought, 'Well, dang! How am I supposed to keep up when I didn't even know you had to plant your whole garden inside your house, months before you could do it outside?' But as I've said before, I'm no quitter.

So I drove to the hardware store and bought the recommended supplies. When I brought them home and began building my boxes, the neighbor came over and suggested a plan — If we could use my truck, he'd help haul all the dirt we needed for both our gardens. We worked side by side, putting in our new boxes. Team work! He put in six, and I went for a more realistic number for myself which was just two.

Once the local nurseries had starter plants, I picked up broccoli, pickling and lemon cucumbers, peppers, tomatoes, and dill. I committed to planting only what I knew my family would eat. My neighbor planted so much more! Beans, cantaloupes, watermelons, pumpkins, etc. He also installed a sprinkler system in his yard and put pea gravel and a fence around that corner of the property.

It really was amazing to watch the transformation of his garden, and I thought about my first envious feelings of comparison, watching his little seedlings under the heat lamp. I could have given up my ambition of growing a vegetable garden, seeing how far ahead he was of me. But instead, I adjusted my expectations and made the decision to be okay with my own level while learning from him. I would never get to a higher level if I didn't just work with what I had right now.

We cannot help but compare ourselves to others, but we can use that comparison to motivate ourselves to achieving greatness.

I started my vegetable garden at the perfect level for me. I was focused on growing my gardening talents, not necessarily achieving the same thing my neighbor could. Had I started this process assuming I could immediately be as good as him (who had years of experience and the schedule of a retired person), I would have surely failed.

Let's not do that, okay?

Comparison isn't bad if the sources you seek bring out the best in you. It's all about what you DO with that information. When you are at the gym and see someone with more experience than you, do you feel defeated? You shouldn't. After all, both of you are showing up and working hard to be healthy. You might learn something just by watching them in action, and you may learn even more if you walk over, introduce yourself, compliment their progress, and tell them you hope to achieve similar results.

Any new goal or intention starts with learning. Then comes the doing. Your ability to learn from others and see the greatness in you is what determines if that comparison is good or bad. Comparison is never bad when the sources you seek bring out the best in you. Healthy comparison happens when we have the intention to become a better version of ourselves, not better than others.

"A good example has twice the value of good advice." — Albert Schweitzer

Who in your life makes you want to be a better person? My neighbor inspired me to finally build that vegetable garden I had been wanting for years, and it was fun (though hard work) all that summer. I got to sustain my family on homegrown veggies and herbs, while learning new skills and achieving already established goals.

A great first step is to write down the names of people you look up to. My number one rule here is that you have to know the people in question. Stop comparing yourself to celebrities and strangers on the Internet. Their lives may look great, but you have no idea how they achieve their goals, and there is little you can learn from their process since you have no access to them.

Your friends, family, neighbors, and colleagues are much better examples for helping you achieve your own ambitions. Ask yourself what it is about them that you admire so much, and what the qualities are that they possess that make them successful? My neighbors were kind, patient, and generous with their time and knowledge. What motivates you to develop the same qualities that the people on your list have?

Once you have a few names written down, along with the qualities that make them successful, ask yourself how you feel when you are around them. The neighbors that helped me with my garden are retired. Just being in their presence, watching them enjoy their leisurely lives, diminished any stress I was feeling. Feeling good is contagious!

Comparison can lead to feelings of envy or inadequacy, or to the Imposter Syndrome. But it can also turn into massive growth. If comparison creates good emotions for you, it's a sign that you are willing to learn and understand the need for mentors.

You can also choose how to feel when in the presence of people you admire. A garden of flowers has no leader, but they all have the same goal: to thrive and bloom. Can you put yourself in the same space as others who share your goals and can motivate you to achieve them?

As a fitness trainer, I'm especially observant of body language. I notice if someone is kind, by their gestures. Are they affectionate? Do they smile and make eye contact? Look around at the people you admire. How do they show their support for others and how can you demonstrate your desire to help others improve by the way you show up?

As you take a deeper look at the ways you compare yourself to others, it may be easy to fall back into negative patterns of envy and failure. Remind yourself that each person has their own set of experiences and expectations. It takes work to achieve our dreams.

But also ask yourself, 'How might I be setting an example for others?' You know from your experience that spending time with positive, successful people is inspiring. You naturally want to embody the good qualities they have, along with mastering similar achievements. Now look at the ways that you set an example for others who may need a little encouragement to be like you.

You also have to continue to guard against jealousy and hopelessness. The best thing you can do to combat negativity is to keep yourself in healthy environments. Instead of scrolling through pictures on social media of lives you have no connection to, reconnect with those you love and admire. A great way to prevent the 'scroll hole' is to set time limits on your phone apps.

Get away from the phone and get back in touch with real people who lead by example — the people who make you feel good about your achievements and those you plan to fulfill.

Instead of consuming, create. Where do you spend too much energy comparing yourself negatively against others? How can you channel that energy, instead, into a new project? What can you do to clear your mind so that your perceptions change?

There will be seasons in relationships, of course, and that's okay. Sometimes you'll feel like you are mastering the act of comparison, and other times you may feel you fall short. But take goodness with you, wherever you go. Remind yourself of your best qualities. Compare yourself to your past self instead of needlessly to others.

I'd love for you to change your phone lock screen to a picture of something that reminds you to improve for all the right reasons. You'll check your phone countless times each day – that's the image you want to see to remind yourself of your value.

But it's also good to reconnect with those you have compared yourself to in the past and you see you've grown as a result. Send thank you letters or call someone you look up to. Practice ownership of the same positive qualities they have for one minute
each day.

A tree is known by its fruit. So as you work to improve and surround yourself with good people, you'll find that healthy comparison is beneficial if it elevates you for the better. Keep growing and begin setting that example for others.

Following and Implementing the good you see is a crucial step in being accountable for who you are, who you want to become, and how you impact the world.

Life Is Unfair

Growing up, whenever friends' parents would drop me off at home for the first time, they would pull up to my house and dubiously ask, "Is this an apartment building?"

It was definitely the biggest house on the street, but not because we had money.

"Nope," I would say cheerfully. "This is my house. My sister burned the house down, and since my parents knew they were going to have a lot more kids, they rebuilt the house bigger!"

But that didn't mean I saw our situation as a blessing. I used to describe myself to high school friends, as, "I'm the richest of the poor, and the poorest of the rich. I'm as middle class as they come!" It was my way of coming to terms with the fact that life isn't fair. We are all dealt different hands and, especially when we're young, we have little control over that.

Where I attended school was very economically diverse. I knew kids who worked to support their whole families, and other kids who drove nicer cars than the school administrators. I was actually right in the middle and not yet aware of how blessed I was — and that my blessings had nothing to do with money.

I give my in-laws a lot of credit for helping me learn this. I met Aubrey when I was in high school and got engaged to him before I graduated. His parents taught me that there was always more to earn, learn, do, and be. I especially wanted to please my mother-in-law, because she always made it clear that she believed in me. She strongly encouraged me to get a college education. She kept saying, "I want to see that diploma hanging on the wall!"

At the time, my own mother (after raising eight kids) was finally pursuing her own higher education, getting a degree and working at the local college. When I told her my mother-in-law was relentlessly bugging me about going to college, mom suggested that we look into federal grants to help pay for it. She also had her employee tuition discount. With the help of her discount and the FAFSA (Free Application for Federal Student Aid), I was able to get an advanced education for free. Time to implement some solid strategies!

The truth is, I never wanted to go to college. I wanted to be a stay-at-home mom (just like my mother had been), but I was guided to improve myself and to take every advantage offered to me. It actually seemed that I had an unfair advantage (with the federal grant and employee discount) provided to better my life and contribute to the world in a bigger, better way, including setting an example for my own daughters at an early age.

Life is actually full of unfair advantages, and many of them just might be available to you. Implementing means carrying out or executing a plan. The good news is that the plans may already be put together for you, and all you have to do is apply!

Getting my degree in Physical Education and Health led me into a fulfilling career and the opportunity to be a positive influence on others. The experience of my college education has shaped who I am, it has greatly enhanced my view of health and the importance it has for individuals and families. Each experience leads to the next.

I would love for you to recognize that proper expectations can be incredibly powerful. It's only when they are misguided, ignored, or ill-intentioned that they become damaging. You have the power to define, determine, and live up to the expectations that you know will turn you into the person you want to be.

It doesn't matter whether you come from money — I certainly didn't. What matters is that you take advantage of what is available to you. That starts with your beautiful mind, your capable body, and your ability to be fully self-aware.

Take a moment to list the advantages that got you where you are now. Consider how you were challenged in meeting the expectations you had, also how you found opportunities that helped you succeed. I graduated college while having children. I learned to ask for help with my kids, communicated my needs to my professors, and took advantage of the family activities offered on campus. My expectations of finishing college without a major break were enabled by services offered to those in my situation.

What unfair advantages have helped you along the way? Write down all of the unexpected blessings that showed up just as you needed them. Don't be surprised, as you do this, that new opportunities will present themselves. Awareness creates room for growth. How are you welcoming more awareness into your life?

Then ask yourself, what do you need now to move forward? What are your current needs, and what opportunities and advantages are available to you? An important first step is to verbalize your goals. Tell friends and family what you are hoping to accomplish. I wouldn't have known about the federal aid available to me without talking to my mom.

There are resources available to help you with your goals, as well. You just need to drop your needs into conversations with friends and family. Once they are aware, they can be a sounding board or extra eyes out there searching for opportunities for you. The only mistake you can make is not asking for help.

What challenges us often makes us stronger, more resilient and more determined to succeed. Originally, I didn't plan on going to college, but I realized how precious support from my mother-in-law was. My in-laws made it easy for me to attend by helping care for my children along the way.

Thankfully, I found the financial aid that allowed a working-class woman like me to get an education, and I was blessed with a love for physical activity and movement, which made choosing my major a breeze. I also had great coaches and teachers throughout my life who helped me see how valuable I was, no matter how much money I had.

I surrounded myself with people who helped me see the value of striving for an education. What have you been blessed with, despite your obstacles? And how have you done your best with what you were given in life?

Life definitely can be unfair, but every time you succeed despite the odds, it's a reminder to celebrate your growth and know that it came from you implementing what was available to you. Be proud of what you have done and show gratitude toward those who offered those advantages — fair or unfair. You had help along the way, as we all did. But be proud of yourself, too. Look back at your past accomplishments and feel fulfilled at how you stepped up. Opportunity dances with those on the dance floor — and you've made some great moves!

It's often hard to see these achievements as they happen, however. When I think back on going to college, teaching classes, serving at church, and raising babies all at the same time, I'm astonished. I'm also ready to take on the next opportunity.

I want you to name your three biggest achievements and compliment yourself (out loud) on them. Mine include, "I had four kids in six years!" "I'm an awesome personal trainer," and "I am the best mom."

Say it with vigor: "I am ready to take on anything!"

If you are wondering what advantages are available to you during this time, let's chat about what your goals and needs are. Go to www. funandsustainable.com/360 and you'll see prompts for connecting with me. Most of all, make sure you take advantage of all that is offered, and implement it in an effective way.

Implementing Contributions

I swear by the parenting method known as "Love and Logic." Time and again, these methods have been proven in my home, as well as in my coaching business. Love and Logic requires using language that all participants understand. Aubrey and I actually took local classes on this method, and one of our greatest takeaways was the concept of *Contributions*.

A *contribution* is a gift or payment to a common fund or collection. In many ways, a family is a common collection. A contribution in Love and Logic is the updated word for CHORES. Chores are boring and hard, whereas the word 'contributions' more accurately describes the household process of taking care of everyone's needs.

Aubrey and I sat down with our kids and a large white board and asked everyone to name the things they most wanted to do together as a family. Once we had our list, we asked everyone to tell us what had to happen to make those wishes become reality.

One of our daughters wanted to have nice meals, sitting together around the table. So we went in a circle and named the things we had to do in order to enjoy family
dinner nights.

Dishes have to be clean, said one of the kids.

My husband said we have to buy groceries.

We each named the ways that make a happy meal come together. Once every person in the family understood all the pieces that make a meal, gathering at the table and enjoying it as a family, it became clearer to each person that we all play a role in making that happen.

Aubrey and I were quick to point out to the girls that the heavy lifting was our responsibility. We would earn money to pay for the groceries and the mortgage on our house, as well as paying for the dishes we eat with and the table where we sat. We would also make sure we pay the utility bills so we could cook food properly and enjoy our meals in a well-lit room.

Then we went around again and asked everyone to volunteer for a contribution to regular family meal nights. Each girl picked responsibilities that would contribute to all of us enjoying meals at home: washing dishes, chopping vegetables, clearing papers from the table, setting timers on the stove.

Then we moved on to other tasks. It was an extensive list: We're a big family living in a large home. Everyone would have to be responsible for their own self, their own room, their own cleanliness. The rest of the contributions needed to be divided up.

Of course, nothing on the list was a surprise to me. I knew full well what it takes to run an organized home, but the responsibility of doing it all had become more than I could manage alone. Here's a secret: Doing it all is hard, but doing none of it is hard, too. You may have heard that lazy moms do it all themselves, because it's easier and quicker just to take care of it than to manage others and teach them how to do it properly. Once you involve other people, your responsibility shifts from simply completing the tasks to now teaching them and literally doubling your efforts, at least for a while.

But eventually you have to show your family how to manage themselves. It's a process, but well worth the effort. The skill of self-mastery begins when you become aware of the mental, physical, and emotional load you're carrying and whether you're fully equipped to handle it all (hint: You're not!).

Introducing the word 'contributions' will be one of the greatest investments that you'll ever implement into your home. Just imagine having set expectations for each member of the family, where they clearly understand their role, and how it contributes to the peace and harmony of the whole family and home.

To implement contributions in your household, start with a family meeting. Be honest. Tell everyone that you can't do it all on your own, and you are asking for their help. Being honest with your limitations, you can focus on what is important, rather than putting out fires all day.

Ask your family what feels out of balance for them. Where could you all be stronger, together? How does your home situation affect each person? Then ask them, What could you change to make things better? Welcome any and all suggestions that are realistic. If you have young children, let them talk while you give them your full attention. A great way to show them that you're really listening is to write down what they say.

Then thank each one for their input, and let them know you're excited to start implementing THEIR SUGGESTIONS (it's helpful and respectful to give them ownership of their ideas). And remind them that it's about working together as a family, not trying to be perfect.

Once you have your list of each person's individual wants, then ask everyone to remember how each gets done. Tell them that not everything is critical. Does the laundry need to get done every day? Probably not. Does the sink need to be empty every night? That would be nice. Does the dog need a walk each day? All these things would be nice and would probably contribute to a happier household, but they're nothing to get your panties in a bunch over.

Let your kids know which responsibilities will be handled by mom and/or dad (paying the bills, making big decisions, enforcing rules), and then let the kids divide the other responsibilities. Letting them choose is important, knowing there will be a few items left over at the end that are unpleasant (cleaning out the dog bowl) or time consuming (raking leaves in the fall).

Ask your kids, "Are these tasks necessary?" and let them answer honestly. If someone wants the house to be cleaner and their suggestion is to hire a maid, ask them what they're willing to contribute financially to pay for that maid. Chances are, they will then be willing to consider a buddy system of cleaning each room, instead, so they don't have to spend their money from birthdays and the tooth fairy on a maid.

Buddy systems, in fact, are great ways to tackle some of the bigger tasks around the house. Nobody feels as if they're doing it alone, and it creates an opportunity to spend time together. I recommend starting with a parent-child team first and then child-child when they become effective working together.

As you work your way through your list of wants and needs and how they're going to get handled, a light will slowly begin to appear at the end of the tunnel. You've just implemented a way for your family to take responsibility — and for you to practice giving up control.

When someone doesn't complete their chosen contribution, don't jump in and do it for them. This is the hardest step at first, especially for clean freaks. Get the hang of saying to yourself, "That's not my job" (although not in ear shot of your kids — they'll adopt that phrase like there's no tomorrow)! Instead, use that phrase as a gentle reminder to yourself not to focus on the little things that someone else needs to learn to take care of.

When the time comes for that contribution to be done, you can offer to help the person responsible and connect personally while finishing the task together. Ask if there was a reason they volunteered for that task, but it was hard to accomplish on their own. They might be in over their head, or they may just need a little extra encouragement.

Now, contributions aren't just ways to get help around the house. They are also a means of communicating your needs and responding as a family. Try this approach for two weeks, and then come together to discuss what did and did not work well. That's a good moment for you to ask yourself how having help around the house lets you focus on more important matters.

I want my kids to take responsibility and to feel good about helping others. I used to give them long lists of things to do, realizing the lists would never end — not for them, or for me. It was more important that I spend time with them than it was to maintain a perfect home. I could empower them to contribute to the household while sharing precious time with my family.

As you figure it all out, be patient with the family and with yourself. Point out what your kids are doing right, not what still needs to be done. Some will struggle more than others, especially those who weren't accountable for doing much. As you reposition your efforts and energy on the big picture, you'll see that working with your family is more rewarding than having a spotless home, and your stress will be reduced, knowing that you are setting yourself and your kids up for success.

Then you can look at using practices for getting healthy, by organizing the parts of your life to accommodate better choices.

Love and Logic — and its concepts of contributions — have been valuable lessons in my household. They also inform the ways that I teach and coach my fitness clients. When you ask for a contribution, the response is much better than when you tell someone they have to do something 'just because.'

Adopting a system for deliberate communication will help you master The Accountability Code faster because many of our goals will include those who live with us. I challenge you to pull out the code and take your family through each step when it comes to everyone helping out ("making a contribution"). I'll give you a quick example:

Reflection — Ask how each family member is doing. Can they find their belongings? Is making a family meal more pleasant in a clean space? Share how things are for you as you are teaching your kids to be responsible.

Humility — Let your family know that running a household and taking care of your health is a challenge at times and that it's important everyone helps out ("contributes"). Point out the strengths each family member has and support them in how they are developing in their contributions.

Planning — Sort out all of the necessary tasks you need to take care of in order to run a successful household. Let each family person have input and decide how often you'll review and change your plan.

Implementing — Put your plan (and reward system, if applicable) in a place where everyone can see it and be easily aware of it. We use a white board that I have decorated with pretty gem magnets. It makes looking at it and paying attention to it appealing. It is located in the family room, and we can each easily know who needs to do what.

Commitment — Next to the contributions, I added a quote that reminds us to look at the board and to get our contributions done. Knowing what needs to be done helps me make a decision when one of my kids wants an extra privilege. They know they must be committed in order to get what they want.

Feedback — It is very clear when someone is not staying on top of their contributions, because all of them pile up on one person when we rotate them. This is a good opportunity to figure out what is going on with that family member. Gather feedback, and then start again and keep going!

Fear Can Motivate

Preparation is one of my favorite things to talk about because nothing feels as good as being prepared. How do I know that? Because I know what it feels like not to be prepared, and that feeling sucks! Being prepared means you have taken action anticipating or preventing an expected outcome. The ability to Implement well is necessary to using and executing The Accountability Code effectively.

I haven't been prepared for a lot of things in my life: the day I started my period in 8th grade, my honeymoon, having an NICU baby, and getting postpartum depression.

Let's face it — we can't be prepared for everything life throws at us, but we can be aware of what our odds are. I remember reading about how many kids drown each year, and that alone prompted me to enroll my kids in swim lessons. I was scared they could drown, so I took action.

I don't love being motivated by fear, but it's one of the emotions we have been given to warn us of danger. It's common to physically react when we feel fear. Why? Because it has the power to interrupt our thought processes, to disrupt the chaos of panic (even if only temporarily), and replace it with action. When you couple a new thought process with the innate need to survive, we tend to take greater action for life-saving change.

Hopefully, though, we act in a positive way. Fear can also make us act irrational if the impulse is strong enough. I learned that I use fear as motivation, and you can, too.

Let me give you examples in each of the four areas of health: spiritual, emotional, mental, and physical. These are my personal fears in each of these four areas.

Keep in mind that these fears aren't always immediate. When our fears are immediately shoved in our faces, that's when we go kind of panicky-crazy. The examples I'm going to share will demonstrate, instead, the perfect way to use fear in a positive and empowering way (think of what could happen, not what is happening right now. NOTE: I don't recommend staying in a state of fear; I'm urging you to take any fearful thoughts that come your way and turn them into action):

SPIRITUAL

I am scared that I will be so numb to the spirit's messages that it causes me to lead my daughters astray.

EMOTIONAL

I'm scared that I will say something I regret because I haven't yet properly worked out how I feel.

MENTAL

I am scared that I will literally go crazy, like many people in my family.

PHYSICAL

I'm scared that I'll develop an intolerance or allergy and have to restrict my food.

My fears are, of course, different than yours will be, and my motivations will be different than yours. The good news is that you don't have to worry about my fears. You only need to work to address yours. The even better news is that you can use The Accountability Code to address your fears and plan appropriately.

Here is what I am doing to overcome my fears:

SPIRITUAL

In order to overcome the fear of being numb to the Spirit's messages and thereby leading my daughters astray, I take time to listen to those messages from the Spirit carefully. I assess if they are encouraging me for good and, if so, I do my best to act diligently.

EMOTIONAL

To avoid saying something I will regret because I haven't worked out properly how I feel, I take time alone to sift through my emotions, to understand them, and to practice how to share my thoughts from a space of observation, openness, and calm.

MENTAL

To address my concerns that I will suffer from mental illness like many in my family have historically done, I keep my physical body healthy, and I consult with professionals to support my mental and emotional well-being.

PHYSICAL

To alleviate my concerns that I will someday have to restrict my diet due to an allergy or food intolerance, I listen carefully to the cues my body sends after eating certain foods. I try to maintain a healthful and well-balanced meal plan and to limit foods that I know can trigger me.

When you take action to address your fears, those fears will grow smaller. They will feel less likely to occur, or less powerful. What you're really doing is practicing discipline in actively changing your life.

When times get hard, you'll have the confidence to meet your fears with fierce motivation and power if you get a handle on taking action when those fears first arise. Here is an example of using The Accountability Code to address, prepare for, and implement action to counterattack my fear of my kids drowning:

Reflection — My fear of my children drowning began when I read multiple blogs about children dying through drowning. Back in 2007-2010 when family blogs were very popular, it was extremely easy to find a family blog to become attached to, see their most popular blog posts, learn every single detail, and then click through to the next one. I found myself in mid-day between college homework assignments, bawling my eyes out over my keyboard. I did not want my children to drown.

Humility — As I read those stories, I gained humble gratitude through learning warning signs I didn't know before. I know it seems like common knowledge for keeping kids safe, but all the mothers of those drowned angels were just like me: out having family fun, creating memories, only to find their kids had suddenly disappeared—and died! I felt blessed to know the need to be hyper vigilant around water. Deeper understanding = increased accountability.

Planning — I recalled my experience of learning to swim, and it was the "sink or swim" approach. I ended up learning to swim, but it was through a traumatic experience in my aunt's pool where my dad yelled at my cousin to stop helping me. I planned to help my kids learn to swim in a different way.

Implementing — I signed my children up for swimming lessons as soon as possible. Knowing I was helping them gain life-saving survival skills gave me peace of mind, as I worked to arm myself with the vigilance skills to be aware of my kids at all times around water. I implemented patterns of counting my girls as often as I saw one of them around water. They had necessary life jackets every single outing around water, and we practiced rules of safety.

Commitment — My commitment to safety seemed over the top to others at times. When I got to the point of handling all four of my kids at the pool on my own, I do remember telling my kids it was time to leave after one child failed to check in with me. Another time, I was told by a stranger that my oldest was too old to be in a life jacket. But I counted off the rest of my younger children to him, and then he understood why.

Feedback — I am happy to say that my fears about my girls drowning have lessened. After four consistent years of swimming lessons, my children not only know the danger-warning signs, but they understand the importance of safety in following rules around water and staying in safe places. The best part about being adequately prepared is that I can honestly relax by the pool on a nice summer day, knowing my kids are well-trained to be safe.

You are going to use The Accountability Code and plug in one of your own fears. I promise that you'll find strength and peace in Planning, Implementing, and Commitment when you harness your fears for good.

Explain to yourself how you usually handle fear and ask, 'What results come from not being aware of how to handle your biggest fears?" Remember that thinking will not overcome fear, but action will.

List your biggest fear in each area of health. Taking the time to do this actually puts you in a state of Reflection, which is the first step in TAC. It can actually feel pretty awesome to revisit what you fear, occasionally, knowing you are empowered to tackle it.

The fears we don't face become our limits. And surprise attacks are less likely if you plan for them. Write down what your biggest fears are and ask yourself, 'Where do those fears come from? Are they rational fears that could come to pass if you aren't aware and careful, or are they irrational fears?'

You are the one that has to courageously face your own fears and take action toward them. Tell yourself, 'I am bigger than my fears!' Don't let the fear of what could happen make nothing happen. Write down each of your fears, as well as what action you will take to prevent or prepare for them.

Here's a great acronym for Fear: False Evidence Appearing Real.

It isn't that the thing you fear cannot come true, but that the fear itself is probably greater than the event and, therefore, is misleading or false.

What is your greatest weapon in defeating fear? It's preparation. If I fear that I'll have to restrict my food someday, I will go through periods of small restriction to test myself. I've seen too many people know what food actively hurts their bodies, yet they are not able to refrain from consuming it. I feel that if I can voluntarily restrict myself in an effort to improve my health once in a while, then I am practicing the ability to eliminate that item if it becomes necessary to do so. Evaluate your fears and put in place and practice the weapons you will use to combat them.

Knowing that some common food restrictions include gluten, sugar, white flour, and carbs, I understand that reducing them is beneficial to my health, even if I don't have to eliminate them. I enjoy finding meals that fit these specifications. And as I work to eat more nutritiously, my preferences naturally become healthier, in general. My plan of prevention is strengthened by the choices and actions I take. What plans will help you prevent your biggest fears from coming to pass?

Putting your prevention into The Accountability Code is preparation. As you work to overcome your fears, I want you to know that preparation will lessen your fears and stress (perhaps altogether). If I ever do need to restrict my diet based on ailments or dietary needs, I'll be capable of doing so because I have prepared myself for it.

It's time for you to face your fears, to prepare for them by creating a plan, and to take action. You have the power to conquer even your biggest fears. Say, 'I am bigger than my fears!' Implementing action is another way of being courageous.

If you are unsure how to tackle your fear, or you need help working through it, please take my Mindset Inner Strength Quiz to begin the process.

Simply scan this QR code and click on free quizzes.

Urgency

I don't like putting things off. Each time I push a task back, I know I reduce my choices and options as the deadline nears. Not being prepared makes my stress levels rise, so I take preparation seriously. The simplicity of using The Accountability Code demonstrates just how easy it is to take action now. That, my friends, is preparation at its finest.

As a life and fitness expert, I like to try fitness events to challenge myself in order to help my clients. These challenges give me a deeper understanding of what it takes to succeed. Recently, I decided to try a half marathon, with six months to prepare. I spoke to a neighbor who had run that marathon, and she told me, "I finished without stopping at all, out of sheer pride, because my family said I couldn't do it."

If she could do it without any training, I figured I could do it with six months of training, and so I began training with time to spare.

Did I mention that I don't love running? I will only go on a run if I feel like turning up the tunes and getting away from home. When I run, I prefer to be dropped off far away from home and then run back. Near my house, we have a fantastic trail that runs along the mountain. This shady pathway goes for miles. When I began training for the half marathon, I used this trail, which exits through a neighborhood opening, and then I found my way home through the streets. I clocked my time, with the goal being to run longer each time than I had the time before. I trusted an online running community that told me, "If you can run ten miles, you can run any distance." I prepared and ran as much as I could before race day, but that comment gave me the confidence to feel ready even if I was unsure how the race would go.

The race would take place in late October, when temperatures were cooler. There was additional preparation I needed to take in order to acclimate to running a marathon in colder weather. I decided to prepare myself for the change in weather by running in the early mornings before the sun had warmed things up.

Anytime I participate in a race or fitness event, I have three goals: stay safe, finish, and have fun. I use these three rules to determine what I need to do to prepare. Every day in planning is golden: when today is over, you can't get it back, and if you fail to prepare, you prepare to fail.

Preparation happens with small, consistent actions, especially when running an endurance race. I had to ask myself: 'Is there a possibility that I could stay safe, finish, and have fun, even if I was not certain of the outcome?' You bet I could!

Your end goal is the start to your plan. When you know where you want to be, you can prepare yourself for each step of the way. My end goal with the half marathon was to complete the race and add it to my list of experiences, gaining expertise to help my clients. I was determined to live by my rules of staying safe, finishing, and having fun. Here are some of the ways I prepared to do that:

- I needed to dress in layers on race day so that I would be warm at the start, but easily cool down as my body temperature rose.
- I needed to be well-fueled, eating nutritiously the days before the race, the morning of, and carrying healthy carb-based snacks, as well as water, during my run.
- I needed good shoes that were broken in.
- I needed to know in advance where the bathrooms were along the way.
- I needed to be in the best shape possible in order to avoid relying upon others for assistance.

In order to stay safe while working towards your goal, what planning needs to occur?

Do you have experience to compare a half marathon to? Before completing this, I believe the longest race I had done before was a Super Spartan Race, which was eight miles and twenty-five obstacles to overcome. I was able to finish that race, so I felt confident that adding just five miles while eliminating those twenty-five obstacles shouldn't be too challenging.

Are you fully aware of the distance and requirements of *your* next goal?

As I mentioned, it was also important to have fun in this half marathon. I didn't have friends joining me, so I had to find fulfillment in other ways. Having fun consisted of remembering exactly why I was doing this, and what the benefit would be long-term. Running itself isn't fun for me, but trying new things is. What sounds fun about your goal? How will you prepare to enjoy yourself while reaching *your* accomplishments?

What must you do today to prepare to succeed? I had to stretch adequately after each run, since injury prevention is a priority to stay safe. I needed to figure out my nutrition for the long distance, which was about two and a half hours of running. I needed to fuel properly with the right supplements. And I needed to get up and run, while increasing my steps daily.

Urgency reminds us of the importance of taking action now. Every day closer to our goals should bring us more in alignment with our plans. Every day that I ran in preparation for the half marathon required me to follow my plans. I had to make time to run. I had to track my distance. I had to push myself and test my limits each time.

But the first time I actually ran 13.1 miles was the day of the race! Up to and including that day, I had to rely on grit and pride to take me the extra 3.1 miles past what my body could complete. What must you do now to achieve the peace of mind that you can finish your goals?

What evidence or determination do you have to prove you will succeed?

Every time you take action toward your goals, you should visualize your physical body creating success. Each time you do that, you increase your level of ability.

And safety should always be part of the preparation for achieving any goal. It's much more fun to plan for success than to stress about healing an injury.

Use urgency as a motivator to actually enjoy life now. As you implement safety measures in your plans, what benefits are you realizing? When you create urgency, you'll find yourself progressing at a faster pace. Future goals will require less planning, plus you'll have evidence of knowing how to accomplish your goals. Do you see why the skill of finishing is something you should put more of an emphasis on?

Lastly, I believe that urgency in having fun is part of what makes life rewarding. Tomorrow is not a guarantee. Tomorrow may be busier than today, and less likely to produce the outcome you're looking for. When you reach your accomplishments, you are happier, and this only contributes to you showing up again and making more of your dreams come true. Think about the last time you really had fun as you worked on your goals. What can you do today that helps you achieve success, while having amazing fun?

Let's do a quick run of The Accountability Code with my half marathon experience so you can see how easy and effective it is to take action with urgency:

Reflection — I am doing this because I want to better help my clients.

Humility — I won't know until I do it, and there'll always be ways to improve.

Planning — Sign up! Pay the fee, commit to the date, & schedule practice.

Implementing — Get out the door now and collect data on your progress.

Commitment — Continue taking action & stay safe, finish, and have fun.

Feedback — Be proud of your progress and efforts, regardless of outcome.

Single Tasking

I used to brag about how much I could get done all at once. I was the Queen of Multitasking and loved hearing people say to me, "I don't know how you do it all!"

I truly believed that doing as much as possible, all at the same time, was the best way to get my responsibilities done — ignoring that multitasking could be just a word for screwing up several things at once!

I used to spend time with my kids to get the chores done. I used the lame excuse that we could have fun cleaning because we would be doing it together. Sad, huh? Imagine someone who wants to hang out with you only if they can get their to-do list done at the same time.

My husband, in his infinite wisdom, decided to show me just how foolhardy my multitasking was. He suggested that for our next date night, we should pick up food and eat it in his office, while I watched him play video games. Ummm, no thanks! Lesson learned!

When it comes to mastering self-accountability and connecting your mind and body, it's imperative that you give both the dedication they deserve. Trying to do it all simultaneously, rather than taking deliberate action with each, could very well be the number one thing that is holding you back from leveling up in the healthiest way.
Let's debunk the myth that multitasking is productive. All important things in life deserve our undivided attention. My kids, husband, family, friends, work, self-care, play time — each merit time on their own to be nourished and enjoyed. If we break that down even more, each of my kids deserves one-on-one time with me, and my husband deserves business talk, home time, and intimacy without them being bundled together.

You also deserve to fulfill each part of you without feeling obligated to shove them all together. Taking action in the right direction will require you to break down which parts of you need the most time and attention in order to thrive. It's time to implement
those truths!

It's taken me a long time to understand the value of *single tasking* and put it into practice. At times, I still feel obligated to get all my responsibilities done at once, but I understand that each will not require the same level of energy or intention.

I've always told people that I can teach every fitness format under the sun, minus yoga and Pilates, because I'm not serious enough for those formats. I am a fun, energetic, and outgoing person. That message, however, stems from the belief that I must be ALL of me in every single moment — and that's neither true nor productive. Waking up and showing up is all about defining each part of you that deserves to grow.

Life is about connecting your mind and your body for a deeper awareness and greater joy. To connect the mind and body, we're going to focus on just one task at a time and focus on putting it into action. The example below can help you apply this concept to your current to-do list.

Make a list of five important things you must get done today. My list today includes spending time with my kids, taking the dog for a walk, alone time with Aubrey, work tasks, and calling my sister.

When you look at the tasks you plan to accomplish today, you'll see that some are more important than others. Assign each of your five tasks a number of 1 to 5, based on its importance. Give it a 1 if it's sort of important and give it a 5 if it's really critical, and you'll have a more focused, more productive, more satisfying day.

5: Spending time with my daughters

4: Spending time with Aubrey

3: Work responsibilities

2: Call Sister

1: Walk Dog

Now ask yourself, 'Which of these five items would be more appropriate to delegate to someone else?' That's an easy answer for me: It's important for the dog to be walked regularly, but it isn't imperative for me to be the one to do it. We can rotate that responsibility in our household to make sure Mia gets her regular exercise.

Look back at your remaining four items and ask yourself, 'Will I do this?' Let me tell you: If it's important to you, you will find a way. If not, you will find an excuse. Do you need to eliminate or reschedule one of your tasks for when you are more likely to tackle it?

If you cut your list back by two, but then find yourself wanting to add more items out of a burst of motivation, hold on. This is a sign that you are focused on quantity rather than quality. If any of those new tasks have to do with someone you dearly love — family, close friends, favorite hobbies — then you should consider adding them to the list and evaluating their importance. If not, when would be a better time to add them to your to-do list?

Now, it's about giving each item the time and attention they deserve. Don't water down the most valuable things in life by mixing them with chores. If you're going to walk the dog, do so with focus and joy. If you need to call your sister, don't do it while watching a movie with your kids.

If you are a recovering multitasker like me, it's tempting to try and go through your list as quickly as you can. But it's important to know your limits. Doing more doesn't necessarily bring more happiness. Take a deep breath and say to yourself, 'I give deliberate attention to the things I care about.'

You can do this lesson for any kind of list. It doesn't have to be about tasks. It could be an intention list or a love list. Define what you want your list to represent and how you assign value to each item on the list. Is your numeric system based on productivity, or happiness?

Once you have your list whittled down to the most critical items, then you need to give each your individual attention. If these tasks are important to you, show each their value through your actions. If your kids are important to you, then show them by spending enjoyable and meaningful time with them. Give them the focus they deserve. Not only will you benefit from each interaction when you're focused, but your body will be more aligned with your beliefs about the importance of these tasks. Your actions express your priorities. What is most important to you today?

As you improve your single tasking, you'll find clarity and purpose in each of your tasks. I urge you to seriously limit technology, if it's not truly necessary, for the task at hand. Don't you find it annoying when someone interrupts your precious time but then just sits there scrolling on their phone? Imagine how annoying others find it when they want to spend time with you, but you've brought your entertainment with you. It's a message that you care more about your device than you do about your loved ones. Turn off the tech if it has nothing to do with your task.

The goal is to improve your relationships, reduce your stress, develop other parts of yourself, and create more happiness in the world you live and work in. The Accountability Code is all about helping you develop the skills to follow through on what you know you really need to do.

Lastly, celebration will solidify your efforts because it reinforces the goodness that comes from making a deliberate effort. After finishing a task, I will tell myself, "I got a lot of work done" or "I did a good job today." And if I fulfill a task that involves someone else, I make sure to tell them that I'm glad we made the time to connect.

I'm happy to be a recovering multitasker who now understands the value and pleasure of focusing on the most important things, one at a time, as they truly deserve. And guess what? My ability to be accountable to what matters most just became easier.

Chapter 5 - Commitment

Commitment – Dedicating yourself to a person or cause

Commitment is your solid, unwavering determination to achieve a specific outcome. In the last chapter, we talked about how you need to revisit your intentions if you find yourself fulfilling others' expectations. I am here to tell you that at times you are going to feel that way about an old version of yourself.

The way you think will change as you learn and grow. You will be exposed to more people, situations, and opportunities that will encourage you to consistently update each piece of The Accountability Code for yourself.

I want to explain this to you by telling you about my 10-year battle with modesty. Yep, religious modesty, as in making sure the private, provocative parts of your body are covered so as not to tempt men around you or not to offend God by showing those off generally. I found myself judging others for showing their stomachs and shoulders, and I was committed to staying covered, no matter the consequences. I never wanted something bad to happen to me because I wasn't modest.

The old me was okay judging others for their lack of righteousness. I was taught that doing certain things brings happiness and that, if you are suffering, it is all because of your choices. I was trained to look through the lenses of obedience and perfection. I was committed to doing what was "right."

Even as a fitness professional, I made an effort to make a statement that I could be modest no matter what I was doing. In my mind, it was a way to prove how righteous I was by making a sacrifice that others wouldn't – forget wearing tank tops, short shorts, let alone just a sports bra on top!

I dealt with adjusting my clothing and even changing angles while instructing, if my undergarments were hanging out or showing. That was until I just about died instructing a water aerobics class in the humidity of an indoor pool. Not only did I have under- garments that went to my knees and covered my shoulders, but I also wore active wear that covered those. As I danced and instructed (all my students were in swimming suits), the humidity got the best of me. I felt trapped in my clothing. Even the highest quality of fabric couldn't help my skin breathe through layers of sweat-soaked clothing.

Escaping a call for an ambulance, I ended class early. The experience stunned me into awareness that something needed to change. Should my commitment to declaring modesty put my life at risk? In an effort to always be covered, I let expectations and teachings of others trump my intention, purpose, and safety. Instead of showing up to instruct others on having a fun and safe workout in an appropriate environment, I had convinced myself that being fully covered, to make a statement, was more important.

My commitment to defining modesty came to life for me. Instead of modesty meaning just being physically covered, I had to go deeper. I had to find out what modesty in action and intention had to do with me living true to my beliefs. Had I been modest in dress while totally abusing what modesty really meant? Unfortunately, yes. Being modest means free from egotism and boastfulness. Wow! What an update for my intentions and commitment! Why not commit to working on the inside, and let the outside follow as we learn?

With so many variables, I realized that only one commitment should guide all others. **I must stay committed to listening to the right sources and act when I receive an answer.** When I journeyed with intention and purpose, my habit of judging others disappeared. I was given the ability to support others in their own journey, always believing that they were doing the same thing.

As I valued my own journey of listening to those internal messages, I dressed in a way that allowed me to show up with honesty and purpose. I realized that my battle with modesty was not in my clothing choices, but how I judged myself and others. No longer did I speculate that I knew others' intentions based on the way they dressed. I treated everyone as if they are learning what is right for *them* – because in reality they are!

At the end of the day, commitment means revisiting your goals and proving to yourself you can keep your word because it's the right thing for you to do. If I dress my mind and body with intention and purpose for what I'm meant to do in life, I cannot fail. Your commitment to the plan you just created is the very piece that will guarantee success.

Here's how to stay committed:

1. Create affirmations.

An affirmation is a statement that represents a belief, intention, or state of being. Throughout the lessons in this book, you'll be given numerous examples of affirmations paired with physical actions. To say you are committed is one thing, but *to take action* is another. Your affirmations should inspire and spark action, whether it be a fresh start, an increased clarity, or an updated sense of urgency to reach your goals.

My affirmations about modesty have evolved as I watch my daughters grow from children into young women who want to express themselves. When clothing tempts me to make a judgment, I think and say, "We are all figuring out what is right for us." Regardless of clothing choices, "We are all worthy of love."

When you create affirmations, you are choosing to keep a desired outcome at the forefront of your mind. When you don't, you're letting old judgments keep their place.

2. Habit link.

Habit linking is your ability to piggyback on something meaningful and to extend the results. Think about the things you do automatically every single day, like brushing your teeth, eating food, going to the bathroom, or sleeping. Habit linking is deciding to pair another action before or after something you're guaranteed to do. After you brush your teeth, repeat an affirmation out loud. Before you eat, count your blessings. After you use the restroom, clean 3 things up to improve your space.

I found habit linking to be incredibly helpful to my fitness and instructing. As I put on my workout clothes, I set the intention of my workout. My clothing choices are purposefully chosen to help me fulfill my physical capabilities to the fullest.

When you habit link, you're creating a chain of events that produce and prolong goodness. When you don't, you'll feel disconnected and find it difficult to create momentum towards your goals.

3. Have a system for checking in.

I am a part of a networking group of 40 business owners that meet in person once a week. It is called Business Networking International or BNI for short. It's been an amazing blessing in my life because of the organized system for checking in. In my group, even though we all run different businesses, we are committed to growing through supporting each other and networking. One major reason people join a BNI or networking group like this is to earn more money and find more referrals, that has been true for me but my main reason for joining was to have a consistent check-in that I agreed to commit to.

As I talk about my business in the weekly meeting, I am reminded of the importance of modesty in all that I do. I want to refrain from exaggerating or thinking that growing my business is always about me, me, me. Pairing my personal goals with an organization that supports me with accountability I have found a higher level of fulfillment and success.

Having a system for checking in gives your life a pattern to follow and ensures you have a checkpoint to recenter on. I find extra strength in my efforts because I am committed to BNI which includes a Code of Ethics. My favorite line in the Code of Ethics is "I will display a positive and supportive attitude." Whether my commitment each week is to my personal goals or a deliberate business goal, the reminders to be supportive and positive go a long way. I recommend visiting a BNI chapter if you need help becoming and staying accountable. This fits perfectly into the fifth step of The Accountability Code, commitment.

When you have a system for checking in, you are reminded of why you started in the first place and it fuels your mind, body, and spirit to keep going. When you don't, it's easy to forget about your goal altogether.

Reasons for resistance to staying Committed —

1. Competing commitment

We have internal beliefs that are set in stone due to how we were programmed as a child, even if they don't serve us well. The way we act reflects our desire to fit in with our society. Competing commitments can hold you back, but once you uncover them, you can update your programming.

One competing commitment I had is about money. I realized this commitment while reading Secrets of the *Millionaire Mind* by Harv T Ecker. He explains that the way we handle money is due to the way our parents treated and spoke about money.

I began to recall my dad always complaining that wealthy people had buildings named after them because of their large donations. He claimed that large donations were only charitable if it was done in secret. His complaints continued by using specific words to describe wealthy people: selfish, prideful, and arrogant. The way he spoke played into how much money I thought I deserved to have or even earn. Deep down, I did not want my dad to believe that if I had money then I would automatically fit into that category, too, so I limited my ability to become wealthy.

My financial situation instantly improved when I got married, and consequently so did my view of money. Compared to my upbringing, my in-laws were rich, but it wasn't due to being selfish, prideful, or arrogant. They have sufficient for their needs and enough to give to help others because they make sound buying decisions, plan ahead, and invest in education and opportunities. Those are all things I failed to learn about money, but now that

I see my dad's opinion was false, I was free to create supporting beliefs that keep me committed to my own personal monetary goals. We should not feel bad when our competing commitments surface. You are human, and you are here to learn.

In order to beat this resistance, continue to question what you were taught and how it plays into your life now. What do you really need to stay committed to, and why?

2. Mental fatigue

Fatigue extends beyond normal tiredness and is a major reason why people don't follow through. It manifests itself through missed engagements, withdrawn mood, lack of desire, and reduced attentiveness. To beat mental fatigue and increase your commitment, the number one thing you can do is get adequate sleep. There are 4 basics of health that I hold every single one of my clients accountable to: sleep, self-care, water, intake, and movement.

When it comes to sleep, I instruct my clients to focus on quality first. The reason for quality is that it can be improved quickly by turning on screens close to bedtime, creating a wind down routine, and introducing breath work to help facilitate relaxation.

Next, we'd focus on understanding your circadian rhythm, or body clock. This means taking note and collecting data on when you function best, when your body signals it's time for bed, and the best time to wake up.

Lastly, increasing the amount of sleep you get is ideal. It is during sleep that our body repairs itself from the damage of stress and prepares for another day. Adequate sleep will do wonders for making sound decisions, performing your best, and, most of all, keeping your commitment in tip-top shape.

I had a client, Jean, who was 5 days into her program with me when she complained that reducing her sugar was not enabling her to lose weight. Upon reviewing her accountability, I could see that she was getting less than 5 hours of sleep, so I suggested we tackle her sleep problem and then talk about weight loss. She agreed, and she admitted that she lays in bed with the intention to sleep, but ends up in sadness thinking about her husband who had passed 3 years earlier. Talk about mental fatigue!

I suggested we include meditations into her evening routine with affirmations about gratitude for life and the experiences she had with her husband. We created intentions that centered around living the kind of life that would make her husband proud. Her mood changed instantly, and within the next couple days she was in tears as she reported having slept for 7 hours. That hadn't happened since before her husband passed away.

As we continued to focus on the basics of sleep, self-care, water, and movement, she excitedly told me that, with her consistency in sleep paired with her food awareness, her excessive weight started coming off!

In order to beat this resistance of mental fatigue and a lack of commitment, put a plan in place to keep a healthy mind and body. Your health is more important than any other goal you can set because if you don't have your health, anything you do have won't
last long.

Fresh Start

My last child, Leah, was eighteen months old when we took her trick-or-treating for the first time. She's a go-getter and has been walking since she was nine months, so I thought she'd keep up with her sisters and quickly learn how this holiday activity goes.

Instead, at every door we knocked on, she'd say "Twick or tweat!" but forget to hold the bag open. Instead, she would reach into the neighbor's big bowl of candy and just grab a handful! She was committed to getting what she could in that moment. That little spitfire would grab the biggest handful of colorful wrapped candy, and little as she was, the neighbor would just laugh and say, "Go ahead!"

But Leah wouldn't let go of the candy and let us put it into her bag. Instead, she would clutch the handful of candy as we proceeded to the next house and it was only after she would see the new enticing candy that she would drop her handful in their bowl and grab a new handful! Everyone laughed, of course, but she had an empty bag, whereas her sisters' bags were quickly filling. Leah wouldn't listen when we told her she had to put the candy in her bag and wait until she got to the next house to get some more. She couldn't let go. She was only willing to do so when she saw something better to replace it.

It's sort of like holding onto a grudge, only willing to let it go when we have something better to be bitter about.

Do you find yourself holding onto experiences or expectations that once served you, but you can't let them go until you find the next thing you deem worthy of your attention? For instance, if someone has wronged you, do you wait until they apologize to forgive them? How is waiting for the next best thing serving you? Or are you missing out on new experiences and exponential growth by holding on to the past? I know I'm guilty of that.

Believe it or not, letting go of one moment and being open to a new beginning is the key to happiness. Luckily, it's never too late to start the habit of letting go, and letting the good fill in. Can we each get out of our own way and create new beginnings that move us right into habits that better help us experience life in the moment, benefit from it, and open us to greater possibilities?

What are you holding onto that's keeping you stuck? Is there a disagreement or conflict from your past that you're consumed with, or a past goal you cannot relinquish? Can you admit that you're the one holding yourself back?

I have been meaning to update my water aerobics class for a couple of years. My students love the format, so it's easy to just tell myself that what I'm doing is fine. But I know I'm capable of more. I'm letting their compliments hold me back from achieving greater success. I tell myself the class is adequate the way it is, when I know the class could be stellar.

What have you failed to do because what you're already doing is 'good enough?'

Just like my water aerobics class, you know there is something in your life that you could improve upon, or something you don't yet have, but want, and something is holding you back from achieving it. That something, by the way, is — *you!*

It starts with releasing your thoughts and committing to move on to the next best thing. Put those ideas in your virtual Halloween bag, and prepare to accept new ones. It doesn't mean that the old thoughts disappear. Just like candy, those ideas were pretty amazing when we got them! As you release each, say out loud,

I am ready for more.

I'm building upon what I already have.

This is going to be so much better.

I know my new experiences make me a better person.

If you're reading an exciting book, you don't want to keep reading the same chapter over and over, no matter how juicy it was. Turn the page! What's coming is going to be better.

What scares you about what may be coming next in your life? Are there particular labels or events that you don't want to let go of because they're comforting, or they have defined you for a long time, and you're at ease with that? Do even the uncomfortable labels (not skinny, not happy) feel so stuck to you that the idea of ripping them off terrifies you? It's normal to feel uncertain about starting a new chapter in life. Comfort zones are — well, comfortable, after all! They're familiar, but not necessarily because they're healthy.

I tell myself that I don't have time to restructure my aerobics class. I don't even know if the students will like the change. I'm tired of teaching so many classes each week. Those are fear-based beliefs that, frankly, are really just excuses. Anytime we step out of our comfort zones, we're going to feel inner resistance.

Say to yourself again, "I am ready for more." I know that I am ready to take my water aerobics class to the next level, and that it only requires me to add one more new song. I don't have to start from scratch, and, frankly, my class would be pretty mad if I did! Introducing just one new song reminds me of my choreography skills and ability to make things fun for my students.
What is your next step? When Leah had the opportunity to get more candy, she went for broke! But we don't have to do that. We can stand back, carefully look at the bowl, and pick our favorite. We can let go of the candy we don't really enjoy and reach instead for what truly excites us. When you get good at letting go of old ideas and habits in favor of new ones, then you, too, can go for broke, "Go all in."

But start small. If your goal is to start meditating, just find a quiet corner and carve out one minute of time at first. You potentially grow just as much by taking that first small step as you do by leaping forward in bounds. If your goal is to create a better start to your day than waking with one eye open and scrolling through your social media feeds, then just try it once! Set your alarm, don't hit snooze, and get out of bed to see what that day might bring you.

Something wonderful is about to happen! You may feel uncomfortable at first, but just by trying a little bit, you're saying **"YES!"** to more fulfilling experiences in life. If you hold onto the past (good or bad), it could prevent you from enjoying all that life has to offer. And if you seek a really fresh start, remember that it's possible only *when or after you start*.

What is the next best thing you can do to see greater results? When you've got momentum, you can keep moving forward. Fill up that bag with candy or whatever you desire, and get ready to do it again the next day!

Keeping your commitment to improving yourself can be much easier than keeping a commitment to hold a grudge. When it comes to committing to a fresh start, let's plug this concept into The Accountability Code.

Whether you feel stagnant due to a negative reason or just a lack of motivation to do something great, The Accountability Code can help you commit to your next phase of happiness, as shown in this outline:

	Getting over negative	Pursuing positive
Reflection —	What is that grudge or offense you are holding on to?	How have you been resting on your laurels?
Humility —	Where were you wrong in the situation?	Determine how your skills can be magnified at this time in your life.
Planning —	What outcome needs to happen for you to move on?	What next goal is worthy of your skillset?
Implementing —	Have that conversation, burn those thoughts, go and make it right.	Follow the same plan that brought you success the first time.
Commitment —	Define how your loyalty to your path is the most important thing.	Share your goals with others.
Feedback —	Notice how you feel when you are done.	Recognize the impact your success is having on others.

Anxiety-Calming Habits

As a mother of four girls, I have learned that my commitment to calmness must never falter. Screams and fights were no stranger to my house, and I've learned that no amount of awesome parenting can guarantee control of growing daughters.

In a house full of girls (or any mixture of kids), it's common to get interrupted, not feel heard, and become overwhelmed when trying to get your point across. In recent years, I began to notice that one of my daughters would frequently leave the room during conflicts rather than fight to be heard.

Liz is my quiet child, which explains why she's often the first to bow out. I wanted her to know that she had a right to her feelings and the responsibility to own her voice. So I approached her with my concerns and learned that she has been dealing with feelings of anxiousness. She tends to get worried easily and isn't comfortable with trying new things very often.

In an effort to help Liz, I decided to learn some anxiety-calming habits so I could accurately explain how it felt to practice them, and then I would share them with her. Reducing anxiety has now become something I'm much more aware of and diligent about, in helping my daughter understand and express her feelings. Staying committed is much easier when there is a solid reason.

Practicing anxiety-calming habits together has enabled us to connect and get clear on how we want to respond to what we are feeling. Liz and I found a deeper connection by spending time one-on-one, meditating together, and talking about how we feel without the interruptions of her sisters.

She can articulate how she feels, when she needs a break, and the appropriate times to yell and scream. My mom taught me a song when I was little, and I've taught it to my girls, too: "Sometimes you just gotta yell and scream, sometimes it's the only thing to do. Noisy as a fire truck, you just gotta open up, and get the crowd's attention turned to you."

Now, I haven't had to teach my girls how to scream or stomp the floor. I have had to teach them where and when it's appropriate, and that slamming doors is not a part of the practice, either! I believe it's okay to yell, but I needed to remind Liz that it's a tool she should use only when necessary.

For instance, we recently went on a walk to the park together. I wanted her to go somewhere she could scream as loud and as much as she wanted. She laughed when I showed her how to do it. I encouraged her by yelling, "Let's scream togeeeeetherrrrr!" and she laughed again. I was grateful that she knew how to raise her voice if she wanted to, but, more importantly, I created an environment where she was happy and smiling and in charge of her expression.

I was also seeing the goodness of spending one-on-one time with each of my children.

I want to share with you more anxiety-calming habits I learned for Liz. These practices can help you learn more about yourself and instantly return you to a calmer awareness, thus increasing your own commitment to your current goal, even potentially reducing the number of times you feel anxious.

Anxiety is defined as a feeling of worry, nervousness, or unease, typically triggered by an imminent event or an uncertain outcome. But in the moment, it can feel profoundly catastrophic, and you may not know how to respond when anxiety hits you. If our commitments are filled with solid anxiety, that can stunt our actions and our achievements.

First, when a situation feels threatening or stressful, remove yourself from it, if possible. Imagine a referee flashing the "time out" (hands in a T) gesture and giving yourself space from the situation. I recommend physically leaving the space and going somewhere you associate with comfort. For me, that's my bed. I even used to work in my bedroom because that space felt so natural and comfortable.

Where can you go to feel safe? You can even take something with you – a pillow, or a blanket, or a cherished object – if that feels right. Remove yourself from the situation, and go someplace where you can be alone.

Once you are in a safe place away from the stress factor, talk to yourself. Give yourself a simple message to acknowledge what you are feeling. Use words that make you feel calm, grounded, and in control of yourself. I usually say the words, "I feel weird," and saying them out loud instantly focuses on my physical body and my emotions, rather than what just triggered me. What can you say in that moment that will bring you back to yourself?

Then pinpoint what made you feel anxious. Sometimes it will be plainly evident, and other times you will need to examine the situation closely to find the trigger. I'll usually work backwards in those moments when I'm trying to figure out what started my stress.

Not long ago, I had a pattern of fighting with my dad and storming out of the house to get away. I'd stay upset long after I returned to my own home, not understanding what got me so anxious. It took removing myself from the situation, finding a place of comfort and security, saying my mantra to myself, "I am doing the best I can," and tracing my steps backward, to finally see that the trigger was my parents' home.

Being in that place where I grew up shifted me uncomfortably back to the feelings and behaviors I had as a kid. Those feelings made me feel anxious because I didn't feel safe there. I gave myself a time out – not only in that moment, but long term. I know when I visit my folks that I'm likely to experience the same feelings, and so I minimize my visits there almost to none.

By the way, taking a time out does not mean to quit trying. It means to regroup and come back with a stronger commitment to doing what is right for you.

The greatest tool I have found in dealing with stress is breathwork. There are many different breathing exercises that can help you find clarity and calm and reconnect you to feeling safe in stressful situations. Here are a few I find helpful:

A. Deep breathing.

Taking deep breaths is linked to improved cognitive performance and can lower stress levels. Taking in more oxygen at once allows your body to fully trade it with outgoing carbon dioxide. This physical response can not only shift your focus, but also relieve unnecessary tension in the body.

B. Begin saying to yourself, "inhale, exhale, inhale, exhale."

This works when you feel so disconnected that you cannot breathe deeply. It is a simple command that brings awareness to your body. Let your body take over when your brain is overwhelmed. Close your eyes, feel your breath, and let it slowly move from contention to harmony.

C. Box breathing.

This is an effective way to become more aware of your breath. Inhale for four seconds. Then hold it for four seconds. Exhale for four seconds. Then hold it again for four seconds. Imagine the four sides of a box or a square, as you breathe in, breathe out, and hold. You'll notice a decrease in stress and worry when you bring your breath into control.

Check out my video tutorial by scanning this QR code and I'll teach you exactly how to implement Box Breathing today.

D. Take your lungs through a range of motion.

I used to wake up in the mornings and immediately my first big breath hurt. I noticed I was only breathing shallowly, and I needed to exert myself more often. Our lungs are like muscles – they need to be conditioned so that they can adapt when we need them the most. Try this lesson throughout the day: Take in a huge breath, and then let it out completely. Fill your lungs as much as you can, and then release as much as possible. Breath is life. You can magnify its usefulness in many ways.

Ultimately, choosing to reduce anxiety takes practice and commitment to feeling well as much as possible. Anxiety, after all, is a powerful response in which our body is telling us we're in trouble. We need that response to recognize danger, but by practicing anxiety- calming habits regularly, you will train your body to use its stress responses only in life-or-death situations.

Make sure that your stress is an appropriate response to the situation you find yourself in. What are the circumstances in your life where anxiety is natural and expected, and which are the ones where stress feels out of proportion to the actual danger presented?

Know your triggers. I know that visiting my parents' home is a big one for me, so I refrain from going there. My daughter Liz has begun to recognize her triggers as we work on methods to reduce her stress and anxiety. Look back over your most stressful events in recent months and ask yourself, 'What are the common denominators?' Then determine how you can best support yourself when faced with similar circumstances.

Don't be afraid when anxiety shows up. It's a warning sign, letting us know when our pace is too fast, or we are out of alignment. Instead, commit to having a plan to use your stress effectively. Try the breathing exercises above or head to my YouTube channel called Fun & Sustainable Fitness. On my channel, if you search the videos with the term "box breathing" a 10 minute video will be there to teach you the process of breathing for relaxation. When emotions are high and your thoughts are troubled, your body can take over, if it's been trained to do so. Let's train it to relax when needed. Your body is like your best friend: there to support you and get you through the rough patches.

What's most important?

"Speed is irrelevant if you are going in the wrong direction."

— Mahatma Gandhi

Continually working towards your goals can be extremely draining. At every step, get real about how you've been failing and/or succeeding and use that info to change.

When I agreed to be on the reality tv show, Ace in the Hole, I was excited to use this as a launching pad to grow my business. I'd been in business, at that point, for six years, and it was still in side-hustle status. I was prepared to overhaul my business model if the experts told me to. And it wouldn't hurt for my business to gain some massive exposure through the show airing on tv later.

If this show has taught me anything, it's about commitment. I have never wanted to quit so much in my entire life, but you should know by now that I am not a quitter.

During prep work for the show, producers mentioned something called an 'uncovery.' I instinctively knew that I'd be put under a microscope, and that it could result in a very emotional experience. Every time I let someone in to know the real inside stuff about my business, I was told where I had gone wrong. So I had to be committed to improving when it was uncomfortable.

Luckily, the uncovering wasn't as triggering as I worried it might be. My mentor made it clear, however, that what I was doing wasn't working, although he encouraged me that with some tweaks I could begin to see massive growth in my business. I'd still be doing the work I love and working just as hard, but my efforts would work for me and not so much against me.

I had a lot of work ahead of me. I not only would be re-strategizing my business, but I'd also be on a reality show, competing against others and vying for the same prizes, resources, and mentorship. It also meant a lot of travel. Thankfully, Aubrey and I have an extended support system that would help care for our daughters while I was zipping around the globe and focusing on my business. I ended up filming in four different locations, including out of the country.

Here is the way my mind works: If I'm going to make these many sacrifices, it better be worth it. I needed to go all in, be entirely committed, and be fully prepared to take the actions my mentors and mindset coaches recommended.

I found myself working from sunup to sundown, never really seeing the end in view. Every time I got a handle on the big task I was working on, another one was thrown at me. The biggest mistake I made was failing to take breaks, rejuvenate, and look at the big picture. I told myself that I am not going to be on tv and suck at it.

I put my personal workouts on hold, told my kids to leave me alone, didn't make healthy meals, and didn't sleep like I should. Keep in mind that getting on this tv show happened right after my family downsized to 1400 square feet, with the intention of traveling around the world. I struggled to make regular meals in a kitchen with only 4 feet of counter space. We weren't supposed to be there as much as we were. As a result, my body quickly wore down: I developed a headache, was constantly exhausted, and, worst of all, I lost my voice!

These were all tangible reminders of the stress I was putting myself through in order to compete. I worked so hard that I no longer had the ability to work. What advantage would that give me? I had to adjust my commitment to what was most important.

I showed up to film the first episodes with barely an audible voice. I was on that show to share my message of Fun and Sustainable Fitness, and I couldn't deliver that message in a way that I wanted to.

Luckily, my life isn't always running at the pace of a reality tv competition show! It was a reminder of the ways that I already know how to adapt and to rebalance myself. Life will sometimes get crazy — in such cases, we need to be prepared to take control of the chaos.

Start with deliberate breaks. You cannot sustain breakneck speed without risking injury or illness. Let the fast times in your life be productive by taking a breather now and again.

Take into consideration how important your body is for the work you do. Whether you have a desk job, a manufacturing position, or something that requires a lot of stopping and standing, your body needs to be maintained with both movement and love. My body isn't wired for the 12-hour desk days I was forcing myself into those first weeks of the reality show, and it quickly let me know.

After losing my voice, I made the decision to take breaks and to return to my workouts. No matter how busy I was or how many demands on my time there were, I chose to step away daily from my computer and head to the gym. Ever since becoming a fitness instructor in 2009, I learned there is magic in moving your body. My worries feel smaller, and my stresses melt away when I'm working on my health in enjoyable ways. If you cannot take an hour break to workout, start with a ten-minute walk.

Say yes to what is most important.

I chose this path, ultimately, for my family. I struggled in the beginning, but inevitably I found small ways to take the breaks I needed and show my husband and kids that I care. If you must multitask, get your family around the dinner table. Ask for help, for feedback, for whatever needs doing, while enjoying nourishment together. We put together a regular grocery order, and I let the kids decide on dinner most times.

Then plan your play. Many times I told my kids, "As soon as I'm done working, we'll go get ice cream or head to the park or play a game." I still had work to do, but I made time for them and still felt on top of my tasks. In order to feel in alignment with myself, I must get work done before I play. If I don't, I struggle being present.

I used to be guilty of working too fast in the wrong direction. At the start of filming the reality show, I once filmed 24 videos in a rush to get to the next steps, only for my mentor to tell me that the scripts were wrong. Had I taken a break and viewed what I had done along the way, I would have discovered the error myself and saved myself over three hours of re-filming.

I'm a big believer that Sundays should be a day of rest. You could choose a different day if you prefer, but you need one day a week off from the daily grind. It gives you the chance to evaluate your progress and reset your body, mind, and spirit. Whenever I fail to take that day's rest, I know I'll feel fatigued by mid-week.

Say yes to what's most important.

I'm putting this in here again on purpose.

What is most important to you? Is your hard work supporting your success? I want to run a successful business, help people transform their lives, and I want to travel and spend time with my husband and children. I can do all of that if I choose my efforts wisely. Worthy pursuits on a big scale are important, but not at the expense of what you value most!

Rest and evaluate often.

When I slow down, I'm able to determine how my actions lead to my next steps. When I don't rest, I often rush through tasks and wind up having to fix them later. Slowing down is critical to catch the mistakes we are bound to make.

Are your sacrifices worth the results?

During filming of the tv show, I had to constantly remind myself that life wouldn't always be this crazy. I also had to acknowledge that the choice Aubrey and I made together to participate in this program did not give my kids a say in the matter. They're old enough to know that mom's going to be away for weeks at a time, but are they mature enough to understand the implications of our separation? It's okay to rely on the kindness of supportive friends and family short-term, but would I continue that practice if this was my permanent state of being? The simple answer is no.

We want to make good choices to avoid regrets later, of course. But "it takes a village to raise a child" (I love that statement!). Throughout the travels I took in support of the show, I knew that I could keep up my commitments because of the love and support of others. That meant, of course, reaching out first and asking for help. We each need a support system.

Who are the individuals who help you with your responsibilities? Who's 'got your back?'

Say yes to what's most important. (Yes, that's the third time I'm putting this here. It's that important!)

If you don't focus on the most important things, you lose your perspective and even your happiness. Focus is the key to staying aligned and purposeful. I ask once again, What is most important to you? How are you following through with your most important goals and values?

Review your 'Why.' This is the most powerful tool in slowing me down in the best way. If I want to grow my business, in order to enhance my children's lives, I can do that. I don't need lots of money or fame to teach them what is most important in life. I continue choosing to do hard things because I know they produce the most growth.

As you work to achieve more and take on commitments that seem larger than life, don't forget to take a step back from time to time. Recognize that you can't be consistent if you are depleted.

Life is defined by the choices you make. If you want something to happen, create strategies that consistently work for you to fulfill your most important value — instead of working against your most important values.

Burn-Out Cure

"The apple doesn't fall far from the tree." The impact you have on your children can last generations. The Accountability Code will help you increase your commitment to breaking negative cycles induced by stress.

I never heard the term self-care when I was growing up. There were always so many people running around the house that I only got alone time when my mom accidentally left me at the park! Nor do I remember my mother taking individual time for herself. She did, however, frequently visit her friend's house up the street for Scrabble games.

I enjoyed accompanying my mom during those days. Her friend had a pool, a Nintendo system that I wasn't fighting siblings for, and animals to play with, too.

But during Scrabble games was the only time my mom ever told me to stop bugging her. She'd be drinking soda and formulating triple score words. Don't attempt to win any sort of word game with my mom — she'll obliterate you! I knew that Scrabble days were a form of fun for her, but I never realized they were also part of her self-care. Nor do I think she thought of it in those terms, but she needed those outings and made them a priority.

I am like my mother in that I choose the same kind of escapes when I need a break: work, games, and friends. I'm lucky that, even as a newlywed, I had strong friendships I made in church. Like mom, I would get together with those friends to play board games, and many of them also had young kids, so it felt good to know that I wasn't alone. At one point, there were about six of us, but as each of our children started to grow up, we drifted apart. Some moved out of the area, and even my closest friendships faded.

Needing the connection of a like-minded community, I decided to start a YouTube channel. I would document our family's life, meet new people, and maybe earn some money while doing it. I loved the new community I was involved in, but producing regular video content was a lot of work. I came across another YouTuber who did book reviews, and she recommended one called *The Burnout Cure* by Julie D. Hanks. That really spoke to me because, at the time, I was trying to figure out what to pursue in life, how to balance family and work, and feeling exhausted. Having babies while going to college left me feeling constantly fatigued.

One chapter of the book talked about the importance of knowing how your parents handled stress. Perfect timing, because I saw my mom's best friend and Scrabble competitor at a bridal shower that weekend. I pulled her aside and asked her, "What are great characteristics of each of my parents that could also be a downfall?"

This friend told me that my dad was generous to a fault, that he would give the shirt off his back to a stranger, and that he was always willing to serve at the drop of a hat. But he often gave away his family's things when we were struggling, and he would leave my mom to fend with eight kids on her own.

I agreed with her assessment of my dad, who is very involved in the community. I remembered times when he helped friends financially but claimed to not be able to afford anything, and I recall feeling that his kindness came at the expense of our family.

As for my mom, the friend told me that mom was so kind and sweet, but she didn't know how to stand up for herself. She said, "I could see that she was struggling inwardly, but the second she interacted with someone else, her smile and positive attitude shined brightly. She didn't know how to give herself space to tune in or assess her own needs."

That was very interesting and very helpful information. I realized that I could see both my father's and my mother's characteristics in me. I have great qualities handed down to me from my parents. But I had the same risks they had by not recognizing their downfall characteristics and suffering as a result, and maybe even passing the worst traits down to yet another generation. I used this lesson to turn inward and define what legacies I would work to keep, and which ones I would discard. This was a commitment to keep, and an extremely important one.

Setting boundaries is incredibly important, and I'm going to teach you exactly how to pinpoint a negative pattern you learned and to create a plan to break the cycle. Boundaries are the key to helping you stay on the right path, consistently helping you keep your commitments strong. This will allow you to reduce stress, to become more aware of who you are, and to live your life with as much happiness as possible.

What are the negative legacies you learned in your childhood? How do your inherited patterns and habits cause stress in your life?

My dad was a yeller. He would accuse us kids of not listening to him unless he raised his voice. I have also been guilty of telling my kids the same thing, using their lack of response to justify losing my temper. My dad constantly told us to "Use your common sense!"

My family wasn't and isn't perfect, but I can't deny the love shown to me growing up. As we each work to progress in our lives, it's important that we don't throw out the baby with the bath water. What are the best things you became as a result of your childhood? What is the relationship between this positive attribute and the more negative ones you were exposed to?

It's natural to want to do better for future generations, so we must stay committed to breaking harmful cycles. As a group of eight kids, we definitely had our arguments. Ever had a rollerblade thrown into your back? Or barely dodged a butter knife that was thrown at you, only to shatter the oven window behind you? I'm also sure I handed out my fair share of aggression, and, in fact, I vividly remember slapping my little sister across the face and calling her a really bad word.

Today, I let my children battle it out sometimes, and I wonder if I'm repeating that cycle. I want to teach them that there are better ways to solve problems than by hitting. While it's not a good idea to let my girls physically fight each other, I do find value in their learning how to throw a proper punch. As part of learning how to break negative cycles from my childhood, I can teach my daughters how to defend themselves without hurting their sisters.

It is always possible to turn the negative into good.

I don't believe children's voices should be taken away. It's hard for kids to express their opinions or emotions, even if it gets a little loud. Aubrey and I are hoping to create a healthy balance that invites positive communication for all.

How can you merge the good and the bad that came from what you learned, growing up? Good lessons can be learned from bad experiences. How did the bad experiences impact you as a child?

I didn't think it was fair that my dad yelled at us to do household tasks he wasn't willing to do himself, like wash his own dishes or clean up his belongings. I never saw him do any household chores and whenever he yelled about a dirty house, I resented him.

Take the negative things others have done to you and consider how they made you feel. Is that emotion one you'd like to pass on to others? What reactions would you prefer to create instead? How can you commit to creating good from the bad?

If you still harbor ill feelings toward a parent or someone else from your past, that can be great motivation to discontinue the same pattern as quickly as possible. I have worked on my yelling, hoping my children see that I'm practicing control over my own behavior. As you address your behaviors, give your parents the same grace you want your kids to have for you. That grace will come in handy as you slip up, here and there. I found the affirmation, "I give and receive grace," to be especially helpful.

How can you find balance in your current environment? You don't have to forget the past, nor are you required to recreate it.

When I realized how bad I felt with how my dad treated me, I made a deliberate effort to treat my kids differently. I took deep breaths before responding, helped my children communicate before things got out of hand, and made my expectations clear by practicing what I preach. I want our relationship to be built on trust, and I'd rather be close to my children than trying to prove I'm right all the time.

This process of identifying the patterns I inherited from my parents, and stopping them before they manifested in my daughters, began by trying to prevent myself from feeling burned out. As an adult, I finally understood the concept of self-care and recognized the examples (or lack thereof) that were established by my parents' behavior.

I hadn't taken into consideration that my mother gave herself very little self-care, until I was a mother myself. We tend to think that each generation has its own problems, but no matter what our challenges are, they produce the same emotions. I wanted to prevent burnout because I wanted to set a different example for my daughters than I received from the previous generation. What are your reasons or motivations to change negative patterns?

A great side effect of this process has been spending much more time with my children because that was really at the root of what I wanted as a child: more time with my parents. By taking time with my kids, I demonstrate a different pattern to emulate, and I reduce my own stress and potential burnout. I'm happy knowing that I'm creating new habits for the next generation, while improving my own health. What are your reasons for breaking unhealthy patterns?

My girls will someday use their childhood as a reference for positive and negative experiences. I know I'm not doing everything right, and as they get older, they get to decide what to keep and what to change. While on the journey of doing your best, be willing to admit your mistakes and shortcomings.

Focus on connection, love, and mutual respect.

The choices you make have a lasting impact.

What is the one message you most want to hand down to the next three generations about reducing stress and creating happiness?

As you get clear on what is important to you, you'll find your commitments come with ease. Emotions are a powerful tool to get us to act. Using The Accountability Code means always intending and working on the change we want to see.

Even though my family isn't perfect I recognize the power I have to change. Watch this 60 second video and use it as a reminder that you can create greatness regardless of where you came from.

Always Ready

Sometimes in your life, you experience massive change in a short amount of time. Your emotions get hit so strongly that you know without a doubt it changes everything. This story about my friend Bee was one of those life-changing experiences that changed my commitment to my own expectations in a fundamental way.

I hope that, as you read this, you can identify experiences in your life that help define your commitments to solid, continuing values for your family and yourself.

Years ago, I sat in church and listened to my friend Bee talk about how her physical limits prevented her from helping people in many ways. She said, instead, she'd offer up a prayer when she could. Bee told me that once she saw someone's car stuck in the snow and, knowing that she couldn't literally help move them out of the way, she offered a prayer on their behalf.

Her words inspired me, and I decided to be like Bee, to pray for those that I couldn't physically help, but I also really wanted to physically help, too. My intention was put to the test when I drove home from the gym one day and came upon a truck which had taken a wide turn that caused a bunch of plywood sheets to slide out of the back of the truck. I was able to park quickly and safely run into the road, and help the driver lift the planks to clear the intersection. I actually found incredible peace and motivation from that incident to constantly be ready for any emergency moment by staying fit.

Bee continued to inspire my service. If you spoke in church, made someone a meal or offered a comment in class that impacted her, you would receive a card in the mail days later, thanking you. I committed to show my gratitude and love through cards, too. I have absolutely loved sending cards. They are excellent ways to offer thanks and lift someone in prayer, even when you cannot physically serve or are unable to call them in person.

Years later, after I moved away, I saw Bee's daughter post on Facebook that her mom was in the hospital. I quickly messaged Michelle for her mom's hospital address, and I fired off a letter to wish her well. Even though she was unwell, she returned the sentiment with some sweet words in another card to me. I have kept a collection of letters and cards that I get from friends, family, and clients over the years, and Bee has her own section.

Sadly, I soon learned that Bee passed away from complications of surgery. It hurt my heart even more to learn that it was weight-loss surgery. I knew how important it was to Bee for her to serve others in the best way she could. It was so sad that her life ended this way. She had taken a big step in her health, but her goodness on this earth was immediately ended. Sadly, no one would ever receive a card from her again.

Bee's legacy will live on, for she touched thousands of lives with her thoughtful cards. I can't help but wonder, however, how great her impact might have been if her physical health was different. Of course, I don't know all the details of her life, but she continues to impact me with her many examples of generosity and compassion.

In grief over the loss of my friend, I reached out to Bee's daughter, Michelle, to let her know how big her mother's impact had been. We had a very tender conversation. She told me that her mom had prayed and prayed to have weight loss surgery, but her family wasn't convinced that she was healthy enough to be successful. They tried to persuade her to change her mind, but Bee was adamant that she needed to go through with it.

To support their mother during her health issues and surgery, Michelle and her siblings started a group chat. They continued to communicate after their mother's passing, and they gained a closer relationship between themselves. To this day, they text daily.

Michelle shared with me that shortly after their mother's death, her brother was contemplating suicide and that he credits those daily texts with saving his life. Michelle allowed me to share her words: "I have no doubt in my mind that my mom traded her life for my brother's. I think she chose to follow the spirit and get the surgery even though we all knew her body wasn't in a good condition to be successful. We had so many tender mercies from the Lord during her illness and passing where we were able to see His hand and know He was aware of us. Knowing it was the right thing is only a small comfort, but it still helps."

It didn't lessen the grief or hurt of loss, but Michelle and her siblings were inspired to be better people because of their humble mother.

We never fully know what our impact will be on others, but we do know how important our bodies and our health are to our service to others. May we be in tune with our spirits and use our bodies to follow through on the good we want and desire to do for others.

I use this mantra: "True happiness comes only when our spirits learn to control our bodies, training them to be governed by the laws of God," as a reminder of what I must do physically so that my body will never hold me back from what is in my heart.

I'm so grateful to Bee for teaching me the lesson of serving however you can, and her ability to empower me with a few short, kind sentences in a card. No matter your physical condition, you have the power to make a massive difference in someone's life!

What ailments or limitations are holding you back from contributing to the world in a larger way? I know that when I'm feeling depressed, I don't show up as my normal self. If I get lazy with my daily health habits, I start to feel depressed more often.

Your body is a vehicle for your spirit. Nobody's body is perfect, but we are all blessed with the means of taking action for good. Knowing the value of eating nutritionally, I invite people over for dinner every other week. This helps me have a sit-down dinner, connect with others, and improves the relationship I have with food. How can you use your body to improve your impact on a deeper level?

I have also learned that when I'm feeling down, I retreat into my shell. This is why I love sending cards in the mail. Sending out words of gratitude relieves any negativity and takes a small amount of effort. I can still use my body to carry out goodness even when I'm not able to physically show up.

Sometimes we don't show up to serve because we don't know who needs us. It's beneficial to pray for service opportunities, and to ask where our help is most needed. Each time I use my body for good, I count my blessings.

Even if you are not on the verge of your own major health challenge, I guarantee that you know someone who is. Choosing to serve them can boost their mood, increase their happiness, and offer motivation to enjoy another day with those they love. Who comes to mind when you think about lifting the spirits of those who are suffering right now?

Do you know your family's history? Depression, anxiety, and mental illness has plagued my family for generations. I know that a good use of my efforts would be to prevent depression and to encourage those I love to seek treatment. What health concerns should you address before they get worse?

Keeping your health concerns hidden doesn't help anyone. The sooner you address what you are dealing with, the sooner you can reverse the impact. Seeking help is always better than trying to deal with it on your own. What health concerns do you need to share with your family and friends? Now is the time to make them known.

Allowing the body to rest and recover is an important part of staying healthy. My body needs movement in order to keep alive. I know that it's not one giant step that does the trick — it's lots of little steps. In order to make those steps, I need the four basics of health. I'll be preaching those until the day I die: sleep, self-care, water intake, and movement. If you do nothing else, commit to these, because they will give you a great baseline of health. Get at least seven hours of sleep, take time to tune in to your feelings each day, drink 64 ounces of water, and practice joyful movement.

You only have one body, and you never know what is coming next. Consider what experiences you've had that increase your motivation to take care of your mind and body. Creating an emotional connection to commitment makes it meaningful and powerful.

Stability

What if I told you that flexibility and stability are not opposites, and that your commitment to achieving them both is possible?

I cannot tell you how many times I have changed up my routine to fit my current season and stage of life. I like changing it up instead of trying to force myself to stick to what doesn't work anymore. Some seasons require me to be more diligent with a specific routine, and other times I can be flexible.

Everything has an ebb and flow to it, and it can feel positive to adjust as needed. The Accountability Code was created to be adaptive and applicable no matter what. Rest easy knowing that no matter what you are going through, The Accountability Code will help you create a plan you can stay committed to.

One summer, I found out that a friend of mine was looking for a surrogate to help her have a child. I was interested and decided to visit my doctor and get a clean bill of health to share with my friend. I wanted her to know, before I went through any additional testing, that I was a good candidate to help her expand her family.

At the time, I was teaching five classes at the pool, plus attending CrossFit for my own personal workouts. With this intense schedule, I needed to eat enough calories and found that eating higher fat foods helps me do that. I was also very busy, so most meals were eaten on the go with little rest throughout the day. My meals that summer consisted of a lot of chicken and cheese taquitos, hard boiled eggs, burritos, and cottage cheese: protein rich, calorie dense, high fat foods.

My doctor ran the tests and the next day, the results came back. I was still considered an above average candidate for surrogacy, but I discovered that I had higher cholesterol than I would like. I was really bummed that my stats weren't absolutely perfect. I had to take a big gulp of my own medicine and remind myself that there is a time and season for everything.

My summers are different from the rest of the year. I don't always need to eat high fat foods to keep up, I don't always teach five classes a week, I don't always continue my own workouts when I commit to teaching and, of course, I don't regularly apply to be a surrogate.

There were so many variables happening in my life that I failed to see what I was consistently doing right. I had to remember that flexibility is the key to stability, and vice versa! And I was committed to achieving both.

Even though any one of us can find a handful of things that we're doing wrong at any given moment, we have to remember the good choices we make, too. When our baseline of health is strong, we create the ability to be flexible on other levels. Regardless of what stage of life or season you are in, you have the power to create stability in your life. Stability will prepare you to shift and adjust, to accommodate the changes that really matter.

When I learned about my high cholesterol, I immediately adjusted my lifestyle. I increased my water intake, enjoyed every workout, stayed connected with friends and family, and worked to keep my body in a healthy condition to nourish a growing baby again if needed. And yes, I adjusted my diet as my schedule relaxed.

I was not selected as my friend's surrogate, but I'm happy to report that she successfully had a baby with another surrogate! I'm also happy to report that my cholesterol is back to normal levels. It was certainly a wake-up call to discover how high my levels were, but I quickly adjusted to reduce my fat intake and prevent further health factors from deterring my path in life.

Had I not become interested in offering my surrogacy services, I might not have gotten the expanded testing that summer that revealed my cholesterol levels. Thankfully, the efforts I have made to be both stable and flexible allowed me to make subtle adjustments to correct my meal plans and bring my cholesterol under control. Commitment to growth is what it's all about.

What are your most important reasons for creating stability in your life? My main reason is so that I can adapt to opportunities and enjoy the season I am currently in.

When stability becomes a habit using The Accountability Code, clarity and maturity also become habits. When I think of stability, I picture coming home to a peaceful home. I have a place to relax and be myself. There are no rules or unexpected demands. My home is a place for me to feel comfortable and to enjoy the freedom to do what I want. What does stability mean to *you*?

Each of us has some form of stability in our life: a home, a phone, income, food, someone to talk to. That stability will also extend into friendships, all areas of health, connection, and career. List which forms of stability are most important to you right now and say, "I have a stable life, and I create stability every day."

What are some action steps you must include in order to stay committed to having stability?

Stable means the strength to stand or endure. Even though things in our life change constantly, often asking us to change or bend, we can do so while holding true to an image that keeps us firm in our position. Imagine a dock by the ocean that remains still, regardless of the rising and falling tide. What challenges are you experiencing in your life right now that represent the changing tide? Reflect on that, and record your thoughts.

What areas in your life require stability, and which require flexibility? When I considered applying to be a surrogate, my overall needs were being met. I just wanted to offer something to someone else. I was enjoying teaching my classes and eating more food for fuel. I still passed the surrogacy health tests. Nobody was asking me for perfection, so there was no need to expect it. Humility helped me improve, even though it wasn't necessary.

If you are financially stable, you can be flexible with your time and generosity. If your health is stable, you can enjoy most foods without major repercussions, and if you have a stable marriage or relationship, you are free from the worries that single folks have. Stability provides flexibility. Can you see how planning enhances your stability in this process?

Pinpoint what areas you would like more flexibility in, and write them down. If I want more flexibility in my schedule, I must arrange it in a way that ensures the most important things are taken care of first. If I want more flexibility in my spending, I must pay my bills first. In order to gain flexibility in the areas you listed, what must you adjust in order to create stability first? How will your implementing skills prepare you for the best position?

Creating stability doesn't happen overnight. It takes practice and a deliberate effort to put all the pieces together and build that core strength. If you wanted financial stability, you would need to save an emergency fund, reduce unnecessary expenses, and plan ahead for planned and unplanned bills. Allow yourself to work towards stability by practicing the small things. Take a deep breath and say to yourself, 'I crave stability, and I am creating it each day. I am committed to being stable.'

There is no stability, however, without sacrifice. You must be willing to create the stability you seek, and that can be challenging in our ever-changing world. You will need to use your feedback to adjust and recommit. Are you seeing the results you want?

All good things take time. As you develop both stability and flexibility through commitment in The Accountability Code, remember that it's possible to enjoy the journey. Watch over time and see how your habits have set you up for success. If you are working on drinking more water, you'll feel refreshed and excited about healthy food choices. If you reduce extra spending, you'll notice that your bank account isn't drained as fast each month and that saving money becomes easier. For you to create stability in your desired area, what is the one thing you must commit to every day?

The world can be chaotic and demanding and even unstable. But the stability we do not find in our world is what we must create within ourselves first if we want to bring stability to the world. We will create an inner peace that comes from mastering what we know we need to do. Believe in your ability to stay committed, no matter what.

Brain—Body Connection

When I was thirteen, my mother started to ask me often to handle small tasks around the house: "Will you take out the trash?" "Will you mow the lawn, please?" "Will you get your room clean today?"

Each time I answered "Yes," even though I didn't want to do many of these tasks and wished my mom would ask one of my siblings instead, I said yes out of love and a sense of responsibility, and I knew they were simple chores that wouldn't take much time.

I said "Yes" each time, and I did each of those tasks, for two reasons: I knew what it felt like to have someone break commitments to me, and I never wanted to be known as a liar.

If I commit to something, I will make sure that I follow through and I always communicate when necessary. And I never wanted to tell someone I would do something and then be the reason they were let down.
There is a difference between committing to others and following through for yourself. We're going to dive a little deeper into why commitments can be easy or difficult to follow through with.

Depending on your personality, who you are showing up for can make a difference. I learned this from an archetype quiz called The Four Tendencies Quiz by Gretchin Rubin. It is a quick quiz that determines how you address obligations in your life. Your obligations can refer to work, home, or personal matters, and there are four types. I'll give you a summary of each, and then explain how to effectively use this information to establish reliability, commitment, and loyalty in your relationships, including your relationship with yourself.

The unique thing about this quiz is that it's based on behaviors and not preferences. It's not about how you feel about yourself but, rather, about what you actually do. When you know what is true for yourself, you'll be able to develop the trait of reliability and following through.

Take a second to read through the different types and determine which one you might be.

- Upholder — meets outer and inner expectations
- Obliger — meets outer expectations, and resists inner expectations
- Rebel — resists outer and inner expectations
- Questioner — resists outer expectations, and meets inner expectations

If you resist inner expectation (rebel, obliger), it does not mean you are doomed for internal confusion. It means you need to be aware of how you place expectations upon yourself based on what others have taught you. Rules you learned as a child may need to be adapted as an adult.

If you resist outer expectations (rebel, questioner), it doesn't mean you aren't a team player. It means you can define your strengths to others and meet the challenge with what you can provide rather than feeling forced to do it. Do what feels right to help, not what others tell you you need to do.

If you meet inner expectations (upholder, questioner), it doesn't mean you are selfish or conceited. It means you can develop a greater level of mastery to show up for others. Your loyalty to yourself can enable you to advocate for others' needs. Focus on serving in ways that feel in alignment.

If you meet outer expectations (upholder, obliger), it doesn't mean you care what everyone thinks about you. It means you go out of your way for others because you know it's important to them. You might translate this skill to your own important items and see the personal benefits.

The purpose of evaluating your current behaviors is to help you improve your trust with the people that matter the most to you. Gaining a deeper connection between the brain and body requires trust. Your brain needs to know that your body will follow through with the tasks assigned, and your body needs to trust that your brain won't lead it astray. Trust breeds commitment.

To develop trust with yourself, I recommend the following three-step process:

1. What are the messages your brain is sending your body right now?
2. What are the messages your body is sending your brain right now?
3. Make a plan to connect the dots on at least one message from each.

The sincerest form of respect is listening to your heart, mind, and body, which I realized even as a teen. When my mother asked me to help around the house, I knew she had a lot of work to do and needed extra help. But I didn't understand initially that I was always given the option to say yes or no. She didn't demand I help her — she asked. I could have said no if I wanted. That empowered me to think about my response before committing. Now, before accepting a new responsibility, I remember that it's my choice to say yes or no. If I say yes, I'm going to follow through because I don't want to break my commitment and let that person down.

I am happier knowing that I have the power to choose. I also see the benefits of my choices. For instance, making healthier meals at dinner takes time, but my family and I get to eat more nutritionally. Helping a loved one with a project helps deepen your connection. How would you benefit from keeping your commitments? How do you grow by becoming more loyal to yourself and to others?

What are the messages your brain is sending your body right now? What are the messages your body is sending your brain right now? My brain is saying I need to stretch. My body responds by saying, I am able to do so.

Those household tasks I helped my mother with when I was younger took about five minutes each. It made it easy to say yes to each one. When you work on keeping the commitments to yourself, understand that each task doesn't have to be an ordeal.

Drinking water takes less than five minutes a day, a 30-minute workout is only two percent of your day, and turning off your phone at the end of the evening takes two seconds. Consider how much time it takes to physically follow through on your small commitments.

I am going to connect the messages between my brain and my body by getting up, taking a break, and stretching. Once I match up the messages, I create awareness, alignment, and trust within myself. My brain trusts that my body will respond appropriately, and my body trusts that my brain will give it the proper guidance.

Once you have pinpointed your brain messages, body messages, and the benefits of taking action, you can pair them together using The Accountability

Code.

Reflection — I am aware and in tune with the messages I received and am capable of listening.

Humility — I am extremely grateful to have a body that works in the way it does. It's not perfect, but I have been given so much to improve.

Planning — Understanding my strengths, I can put my efforts to work in the most effective and fulfilling way.

Implementing — I will participate in a quick movement meditation where I move my body and recall in my mind what I am really supposed to be doing with my day.

Commitment — I take regular breaks to stretch, check in, celebrate progress, and thank myself for my efforts.

Feedback — I get more done when I understand how my body works. I am committed to the process and not the obligations of people who are not important to me.

Personal power is the ability to take action, and using The Accountability Code is the perfect process. When you have learned to trust yourself, you develop commitment, and that commitment allows you to say yes to the things you care about, and to take action to fulfill them.

Chapter 6 - Feedback

Feedback – Information used as a basis for improvement

Take a deep breath as we talk about feedback.

Feedback is crucial when it comes to mastering accountability because we'll honestly never be done working on ourselves. However, happiness is gained in the ability to follow through on our ultimate purposes. Because the very best version of ourselves is in the future, it's imperative that we change how we view feedback, or should I say *feedforward*?

My amazing mentor, Marshall Goldsmith (bestselling author), taught me that *feedforward* is beneficial because it focuses on the "infinite variety of opportunities that can happen in the future." I love that because the word forward indicates ACTION THAT AFFECTS THE FUTURE!

The best part about the last step of The Accountability Code is that it seamlessly overlaps with Reflection, making the entire Accountability Code easy to apply when set up and used properly. Feedback is commonly understood as a tool to improve, whereas feedforward isn't as commonly known. Going forward, please keep in mind how feedforward can benefit you whenever I use the word *feedback*.

What is the process of using feedback and feedforward to learn from our mistakes?

Marshall Goldsmith taught me a great system that gives us hope and encouragement to change, and this system is what I have based this last step of The Accountability Code on. If you are familiar with Marshall's process, you will recognize a couple different parts, but keep in mind that applying The Accountability Code to your own life is a personal matter, and this step reflects the intimate parts of choosing to change starting on the inside.

The importance of the feedback step is that it's all data! You cannot change the past, but you have the power to change the future. When you look in the mirror, you are collecting feedback and data in both negative and positive ways. We want to make this step anything but painful, embarrassing, or uncomfortable. Those feelings aren't often motivating to help people improve, so let's learn a better way.

How to gather specific and helpful feedback:

1. Pick a behavior you'd like to change.

"I want to be a better listener." "I want to be present." "I want to stop yelling at my family." Express this desire to 6-10 people. They can be people who know you well or just know of you. You can even make a post on your social media sites. When I was dealing with feelings of resentment and anger towards a trainer who used to work for me and then quit to rip off my sales process and programs, I asked on my Facebook wall, "How do I forgive when I am still so mad?" I was actively wanting help to learn forgiveness.

When you pick a behavior you'd like to change, you are choosing to take on a battle you are committed to because it means something specific to you. When you don't, you will only find opposition that others throw your way, and it's never fun to be told how to improve if you aren't interested in making a change.

2. Ask for feedforward.

Explain that *feedforward* relates to ideas for the future only and that there are 3 rules in this exercise:

    A. Responses should not focus on what has happened in the past, only suggestions for future actions.

    B. You are not allowed to critique their suggestions, to ask for help applying it immediately, or even to indicate if it was good or bad advice.

    C. Say, "Thank you, very much" for every piece of advice you are given.

My Facebook post brought in 24 comments that were extremely helpful, not only because they shared good things, but it also proved that people are always willing to help you improve. I will include some comments that focus on what I could do in the future. Some responses included, "Let it go or be dragged." "Be mad. Feel it. Process it. Take a deep breath and find meaning in it." "Pray for forgiveness, both for them and so that your heart will be softened."

When you ask for feedforward, you are validating your need for change. That expression keeps you in an ever-growing position. When you don't adopt that position, you may find yourself reliving past experiences that cannot be changed and therefore stunt your growth and diminish your focus.

3. Have fun with it.

Rest easy, knowing that all you have done up to this point is valuable!

Keeping the process fun is an amazing way to keep a positive attitude about your goals and dreams.

Knowing that you will not be put down during this exercise opens up your brain and spirit for many possibilities, and therefore your ability to act increases. I wish I could tell you that trying to forgive a past trainer and ex-friend was fun, but back then I didn't know how to formulate feedback into what I have now developed as The Accountability Code. One way to have fun with it is to know that the changing process is up to you. People are not giving you feedback based on you; they are giving you feedback based on the process and current goal.

When you have fun with it, you keep your abilities strong and worthwhile. You sincerely work to change the outcome. When you don't, you'll keep your problems as problems believing that no one can help you. Alastair Santhouse (author) said, "If the only tool you have is a hammer, then every problem becomes a nail."

4. Topics for reflection.

Now that you have been given ideas on how to improve, it's time to integrate and update them into The Accountability Code. What is this new info teaching you? What does that mean for the rest of your plan and how you'll now wake up and show up?

After feeling like I was stabbed in the back, I worked through my problems with this trainer. We were able to come to an agreement about where to go from there and what it meant for our relationship.

Going through that experience allowed me to restructure how I bring people into my business, how I might separate friendship and business, and ultimately how I handle my own emotions. While I loved having a team of trainers work for me, I learned that I made a lot of mistakes! That time in my life has provided me with priceless feedback to move forward.

When you take the feedback and use it as a topic for reflection, you will see significant progress in who you are as a person. You'll find it easier to demonstrate the qualities you desire. When you don't, you'll find any means of improvement as an inconvenience that threatens your current self.

Reasons for resistance to feedback —

1. Not trained to give useful feedback

If you were raised in an environment where you were constantly put down and ridiculed for not knowing any better, it can be difficult to openly ask for feedback.
The great thing about using personal feedback and feedforward is that you get to choose who you involve in your process. You are an adult. You do not have to take any information from anyone you don't want to. As you use this step in The Accountability Code, utilize people who are working on bettering themselves as well, and you'll find this exercise much more useful.

In order to avoid getting feedback from the wrong people, determine who you ask for help from in the first place. Asking on my Facebook wall might not have been the safest place at the time, but I did receive helpful feedback that I could trust.

2. Fear of others' judgment

Many people don't like sharing feedback for fear of rocking the boat.

We all know how easy it is to spot the mote in our neighbor's eye, even with a beam in our own. If you set the stage with the three rules (focus on future, not critiquing, say thank you), then neither you nor the other person has to fear the outcome. It's all about improving as a person.

In order to beat this resistance and utilize feedback for good, keep it fun. Understand that any feedback you receive is only a topic of reflection if you want it to be.

3. Unstable emotions

I know how hard it can be to ask for suggestions when you already know full well what you need to improve.

That is exactly why *feedforward* is different: It is not about changing the past, it is about improving for the future in a fun way. If you are still worried about adding more to your plate, then just practice saying, "Thank you very much." Move on and take it to your reflection when you have the mental capacity to do so. Work at your own pace.

In order to beat this resistance, practice feeling out your emotions and use external feedback in a broad sense sparingly. Work with a trusted individual more often to get a sense of how you take feedback.

As you work with this book, know that YOU ARE AMAZING and 100 percent capable of applying The Accountability Code in your own way so that it makes sense to your personal progress. I know, without a doubt, that when you use The Accountability Code consistently in your life, you will experience significant improvements to your confidence, productivity, purpose, and impact in the world.

How to Turn Your Weakness into a Strength

I am a recovering Workaholic.

It's not easy to admit that I put my business responsibilities ahead of my personal needs and my family, but I can share that now that I have found steps to overcome my overachieving ways.

In his book *What Got You Here Won't Get You There*, Marshall Goldsmith identifies a genius process of self-improvement that he calls *FeedForward*. It's a fascinating role-playing exercise in which two participants are asked to listen to each other, to ask for what they need, and to offer real solutions for the future. You each identify ways that you wish to change or improve, ask for feedback, listen, and then switch roles.

Goldsmith elaborates by suggesting that you expand this Q&A session into your relationships. In fact, the closer the other participant is to you, the more effective the answers may be, and the more honest the questions might get.

Each of us has ways that we would like to improve. Asking for help can bring answers that help us to be better. But we can all relate to being prompted by unsolicited advice or criticism. We change then, too, but not usually for the better.

Instead, when we interact with a unified feeling of good intention to deepen the relationship, the other person will generally offer practical, well-intended solutions. Your job isn't to be a slave to what they say, but to ponder their words, say "thank you," and consider how effective that advice may be. And then, as Goldsmith explains, move on and ask another person how you might improve this area of your life.

When I began this exercise, I knew I'd have to ask for help about my workaholism. It is good to have a dedicated business mindset, and to persevere at pursuing your dreams, but not at the cost of your relationships, your freedom, and your well-being. The people in our lives can provide solutions, if we are willing to ask for help and to listen meaningfully. You'll get feedback that may improve your weaknesses from a place of love and support, rather than guilt, shame, or resentment.

Start with a trusted friend. Tell them you want to make an improvement in your actions, behaviors, or interactions. Trust me, this process isn't as bad as you think it is! When you approach someone and ask for help, most are willing to provide answers and to offer kindness. They may even relate to your struggle and offer ideas that they have been considering for a similar problem. We're all human, and unless you're asking to stop murdering people, chances are you're going to find common ground!

Change happens easier when we are met with love and support. It also happens easier when we are honest with what we want. Look at yourself clearly. What negative experiences could you have handled differently? Do you easily get offended or take more from relationships than you give?

I had to be honest about being a workaholic. I would get so wrapped up in my business that I was constantly multitasking. I wasn't putting in the same time and effort to my relationships as I was to work, and it left me feeling disconnected from those I loved most.

You may have many things about yourself you'd like to change, but start with just one. If you want to increase your chances of success, then focus on one area for now. You will see that the improvements will flow into other areas of your life. My workaholism also affected my health — I wasn't taking critical breaks during workdays to replenish myself. My health wasn't the immediate focus on my attempt to make change, but it did improve as a result. Now I know that if I take a break or even a weeklong vacation, that everything will be waiting for me when I return, and I had to admit that my deadlines weren't as critical as I treated them.

Recognizing that I was a workaholic was the first step, and it wasn't easy. I enjoyed my reputation as a dedicated entrepreneur. I didn't develop this habit without reason. I'm frequently complimented on my grit and determination, and it opened a lot of opportunities for me. But I was compromising on the one thing you cannot replenish — and that is time. I needed to slow down, and enjoy the life that I was having.

I did, and in so doing I turned my weakness into a strength.

You, too, are capable of change, and you are worth investing in. So reach out to a close friend, tell them your weakness, and ask them for ideas on how to improve. There is no judgment in FeedForward. Regardless of what feedback they offer, you only have to say "thank you" in response. They might be spot-on, their advice might be extreme, they may really be talking about their own issues, but either way they provide you with an answer. Once you have that answer, you have options. You get to decide what to do with that information, and if you decide their advice was valuable, then you need to act on it.

However, you should be selective about who you trust to share your vulnerabilities with. Who are the handful of people who have earned the right to weigh in on your choices? Mine would include my husband, my sister, and a friend of several years. The longer they've known you, the better.

Say to them, "I would like to improve my ability to (fill in the blank). How would you suggest I do that?" Collect their answers and ponder some action steps. When I asked how I could improve my workaholic tendencies, my sister told me to express gratitude for where I was at the time. My friend sent a link on how to be present in the moment, and my husband simply applauded me and told me I was doing a great job. Each of their answers were valid and came from a place of love and trust. With those options, I was able to make small steps toward improving my overachieving, overworking ways.

Your ability to change is increased by the internal desire to improve at a level and pace that is right for you. You also have to assess yourself from time to time, watching to see how your behavior has changed. For me, it meant slowing my roll: hustling less, and carving out precious time with loved ones more. I could measure that time with treasured activities we will remember for a lifetime.

A concentrated effort produces results every time. I suggest keeping a journal of your progress. Notate your observations about how you master making deliberate change. Score yourself from 1 to 10 on listening to advice, considering it, and making change. Any time you give yourself a 10 from great results, validate those efforts by sharing your progress with those in your inner circle. Don't just tell them what you're doing, tell them why and how. If they contributed to your success, let them know how much you appreciate their willingness to be involved and to care.

Anytime you have a weakness that you want to improve, use these techniques. You'll also find that your ability to listen and receive feedback on any topic will deepen. That's a powerful trait to have.

The wonderful thing about people is that we are made to grow. You have the power and the support to change your life — if it's something you truly care about.

I was incredibly blessed to be coached by Marshall Goldsmith and am thrilled to say that my programs have his stamp of approval.

Behaviors

English poet John Dryden said, "We first make our habits, and then our habits make us." To that, I would add the following:

> *The body doesn't lie.*
>
> It's a physical representation of what is happening on the inside. Behaviors determine results. If you want certain outcomes, you have to act accordingly. The body is constantly providing feedback based on the stress it's put under.

Look at yourself. Are your shoulders slumped due to prolonged poor posture, does your body language or attitude send people away, is your low energy a sign of an imbalance in your life? What do your behaviors tell you about yourself?

Using Feedback in The Accountability Code is crucial to changing habits and behaviors. You cannot change what you aren't aware of. It's time to gather that data and then use it to become better.

In an effort to collect more data on my behaviors and my ability to be accountable to the right things, I recently completed Gallup's 'Strengthsfinder' Quiz and was rather surprised at the results. I felt confident that my number one strength would be discipline or leadership. Instead, in order, here were my top five:

- Communication
- Harmony
- Input
- WOO (Winning Others Over)
- Activator

Three of these strengths fall in the influence category. Having influence or being an *Influencer* is a loaded word these days. We can all cite examples of those who use influence for good, or for bad. In middle school, I was student body president and would often get reprimanded by faculty for setting a bad example by acting like the class clown to make my peers laugh. I remember fighting back, saying, "It's not my fault if people are watching and copying me!"

Oh boy, was I wrong! I get it today, as the mom to four daughters who now follow my every move. My behavior is more important than ever. And observing their actions provides massive feedback that can help me improve. The fact is, we are all influencers, affecting those around us. What sort of impact do we want to have? How do our behaviors communicate our message in the strongest way?

After sifting through the information from the Gallup quiz, the strengths they assigned to me based on my answers made sense. I learned that what I truly believe, I will live through my physical actions and, in turn, what I improve in my behaviors will solidify my thoughts and beliefs.
It validates my personal belief that I use my physical body to help others. I keep in shape with the intention to serve, and I know that I receive divine messages more often when my body doesn't distract me by feeling ill or by fighting fatigue.

Your behaviors and habits reveal your strengths. Sometimes, though, a strength can be a weakness. My focus on the physical body sometimes meant being too focused on what others thought about my appearance. It has taken a lot of time and care to separate my worth from my body mass index, fertility, or skin complexion. I now focus on keeping my word, following through, being a light, and encouraging others to be their best selves.

Inserting useful Feedback into The Accountability Code can help you see progress in how your behaviors determine your success. It will teach you to understand which behaviors produce what results. This is feedback in action.

Think about some of your current habits — the ones that have stuck around a while. How have they paid off for you? The best way to improve is to build upon what you're already doing. It's hard to start a new habit from scratch, and habits are the foundation of success.

It would be unwise to change all of your habits at once and to ignore the fact that you're already doing great things to produce desired results. So before you start setting new intentions for a massive overhaul, I want you to acknowledge how successful you have been at past ones, and then we're going to build upon that.

Your strengths make you unique, and I'm a firm believer in developing more of the good you, instead of trying to trade it for someone or something else. You don't have to take a quiz to know your strengths, although it never hurts to seek data from trusted sources. You already have an idea of what makes you so unique and powerful, and validating that can help you magnify it.

Are you a good leader, trustworthy, hard-working, reliable, adaptable? Write out your own best strengths. But define them the way that you know best. Leadership isn't only demonstrated by being bold, and confidence doesn't just manifest in how we are seen. What are your top strengths, and what are the ways that you uniquely embody them? How have those strengths turned into habits that bring positive results?

People don't decide their future — they decide their habits, and their habits determine their future.

How might you improve your habits so that you get better results? What feedback are you getting so far? For example, I like to communicate. In order for me to improve my communication, it would be wise for me to learn how my words impact others. I might ask friends and loved ones for feedback on how I speak to them. Based on their answers, I could find ways to refine my messages in order to get better results.

Another thing I can work on is listening. When I speak with my kids, I put down any work or devices I am engaged with, make eye contact, and sometimes hold their hand to take the physical connection to a deeper level.

A change in habits leads to a change in lifestyle. It isn't hard to make those changes when you're building upon what you know you're already doing right. As creatures of habit, we thrive on doing the same thing over and over. So when we change that just a little bit, we can gradually get different results.

Let's say you want to get up a little earlier each morning. If you usually wake at 7:30am, set your alarm for 7:15 instead. It's not a drastic change, but those fifteen minutes can really add value to your morning routine if it's planned and deliberate. Improving your morning routine comes when you not only set that alarm earlier, but you decide in advance how you will spend that time. You could drink a glass of water and meditate. Or you could go outside and enjoy a nature walk.

Evidence of the impact of changing habits will show up when you're consistent. I've tried getting up earlier in the mornings and learned one valuable truth: I get more done throughout my day when I wake up earlier. Don't be too quick to dismiss change. It takes physical movement, but also an emotional conversion to achieve a reward.

When you look at your habits and behaviors, which ones continue to serve you? Do they highlight your natural talents and abilities? I make a habit of talking to myself each day. It's an extension of my strong communication skills and helps me refine my message to myself and others. If I want to be effective at complimenting others, for instance, it helps to first compliment myself.

By waking up earlier in the morning, I use that extra time to fill my bucket. And filling my bucket often means communicating with myself more, and better. The improved communication not only helps me get more in touch with what I'm feeling, but makes me more effective at teaching my clients and children.

What are your strengths, and what areas of your life can you apply those strengths to? What feedback have you received that validates what your strengths are?

Developing your skills and habits will benefit everyone around you. First, by being in harmony with yourself, you become more aware. You'll see people more clearly. If I learn to be patient with my own mistakes, I'm going to be patient when my husband makes one, too. When I understand the benefit of optimizing my own habits, I show up better in my life. How can improving your habits and behaviors help others?

We are each ultimately responsible for maintaining our own good habits and changing our behaviors if they're not paying off. We can ask for help with this Feedback step in sticking to those changes, but we have to take ownership of our habits. Look closely at yourself: What do you see? What happens on the surface reflects what's happening underneath. If you want a different outcome, how are you going to behave differently?

If you haven't noticed yet, I'm all about Accountability, and I would love to help you break free from the damaging habits you've had for far too long. Trust me — you can change and create a life with more joy than you ever thought possible. You are in the right place, and now it's time to take the next step. Take a deep breath and say, "I am capable and ready for change."

Shift Intentions

I have had the opportunity to attend several retreats during my career, and each is a learning experience. I have participated in retreats as an attendee, a speaker, an organizer, and a facilitator. Today, I want to tell you about a couple of experiences that gave me powerful feedback to help me recognize when I'm not in the right space.

Plugging Feedback into The Accountability Code is the only way to catch or avoid or omit damaging patterns from your behavior. You can't expect to change if you aren't updating what is working and what isn't.

I was invited to my first retreat (we'll call it the Goddess Retreat) as part of a business mastermind group I joined. The retreat was a bonus for purchasing membership in the mastermind group for a whole year. This was an expensive, elite group, and to maximize the value of my membership I tried to take advantage of everything given.

On the first day of the Goddess Retreat, everyone was asked to give their reasons for being there. I answered honestly, "to honor my investment in my business." Other women had different answers, such as, "to connect with you beautiful women" and "to make lifelong friends." I was there out of a commitment to my business and the work I had put in to succeed in it. I was not there to party, although I did relish the idea of a weekend away from home and my responsibilities.

My mentor was not thrilled that I wasn't contributing to the life of the party, so she pulled me aside to warn me to loosen up. She didn't ask how I was doing, or how I felt. She just wanted me to be peppier. Normally I am, but the vibe of the group was to party with alcohol and lotto tickets. When I explained that I came ready to network and learn and take advantage of every minute this event presented, she disinvited me from her mentorship, claiming she had never asked anyone to leave before, but she felt like I didn't want to be there — ummmm, okay?

But I paid a lot of money to be in that mastermind group, and I continued to work the program, outside of that mentor's influence. I told you I'm no quitter. I was still committed, but now I had a solid experience of what this person really expected of me as part of her mastermind group.

I hope no one ever goes to a retreat and feels alienated the way I did. I was there to work my business and relax away from the kids. If she was going to pull me aside, I had hoped it would be for encouragement, not a lecture on her expectation of how I showed up.

As I pondered on what had just happened, I realized that this wasn't the right space for me. There was a lot of partying going on, and I wasn't interested in getting drunk just to hang with the cool girls. Nor did I want to gamble, and the clincher was walking into the main room to find someone doing a 'spiritual awakening' that involved releasing traumatic spirits, crystals, and incense. Let's just say, that isn't my idea of a successful or productive business retreat for me! This is all great feedback!

As the retreat continued, I found myself less and less involved. Cue exercise: I put on my shoes and headed out for a run. As I got some air and cleared my head, I saw the situation clearly: I felt disconnected because I felt deceived. I felt the retreats were just sales gimmicks and that the organizers weren't considering each of our serious expectations. As soon as I faced that feeling, it began to dissipate. I remembered that I had met some amazing women in the past few days, with incredible life stories that were all independent of what this mentor had tried to tell me what to do. I decided to return to the retreat after my run, and I left the poor attitude at the door. I spent the rest of that trip connecting with others and creating memories that will last a lifetime.

The next retreat I had on my books (we'll call it the Journey Retreat) was to deliver a talk as a keynote speaker. I was excited to share my story of fun and sustainable fitness with the other women, and I felt that I had made the most of my mastermind group while it lasted because I was, in fact, growing my business by finding more clients, especially in the retreat space. I was looking forward to inspiring others to improve their health.

I arrived a few hours late due to my travel schedule, and, upon checking-in, I immediately felt apprehensive when I walked in. Memories flooded of the Goddess Retreat, and I was worried about how I was supposed to show up. I thought, 'Nobody knows me here, there wasn't a friendly face to greet me, and because I missed a meal, everybody else would already be buddied up and I'd be alone.' I also noticed that there were women at the retreat in way fitter shape than me. How was I supposed to stand in front of them and present myself as the expert when I didn't have the same presence of muscle they had?

It threw me off my game and out of alignment with how I normally show up. I don't like that feeling. It has the potential to make me shrink from opportunities and to feel less than my best.

The highest functioning version of myself goes out of the way to meet people. I shake their hand, learn their names, and take a few seconds to connect in ways that won't be forgotten easily. My higher self refuses to accept that anyone is unapproachable, and I'm fantastic at getting shy people out of their shells.

My higher functioning self knows that while I won't click with everyone immediately, I'll still leave a lasting impression and an opportunity for relationships to form. And my higher self understands that my ability to connect quickly loosens people up, makes them feel special and more comfortable in their own space.

In my higher functioning mode, I am comfortable reminding myself of my true power, and I position my mindset to fuel my physical actions accordingly.

For a short second, I realized I had to shift to the power of my higher functioning self immediately. I was waiting to give a message of light and hope to a captive audience of seekers, and I needed to remember something important:

SNAP OUT OF IT!

I had to shake myself back to reality, wind up my charm dial, and go mingle with the other attendees, as I always do. I had to remind myself that this is the type of environment where I can thrive. I had to go make some fun so I could take the stage the next day and give a speech that would transform lives.

I am so happy to say that because of that first retreat experience, I learned exactly what I didn't want to happen at this one. I had to utilize the vital feedback to shift into the right headspace. Not only did I need to be more deliberate about what environment I found myself in, I needed to engage my Accountability for showing up as the best me.

It takes time to define our best environments, our favorite skills, and our internal and external rewards. We cannot always control the situation around us, but there are ways to at least distinguish our behaviors and remove the stumbling blocks in our way.

Alignment is key, and it is defined by acting how you know you need to be, not how someone else expects.

When was the last time you got thrown off your game? When you know what puts you in a negative cycle, you become aware of the triggers that alter your mindset and behavior. It's important even in an unfamiliar or uncomfortable environment to recognize what your intention was and how the event failed to meet your expectations.

At the Journey Retreat, I was there to live my brand of fun and sustainable fitness. I was there to make new friends and help others feel welcome. That was my intention. At the earlier Goddess Retreat, I was there because I felt obligated to be there — and we know how well *that* turned out!

What situations trigger different behaviors for you?

It's okay that sometimes you show up in a different way than usual. You may behave differently based on those around you, and that's okay — but only if you are aware and are choosing to express yourself in a different way. There is more than one side to you. When are you bubbly and fun? When are you more serious? What sort of experience calls for a calm and collected version of you? You should define it, and you should choose it.

To remember who you are, you have to forget who others tell you to be. Don't ever feel obligated to show up as some perfect version of yourself or someone you're not, especially when the environment shifts away from its initial intention.

When this type of situation presents itself, do as I did — step aside for a moment and clear your head. You don't have to run, as I did. You can do a meditation exercise, breath work, and put some distance between yourself and the chaos.

How will you change the next time you find yourself in an uncomfortable situation? I love the fact that I now recognize what throws me off — feeling small or less than I'm capable of, or in a place of low energy. I remind myself that I expect myself to be authentic, and I shift my behavior so I can be present. Experience tells me to do this, but it's confidence that gives me the power to do it.

I firmly believe that we find lessons in everyday life. Part of those lessons is to observe carefully and filter information so that we understand what is expected of us and what we are expecting of the situation. I love retreats, now, and I have learned not to waste my time and money in places that cause me to disconnect or not to fulfill obligations.

At that first retreat, it was my fault for not understanding what my mentor was expecting or whether that was the best thing for me. At the time, I needed support and a break, and I got neither. Lesson learned.

Feedback collection: Based on your learning experiences, what are the red flags and stumbling blocks you now watch out for? How will you plug those into The Accountability Code?

It's important to understand that we aren't one dimensional and shouldn't be known as just one thing. Different circumstances will creep up on us and ask us to shift. That can result in feeling blindsided or empowered. Just remember that it's your choice to adapt, when appropriate, and to stay in alignment with your values when it's not.

I invite you to take my free Mindset Quiz. After you answer a few questions, it will reveal your inner strength and areas to be aware of. This will give you valuable information on what to work on, so you can avoid all the pitfalls faster.

I invite you to take my free Mindset Quiz by scanning the QR code and clicking on Free Quizzes.

Recognize Patterns

How do you know what feels 'OFF,' if you don't know what 'ON' feels like? By maintaining daily habits to check in with ourselves, we can often prevent little problems from turning into chronic or traumatic crises. Checking in is exactly how you'll gain important Feedback for change.

One spring night after her bath, my daughter Liz asked me to braid her hair. She's a big fan of a few braids on the side while letting the rest of her hair sweep to the opposite side. She came into my room with a comb and laid down on my bed with her head to the side.

When I was halfway through her braids, I saw a small dark spot next to her ear. I folded her ear forward and found a tick! I yelled for Aubrey to come quickly, and he ran in the room along with Liz's three sisters. I tried to keep a calm voice, but I could feel Liz freaking out. I told her to stay still and asked Aubrey to bring me a pair of tweezers, a cotton ball, some oil and a Ziploc bag. When I had everything and Liz was sufficiently calm, I began to remove the tick.

I know there will be a debate about my methods, but I'll just tell you that I have prepared for this moment my whole life, ever since I started attending youth camp and had to pass off First Aid Safety. I grabbed the tweezers, gently but firmly squeezed the tick at the base of its head and pulled away slowly. The tick held on for dear life, but I continued to pull at a steady pace. The tick pulled Liz's skin away from her scalp and eventually tore a little bit, but it did release. She bled minimally and showed no signs of a bullseye rash. The girls watched as their dad killed the tick inside the bag with alcohol, and I disinfected the area behind Liz's ear. That night, I also texted all our neighbors to tell them what happened, and where Liz had been playing that day, so they could check their kids, too.

I continued to check Liz's ear over the next several days, and she was clear of any rash, but I couldn't help but worry about Lyme Disease. What if down the road she developed health problems because of that tick? What if she hadn't taken a bath that night or wanted braids? What if I had missed seeing the tick because I was distracted or careless?

Understanding what is normal and healthy requires recognizing patterns. When your body needs attention, it will break a pattern. This may include physical habits, emotional phases, and social patterns. I want to share some of the ways that you can begin to recognize your patterns so you may know when something is off.

Journaling

Rather than sharing the details of your life on social media, I suggest keeping a record. Using a lined notebook or journal, begin writing down things that are important to you and how often you experience them. Collecting data is a great gauge of how you are doing in different areas of your life. You could track your water intake, menstrual cycle, income, moods, family activities, birthdays, and special events. Where do you think you need to look for patterns in *your* life?

Journaling helps with good decision making. When you document your thoughts or actions, you reveal the patterns they make. Then you can decide what plan of action you should take if those patterns demand a need for change.

Journaling is an exercise in values, safekeeping memories, and awareness. As you take time to document your life, do so out of love. Record the things that bring up good feelings, and when you record the things that you are concerned about, be kind to yourself. Effective documentation increases awareness of how you treat yourself
and others.

Relationships

Liz wouldn't have found the tick on her own in time to prevent it from affecting her health. She needed her mother to spot that tick, and now she and her sisters regularly check their bodies during bath time. They have created patterns in their life to benefit their health, because they learned it from a trusted source.

You will also learn patterns from others, and you need to know that someone has your back. It's important to cultivate friendships and relationships with people who will be loving, but honest, with you. I used to complain that nobody ever called me to hang out or go on girls' trips, so I was extra sensitive about offering my time to others. Then I heard a friend complain that nobody ever asked her to do anything. She said nobody calls to reach out and check on her, and I felt offended because I was pretty sure that I had!

I realized that when I felt lonely, I probably did have friends checking on me.

It's just that I wasn't appreciating or paying attention to them. I had to work harder to reach out to my friends, to let them know I was paying attention and wanted to share time with them. But I also needed to reach out and directly ask people when I wanted time with them.

The best thing about the world we live in is that you can find new friends all the time with a click. Go to your favorite social media sites or Facebook groups. There are potential allies hiding in the crowd, and until you make the effort to get to know them, you never know who might wind up being a great friend. Make a habit of reaching out on a regular basis to someone new.

Once you have your trusted tribe, decide how and when you'll check in with each other. When I'm traveling, my sister and I send funny Instagram reels to each other. Another sister and I cheer each other on through our Apple watches when we finish our workouts. Give generously of your time, but initially expect little in return. Just reach out, make it fun, and respond to new friends the way you'd like to be treated. Practice opening up, if you're shy. Maybe it starts with text messages and eventually grows into a regular lunch outing with someone who 'gets' you. Practice checking in when you need support, and be ready to listen and respond when others ask that of you.

We repeat what we don't repair. If you fail to put a plan in place, you can't expect anything to change. What habits are depleting your energy? What feedback is helpful as you look to improve? Look at the patterns in your life and determine which of them needs your attention.

Health Patterns

Mental patterns might be hard to recognize at first, because you can never get away from your thoughts. Trust me, I've tried! What you can do is set a timer on your phone to track the time you spend thinking about any one thing. When the alarm goes off, it's time to shift your focus elsewhere. What else can you be doing that matters? If you're scrolling through social media or replying to text threads that you don't really care about, walk away from your device and do something productive to break the pattern.

Emotional patterns are the easiest to detect, because your mood will tell you what you are feeling. Try defining your moods. My daughter Lexi and I were headed to the mall recently and she said, "I'm happy!" Defining your emotions is a good practice for self-awareness. It allows you to address any issues at the root of unpleasant feelings before they get out of control. If you keep your emotions hidden, you fail to validate them. And that failure to validate causes a disconnect.

Social patterns are different for everyone, and so everyone will have differing ways to detect those habits. I'm more social than my husband, so I tend to use social patterns as a form of measurement. When I'm not feeling myself, I go inward in order to reset. My husband expresses his feelings of disconnection in an outward way (to me or to another person). How can your social behaviors be used as a gauge to determine when you don't feel your best?

Life really is all about patterns. Once you understand them, you'll see them everywhere – in nature, in design, and even in your behaviors. And once you know your patterns, you'll learn exactly what each means.

Take a look at my post about creating emotional recipes for desired outcomes. You can easily plug your feedback into The Accountability Code and create a plan around recognizing patterns and creating the exact outcome you'd like.

Feed Your Focus

During a college course called "Teaching and Coaching Aerobic Conditioning," I fell in love with step aerobics. It combined movement and music in a way that took me back to my childhood. You see, my parents actually met in a disco!

I was pregnant with my first child while attending this class and, even with my expanding belly, I was able to capably keep the beat and create moves all over the step platforms with hops, jumps, and perfect synchrony. My professor told me, "You need to teach group fitness classes here at the college! You'll have to get certified, but that'll be a piece of cake for you."

I went home that night and told Aubrey the exciting news. I was enthused about finding a way to stay in shape while expecting. After my first baby Leila's birth, I spent a whole Saturday getting certified.

I was hooked! I had found a way to grow my knowledge in the field of my degree, had a fun break away from the baby, and was essentially getting paid to workout! I absolutely loved teaching at the college and wanted to find even more places to teach at.

I drove past a new gym on my way home and thought, 'Hey! I bet they need an instructor!' I stopped in and discovered the head trainer was someone I knew from childhood. She introduced me to the gym owner, and the next thing I knew, I had multiple AM classes on the schedule.

Another friend told me about a substitute position at the community gym she attended. It was for an aquatics class, and I enthusiastically jumped at that position. I loved teaching water classes, although they were hard to come by. Through that process I was able to introduce the aqua dance program at the college, too.

Teaching fitness became addicting to me. I loved teaching and talking, but I really loved starting something new and challenging myself to get better at it. I was great at promoting the classes, helping people get comfortable in the gym, and expanding my fitness knowledge. I became quite the expert on different ways to exercise and to have fun and stay safe while doing it.

Then I saw another new gym open up, and I mentioned to Aubrey that I was going to stop in and see if I could get a job there. In his most tactful way possible, he said no.

At the time, I had two kids, was working at four gyms, still in school, and had other obligations. I was 20 years old, looked amazing, and my ego was a bit inflated. I was so distracted about the concept of free memberships at gyms (essentially, I was getting paid to work out). But I hadn't yet mastered the art of taking a break, when needed.

Aubrey could see that I was overdoing it. I had a bad case of *Shiny Object Syndrome* – chasing the newest, flashiest thing that came along. I'm so grateful that my husband is the yin to my yang. He helped me become aware of how my behavior was impacting our growing family, my health, and our long-term plans. He didn't demand that I stop teaching altogether. He simply said, "Do you really need another class on your schedule?"

He was right. It was time to learn the concept of starving my distractions in order to feed my focus. I had to develop some self-control before I burned myself out completely. I certainly needed a level of accountability to stick to what I really needed to do.

Here is a simple way to determine if your priorities have gone off track. This process will help you make future decisions because it will be clear if the option fits into your YES list or not. After you gain this information, let's plug it into The Accountability Code as an example of how feeding your focus is improved by taking an organized approach.

To get the results you want, you don't have to be extreme. You just need to be focused, and that starts with identifying your primary goals. What is your main goal and focus right now? At that time in my life, it was school and babies. Aubrey had embraced my idea of having a big family and getting an education. Those were my primary goals. I had to recognize that teaching was a secondary goal.

Then, once you have your goals, you need to set a timeline for them. When I was 20, I didn't know how many children we were going to have, but I knew we wanted several, fairly close together in age. As each child approached one year, we'd know it was time to start trying again. If you work closely with your scheduled goals, you'll find more success in making them happen. I know that family planning can be a sensitive topic. I don't want to sound like I just made a plan and boom — my babies were here. I firmly believe I manifested this life goal throughout my entire childhood. There was nothing I cared about more than getting married and becoming a mom. It was a huge part of the way I was raised and where my focus was even before I was married. I tracked my cycle, ate nutritious foods, avoided birth control as a new wife, and revolved my life around this primary goal of motherhood.

I also understand that infertility is a major struggle for many. I don't want to send the message that if you just focus on it, it will happen. If you are in the midst of trying to start a family, don't give up. If your plan doesn't work, change the plan, not the goal.

Whatever your goals, how do you keep the focus and accomplish them? You plan what is necessary first. There are really three necessities in life. You will be required to care for each of these necessities in order to support your goals.

Health

A strong body and clear mind will help you fulfill your wishes. What physical strength will you need to accomplish your goals? What mental clarity is required to focus? As a physical education and health major, I needed strength and great health. That was especially true since I was either nursing, preparing to be pregnant, pregnant, or recovering from delivery throughout my entire education. Optimal health meant that I needed fewer breaks between the babies so I could pursue my degree. Since family was necessary, that meant that finishing school was still in second place.

Write down your goals and how your health impacts your ability to focus and fulfill them. Then ask yourself, 'How can I shift my focus to my body, in order to support
my goals?'

Family

Personal relationships (whether related by blood or soulful friendships) are the basis of life. Feeling connected and supported is one of our basic human needs, and most goals are geared toward improving family life. Use your family (birth or chosen) to understand your most pressing needs and desires. Will pursuing your goals require a sacrifice in your relationships? Is reaching your dreams worth losing what you have now, including your connection to loved ones?

Faith and Feedback

If we get so consumed with our goals, we may become tempted to pursue them at an unrealistic pace or to sacrifice our values in order to make them happen. I know that I've been tempted to put all my time and energy into what I want, now, rather than on the long-term goals ahead. Every time I do that, I make poor decisions and get burnt out. When I turn to my faith, it recenters my focus on what matters most. How does your faith help you focus on *your* goals in the right way?

Too much of a good thing can be harmful. A great way to know if you're pursuing your goals in an unhealthy way is to ask someone who has been where you are. They will understand the impact of what you're doing in light of what you are trying to accomplish.

I gained more insight into my own fitness career goals after I talked to other instructors. I listened as they told me about feeling burned out, not making enough money, the inability to find subs when they were unable to teach. They warned me about offering too many classes without the proper set up. Talk to someone who understands the goals you have set for yourself. They can help you avoid turning that goal into something detrimental.

It's also important to evaluate your plans, especially when they throw you off balance or alignment. My Shiny Object Syndrome distracted me from seeing the value of what I already had. What have you been pursuing at the cost of what you have? It's tempting, for instance, to rush through your tasks in order to accomplish your goals. But there's a price to be had for going at a faster pace than you can handle. Often, that rush results in failing to recognize the warning signs that you are stumbling away from your path.

It is in these situations that it is so valuable to have a trusted loved one who knows you well enough to recognize the signs. What are the red flags that you recognize in your pursuit of your goals? How can others support you by helping you respect those warnings?

Your attention is best spent on the only path that matters, and only you and those you love can determine that path. Having a support system is an excellent way to keep focused and follow the process that results in meaningful success.

Listen Up

"The energy of the mind is the essence of life."

— Aristotle

Your body is constantly sending your messages with valuable feedback. Are you listening?

One of the best things about my Fun and Sustainable Fitness program is that clients get to eat the foods they want. I've never told any client that they have to eat perfectly. Instead, I train them to listen to the cues their body is sending and nourish themselves.

Tracking apps are great tools to help you understand the value of what you put into your body. But the most important information is how your body responds and how well you pay attention to those messages.

When we listen to the messages our body sends us, it creates awareness. When we respond to those messages, we create accountability.

If I eat a donut, my brain is initially going to say, "Wow, that tastes delicious! Remember when you were fifteen and worked at a bakery? Those sure were good times — we love donuts!" But if you eat too many, your body is probably going to say something like, "Uhhh, that was too much sugar. I guess that's why we don't eat a lot of fried food. We sure do feel bloated and tired right now."

I have the ability — just as you do — to process both of these pieces of information, the tasty reactions right after I eat the donut, and the let-down later when I'm sugar crashing and tired. The trick is to recall both of those cues before I eat my next donut. This will allow me to make better choices, ones that will satisfy both my brain and body. I might only eat half a donut or a donut hole. Or I might sprinkle a little cinnamon on a nutritious sweet snack, to simulate the flavors in the donut.

Food is powerful. It has the ability to help us function better, or to hold us back from doing what we need to do. Everything we eat goes through our digestive tract and gets broken down into their simplest forms. If we are eating nutrient dense foods, our body will work to absorb them. If we are eating substances with no nutritional value, we have more toxic waste to get rid of and we're just not going to feel well.

One day, leaving the gym, I stopped in the nutrition shop and ordered a Snickers protein shake. When the boy at the desk began making it for me, I asked him to hand over the bag so I could read the ingredient list. He asked if I was tracking for a bodybuilding show. I laughed and said, no, that you shouldn't only be interested in tracking food for a fitness competition. You should be interested in what's in your food so you can be more aware of how your body reacts when you eat a certain way. You should know the fats, carbs and proteins in your foods so that the cues your body sends you will make sense.

Now, I don't track my food all the time, but tracking for a while and teaching others about it was extremely eye-opening. The food you eat is literally fueling your body, and while the anti-diet culture will try to shame you for learning more about calories, macros, micros, meal timing, and eating styles, you owe it to your body and mind to understand how your foods make you feel.

The purpose of this message is to ignite a fire in you, to take more control of what goes into your body. You don't have to eat perfectly. But when you listen to your body's cues, knowing what it is responding to, you can take better care of yourself. I suggest trying some of these suggestions, to learn more about nutrition and how to gather data in support of your well-being.

Intentionally including variety in your diet can broaden your horizons. When you work to improve your nutrition and energy levels, you're more likely to branch out into new food groups and cuisines. Variety of foods equals less picky eaters.

First, eat to nourish your body. Understand portion control, including the serving sizes on food labels. Some are not accurate (some are downright outrageous), but take the time to learn about servings. You will gain an awareness of how your body feels not only in response to certain foods, but also to quantities.

Eat with the intention of pairing foods together. If you eat just one item (ribs, let's say), you are limiting your food preferences, and you are more likely to overeat. You may have heard the phrase, "Eat from the rainbow." When you pair foods together, you're more likely to receive all the nutrition you need. When we fail to include or introduce more options, we may become deficient in some areas. Aim to include at least three to four different foods in every meal.

When you eat, take breaks and pay attention to your body. A good rule of thumb is to eat until you are satisfied, not full. Recognizing the difference between both these feelings requires you to pay attention to your body.

Satisfied means adequately nourished, and full means uncomfortably indulged. A level of satisfaction is ideal for managing weight and energy levels.

I encourage my clients to snack throughout the day. You might think that's dangerous, but when your body knows that food is available, you are less likely to overeat at mealtimes. When snacking, choose from the basics, the items that come directly from the earth — nuts and seeds, fruits and vegetables. Rarely will these foods lead to poor health.

For meals, eat real food. Nutrients are the basis of function. Don't disregard 'whole foods' because they don't come with a flashy claim on the front of them. Plants, hearty grains, and animal proteins provide all the nutrients we need. Plan your meals around these basics, and add in a few of the other foods you enjoy as the spice of life.

While paying attention to how foods make you feel, pay close attention to your blood sugar. Processed foods are full of man-made ingredients designed to keep your tastebuds hypersensitive. They pack more flavor into fewer bites, to entice you to eat more. Very deceptive, huh? This is a major factor in the rise of diabetes, as the average human gets conditioned to ignore their fullness cues and instead, reward their brain with empty but flavorful pleasures. When considering meal choices, choose foods that are great for the gut, which means great for the entire body.

Don't overcomplicate it! Eat at home as often as possible, where you can control your foods and portions. Again, you don't have to become super healthy about what you eat. This is more about making deliberate choices to take control of how we feel. By dining at home, you will save money, eat together with your family, increase your understanding of choice, and develop more confidence in controlling your eating habits. You also set a great example, particularly for your children. Eating at home and preparing healthy meals together is a great way to exemplify taking care of yourself and others. Everyone needs to know that home is a safe place to be nourished. Eat specific meals at regular times. Sit together instead of eating on the go. Take the time to savor your food instead of rushing.

When it's your home, you set the rules. You get to decide what foods are available to you. When you set up your environment for healthy eating, you'll make better choices. Consider what foods will help you make better choices and which ones only get to show up every once in a while.

Control portions and maintain nutrition. When serving yourself, take only what you will eat. This allows you to be more aware of your daily choices when it comes to how much food you need to survive and to thrive.

Take time to fuel your body, to listen carefully to the cues your food sends your brain, and to nourish your entire being. When you listen and learn, it makes The Accountability Code in your life all that more powerful.

If you need accountability AND nutrition education, I totally have you covered. My Healthy Eating Challenge has helped thousands of women enjoy their food, enjoy learning what's in their food, and enjoy the benefits of a healthier mind and body from solid nutrition.

Check Ins

I put a new car on my vision board a couple years ago, and it was a great way to motivate me to work harder. Luckily, I was able to make it happen. I got focused and organized, and I purchased a nicer car to drive for the next ten years or so. I also got the highest model of the vehicle, and it has a few features that I absolutely love!

I want to talk about some of the features that demonstrate how important feedback is. The Accountability Code will only be useful if you are willing to work with the ever- changing factors in your life.

First, adaptive cruise control.
You can set the speed you want to cruise at, but you also set the distance you wish to keep between you and the car in front of you. That means if the car in front of you slows down, your car will keep the pace all the way down to a complete stop, if needed. When that car speeds up, my car will accelerate as well.

This adaptive cruise control has assisted me in quickly finding and following the correct speed limit. I speed less and am more relaxed when I drive.

The second feature I love is lane assist.

The camera sensors on the front of the car can detect the lines on the streets, so if my car begins to move out of the lane without using a turn signal, the car will turn the wheel to move you back into correct alignment.

The nudge to get back in the lane can be minute if you are paying attention. I have tested this feature, driving without my hands on the wheel and allowing myself to drift into another lane when it's clear and safe. I found that if the correction needed is too great, lights on the dashboard will activate, and the car flashes red lights internally for me to take the wheel again.

These features have enhanced my driving experiences and capabilities. Not only am I more aware of my driving habits, but I also now view my road to health similarly. Not everyone is blessed with top-of-the line cars, or health. Some of us grew up in homes where health and fitness was talked about and a priority. But that was not the case for me, and many of us grew up needing to figure it all out on our own. We did not have an adequate presence of health to emulate.

Whichever group you fall into, we are all blessed with the opportunity to improve our health for free. Walking, water, meditation, self-care, and sleep are all free! Regardless of your income, there are ways to know whether you are going too fast, too slow, or veering out of your lane. It just takes a little bit of strong feedback to help us become aware.

Let me introduce you to the concept of doing quick check-ins for realistic and immediate feedback.

Just like I don't depend on my car to do 100% of the work to get me to my next destination, I can't expect to give away my responsibility to my well-being, either. I have to have a plan for health and use check-ins as a way to keep me going and to get the feedback needed when I have to take control. I'm going to teach you how to solidify your check-in sources and how to ask for help when you are driving toward your goals and looking for feedback.

What are the situations you know that you need warnings about when it comes to improving your mind and body awareness? When I discovered that mental illness runs in my family, I took corrective steps to make sure that I keep my health in check, including my mental and emotional health.

Now, when we test drove my newest car, we knew that it was used and had some work done. We discovered that the lane assist camera in the front was not functioning properly. The vehicle could be almost a half a car's length off the side of the road before it would detect the need for a correction. It needed to be recalibrated.

So, too, do we need to recalibrate our sensors from time to time, particularly when it comes to our health. Do you overreact to situations? Is it hard to ask for help? Is your mood generally happy and content? What are your greatest strengths?

When you know your strengths, they become the basis of your daily expectations. If you were driving and in danger of going off the road, you'd want to detect it as soon as possible. That trajectory has the potential to be a life-or-death situation. So is your health. If I am feeling down, I let someone know so that further unsafe movements can be addressed. If I'm angry, or creating dumb stories about people's motives, or I believe someone is intentionally trying to hurt me, then I know I need to be reined in. What are the warning emotions you often receive in times of danger or distress?

If you know that certain situations, like perilous roads in winter, are more dangerous for you than others, you will choose to avoid them whenever possible. Don't force yourself to handle anything that feels unsafe. There is always a different road to take. What potential people or situations do you recognize are unsafe, particularly as you work on your goals?

I find it helpful to talk to people with experience in these situations. When I struggle with a family member, I know my siblings can relate. And the more I tune in to what my real struggles are, the greater my communication is with others. Loved ones can sense when I'm not my usual social, upbeat self, and they will reach out and check in with me. But it's incumbent upon me to express my emotions and not hide them. I have to send feedback to others if I want feedback to support me in return.

It's also important not to commit to things if we know there's something that needs to be fixed first. Is there something in your life that needs to be addressed before moving forward with your goals?

It's a necessity to halt your progress toward a goal so you can address safety. Hey, I could have purchased my car with the existing problems and maybe just talked the dealer down in price, but safety was more important to me. When we acknowledge our safety, we protect ourselves from getting hurt. I want you to take a deep breath and say to yourself, 'I choose to be safe, first, before all else.'

Neglecting the warning signs can be detrimental in the long run. If you want to lose weight and continually follow different diets without addressing your disordered eating habits, those problems will continue to exist. Start by telling yourself the truth. When you are in alignment with the desires of your heart, things have a better chance of working out.

Use feedback to tell yourself and others what is happening in your life. When I get in my car, I have every intention of driving it correctly and safely. The features of my car are meant to correct me when I fail to do it myself, but they can't do it all for me. I have learned that I am happier by staying on the path instead of receiving constant corrections. Would you rather wait for someone to tell you what to do, or do you prefer to guide yourself? Who are the people that have earned the right to know your journey and offer constructive feedback?

This process is necessary for everyone. Gain comfort knowing that when you share your little and big mistakes, others can relate. You should never feel alone, and the best way to safety-proof your path is by practicing those little check-ins. Inhale nice and big as you say to yourself, 'My pathway is safe. I have loved ones who can help. And I'm never too far off track.'

We are all blessed with the opportunity to improve our health for free, and that includes sharing your experience with those who can give you the feedback you need to make improvements to keep you safe and on track.

Results Determine Shift

As we continue to talk about the importance of Feedback as the last step in The Accountability Code, I'd like to share with you a statement that gave me numerous opportunities to pause and adapt my actions. All my life, my dad repeated a lesson that he learned from his father: "You won't know how you did as a parent until you see how your grandkids turn out."

At face value, this seems like a really logical statement. It won't be until we see how your children run their adult lives that we can determine if what we taught them was taken to heart. But like many things I learned when I was young, this statement came into question in recent years when my dad rejected me for choosing to live my life differently than he wanted.

I decided to explore this expression, to understand it. Did my grandpa end up thinking he was a good parent? Did he even know how I turned out? Does my dad believe he is a good parent? Does he get to judge my children to determine his worth as a father? If my children are happy, healthy, good people, does that mean dad takes credit?

Is there some truth to what he said, or is this statement altogether false? If it is false, why did my dad repeat it over and over again to me? If he believes this statement to be true, then what does that say about the way he was raised considering that he believes that I have gone so far off the right path?

When something is repeated to us over and over, it can become part of who we are. I need to do everything in my power to make sure that the thoughts that live in my mind push me to actually do good. I don't want to believe that I cannot be accepted by my dad because I don't choose to obey him as an adult.

I am happy to say that I have made peace with this statement and have turned this life-changing lesson into a system that allows me to accurately gauge my actions and how they will impact my parents, my children, and all those I come in contact with.

My practice involves a nightly check-in to plan my day ahead and assess my progress. I know without a doubt that when I take the time to evaluate how I am acting, I can honestly say if I've done my best each day. I accept that the actions of others are irrelevant to what I do. When you have faith that you are doing your best and commit to improving each day, you prove your imperfect human qualities and will find the reassurance that you are loved along the way.

I created a little booklet that helps me plan and execute my day according to what I want to accomplish and who I wish to become. There are five steps I try to complete daily. I am not always perfect in performing those five steps, but after using this form as often as possible for the last four years, I can honestly say I am doing the best I can.

Before I share the steps with you, I want to emphasize one perspective that helped me remove the shame in saying "I'm doing the best I can" — No one has the right to decide how well you or your children turn out. No one has that right but you and God. Period.

Follow these steps and take comfort in knowing that your path will adapt as you call for guidance from your loving Father in Heaven, who knows everything about you and wants nothing less than for you to choose ultimate peace and love.

Here are the five steps:

1. **Make Your List.**

    Each morning, make a list of your to-do items. Add in the names of people you wish to serve that day. Limit your To-Do and To-Serve list to no more than 15 tasks, so choose wisely.

    When you make service a forefront of your intentions, you keep your heart open to new experiences. Becoming the best person you can be does not just mean you are successful at accomplishing your goals, but that you also share your light with others.

    Working on yourself is only preparing you to more effectively hear the messages to help others. Take a deep breath and say to yourself, 'I love; therefore, I serve.' Your service to others, not your accomplishments, is what leads to greatness.

2. Pray for Guidance.

As you review your To-Do and To-Serve lists, pray for guidance to align yourself with the purposes of God. Now, having a plan for the day already creates a positive attitude for positive action. And asking for guidance through prayer will not only help you get things done, but to do them with the best intentions.

I recommend finding a quiet place where you feel comfortable and relaxed, and then you can talk with God about why these tasks are important to you. Explain how good will come from following through. Take time to listen, and pause to create space for messages or guidance to come through to you from Him.

As you state your intentions, know that you are part of a bigger plan. Each day that you pray for guidance in your tasks, you'll find you are ensuring actions more in line with what you are meant to do.

3. Set Your Priorities.

Now you have to prioritize that list for the day. On each list, write the number 1 for those that are most critical, a 2 for the next in priority, and so on. Once you have set the priority level of each item, you can plan your day accordingly. Some lesser priorities might come right behind the more critical ones if they involve using the same tools and resources. Some of your biggest tasks might have to wait until later in the day when you have the assistance or energy required.

Know that you may not accomplish every to-do list and assist every to-serve person. The tasks with lesser priorities may not get completed, but they are also not as important as your number one, two, or three tasks. Focus on those that must get done, and then allow the others to come as your day progresses. Take a deep breath and say, "I use my time well." Let your emotions guide you as you review your lists and decide what must be accomplished and who
to serve.

4. Start Doing Your Goals.

The best way to get things done is to simply start. You have a plan, you've asked for help, and now it's time to do the work.

As you complete each item, check it off the list and find a way to celebrate. Take a deep breath and say, "I am great at following through," and don't forget to take time to breathe, to stop and smell the roses as they present themselves. Continue to listen to the Spirit throughout the day as you work.

Don't let checking boxes distract you from feeling the benefits now. Give yourself a pat on the back as you practice the actions that help you become who you are supposed to be.

Not everyone is going to give you credit for your work, including those you serve.

Do it anyway.

5. **Pray Again.**

Each night, after you have accomplished your tasks and service, report to Heavenly Father in prayer. Ask questions, listen, repent, and feel His love. After you have prayed, write down the main emotion you felt afterwards. A nightly check-in is beneficial to see how you did, regroup after a long day, and consider how tomorrow might be improved. Take a look at your list — all that you accomplished and things you may not have — and be glad. Take a deep breath and say, "I did a great job today."

Don't forget to thank those who helped you accomplish your tasks, and thank those you were able to serve by allowing you into their lives and helping you strive to be a better person. Thank God, as you share your progress and feelings with Him. Let Him rejuvenate you and show you love. A greater awareness and love will come as you pray and commune with the Lord on the ways that you can serve, and the successes you may find.

Then every day, every way, get a little better. Remember that you are responsible for your own actions, and others are responsible for their own, too. We may see reflections of our best and worst efforts in our children and even our grandchildren, but we do not own their successes and failures. We can only claim our own.

Conclusion

Boundaries

Boundaries are a way of defining what you will and won't allow in your life. As you embark on using The Accountability Code, you will have clarity on what sources lift you up and which ones bring you down.

While you define each step of TAC — Reflection, Humility, Planning, Implementing, Commitment, and Feedback — you'll see that setting boundaries allows you to accurately define your action and intention.

To illustrate this point, let me tell you a story I heard many years ago. Then afterwards I will use The Accountability Code to accurately describe why setting boundaries is necessary to master self-accountability. Although I no longer remember who told this story to me, the sensibility of the lesson of this tale explains why we align limits with the most important issues in our lives.

Once, there was a man who needed to transport a load of precious wood to a faraway town. He was an expert in chopping, milling, and refining the wood, but he knew he needed a professional driver in order to transport it safely and on time. It couldn't be just any driver. It had to be one who was knowledgeable and safe for the road, which was very dangerous. It included many ups and downs, twists and turns, and bridges, but it was the quickest route to the destination.

There was another road, but it would take much longer to deliver the load. Most drivers didn't consider this longer road because they wanted to make the sum of money as quickly as possible and move on to the next job.

One particular turn was known as 'The Place of No Return.' If an inexperienced driver didn't know the conditions of this road, they could potentially risk going over the cliff and being swept away during a storm.

The woodman was determined to find the best driver, no matter the cost. He understood the value of keeping the load rather than replacing the load, truck, and driver. The sum he was prepared to pay gained the attention of many people in that small town. Applicants who believed they could make the journey with such a large load were encouraged to apply. The man took the time to interview each one to ensure he would make the right choice.

His only question was, "How will I know my load will make it safely to this town?"

Driver one said, "Sir, I have carried over 100 loads and have come so close to the edges on that road, yet I have never lost one."

Driver two said, "I am an expert with great precision. I can get one inch away from the edge of the road and will not let the load fall."

The final driver said, "I can see how much you value your load, and I will stay as far away from the edge as possible. I will avoid the road if the weather is bad and take the alternate route regardless of the days it takes, for I know that is the safest way for me, the truck, and the load."

The woodman instantly knew which driver had the best qualifications because he was very clear in what he would and would not do. Setting boundaries is choosing to put in place a standard that keeps you safe and in the best health possible. We cannot always rely on someone's word if we haven't prepared a plan to stay safe. In this story, the first two drivers came up with some good arguments. But the last driver best understood the importance of the task.

I think you know what it feels like to live on the edge, and you may be yearning for the protection that comes from staying away from danger. What is the safest position, and how do you know for sure? I feel that the most dangerous situation I've experienced is one where I question my self-worth. I've had multiple arguments with my dad who says things to me that make me doubt who I am. Without a proper boundary, I allowed him to dictate my perception of myself. I have come to realize that the safest position for me is one of minimal contact.

A lack of boundaries invites a lack of respect.

You can apply boundaries to many different situations. Let's say there's a particular food that makes you feel crappy after you eat it. You think, 'Eating Betty's Burgers makes me feel sick. I'm not eating that anymore!' That is a boundary. You are deciding what you will and won't allow in your life. First determine the situations or triggers that make you feel unhealthy. Personally, I feel like crap when I sit around all day and eat lots of junk food. I also feel sick when someone is rude to me. What makes you feel like crap?

When I experience that yucky feeling, it isn't easy to turn it around. It takes a while to settle, and then to pass. But during that time, I'm not very happy or productive. I start to feel bad about myself and my actions. That's the impact of feeling unhealthy — it creates more unhealthiness and unhappiness.

I hate thinking that I'm not measuring up, that I made bad choices, or that I'm not where I need to be. When I'm in that space, I don't show up for myself or others the way I should — I lack accountability, and that's a dangerous position for me to be in. What is the cost of lost time for you, when you are dealing with poor health or low self-worth? I hope that you are hitting that point right now where you recognize that it's not okay to treat yourself like that anymore.

It's not okay for others to do so, either. How do you feel when your boundaries are violated by others? Do you want to escape, or do you sink into despair? Stop asking why they keep doing it and start asking, instead, why you allow it.

Every emotion is a gift, even the negative ones. They provide powerful feedback and motivation to make positive change. Start by saying, "I don't like the way this makes me feel." Pronouncing your feelings will validate them and motivate you to choose something better. Empower yourself to take a different path.

That's also the time to reduce the triggers that brought on the unhappy feelings and replace them, if necessary. Once I realized the damage caused by my relationship with my dad had demeaned and diminished me, I found the strength to protect myself. I recognized that the damage I was feeling outweighed the benefit of trying to keep up the relationship, so I decided to reduce my exposure, and it has helped me tremendously, especially as I've applied The Accountability Code to keep me in check. I can choose the healthiest option even when all the choices aren't perfect. I created boundaries, and I'm only in the presence of this family member when it is safe for me.

For further clarity, let's plug in the personal Accountability Code process I went through:

Reflection — I don't like visiting my dad with the intention to catch up only to have the conversation turn to how evil and dishonest his family has been to him over the years. When discussing what is going on in my life, my dad is constantly trying to teach me a lesson instead of really hearing what my family is up to. When trying to change the subject to something lighter, especially with kids around, I am accused of not seeing the truth of the situation in the media or politics. I often have to compete with the TV for his attention and when he does call me, it's to ask me for something. This has been going on for years.

Humility — I love my dad and want to spend time with him. I miss the days where our whole family could get together and just enjoy each other's company, play some games, and watch the grandchildren's latest impromptu play. I will pray that my dad gets the justice he is searching for and that he values all that he does have. I continue to live the values he taught me and sincerely thank him for the confidence and leadership skills he taught me. I am a good human because of what he and my mom taught me growing up.

Planning — I must resolve any family conflict that arises so I can avoid feeling about my siblings the way my dad has experienced. I plan for my own success in hopes of never having an issue if splitting of assets doesn't go my way. Aubrey and I stay open to the promptings we have to love and serve, when appropriate, and I spend adequate time trying to be a good parent to my own children.

Implementing — On a regular basis, carry out my plan and intentions I communicate with each of my siblings, plan family gatherings without any bossy expectations. I send uplifting cards in the mail and I make an effort to listen to my kids individually.
Commitment — I use all triggers, good and bad, to remind myself that I have the power to break negative cycles. I do not need to believe my dad's opinion of his siblings. I do not have to agree with his political views and I must keep myself in a place of humility so as to not put being right over having personal relationships with those I love.

Feedback — I have developed a closer relationship with each of my siblings. My mother has benefited from my expertise as a life and fitness expert. Sharing my struggles has empowered others to seek help with their toxic relationships. I speak with more surety to my dad about seeking professional help for his issues and I am much more aware of how my actions impact those around me.

Using The Accountability Code is the perfect system for processing your concerns, handling them in a realistic way, and becoming a better person despite what the world is throwing at you. It will help you sift through all factors that impact your progress and move you towards happiness and great health.

Each issue or event is a trigger that you can put into The Accountability Code and see progress in your life because of it.

As you begin to reduce your negative triggers, you'll feel less stress, but it requires adjusting your thoughts in response. I had to choose to find a path to wellness as fast as possible after interacting with my dad.

Boundaries are essential to our well-being, physical and emotional. Once they've been in place for a while and you've acted on your commitments, you'll start to notice that you feel happier about yourself. That means the boundary is effective and so are you. As I placed distance between myself and this other person, I realized that I had not felt down in a long time. I made the connection that interacting with this person went hand in hand with negative feelings about myself.

Emotions change, and so do people. The longer your boundaries are in place, the more confident you will be about them, and the easier it will be to explain them to others. You never need to explain why you feel the need to protect yourself, but communicating about your boundaries can create healthy new relationships. Those who support you deserve to be on your team and those who don't care to listen might as well be holding up their own red flag. Take the time to describe to others what is necessary to enter your space in a safe way.

My hope is that as you define your boundaries, you'll find yourself further away from the edge and immersed in The Accountability Code. Nothing is more important than your well-being. Take heed to what your mind, body, and spirit needs for it is truly the only thing you have.

Charity

Mastering accountability allows you to fully feel into your experiences. And the greater your experiences, then the stronger and more connected you will be.

As I have worked to be more accountable in my life I have reflected on why that's important to me and how I came to care at the level I do.

When I unexpectedly made the cheerleading team in high school, I got a rude awakening when I learned what the monthly costs would be. I left my first team info meeting in tears, hearing that I would have to come up with at least $500 each month!

I come from a large working-class family, and we were always on a tight budget. Even as a teen, I was expected to cover my personal expenses like gas, car insurance, phone, schoolbooks, and recreation. Realizing that in addition to all that, I would now also need to pay for practice shoes, competition shoes, matching bags, sweats, uniforms, jackets, hair bows, tumbling lessons, more gas money to drive to competitions, plus the cost of my time, which took me away from other potential earning gigs. I was overwhelmed.

I tried out for the team to prove myself, but after that first meeting, I found myself asking if I really needed to follow through. I'm not a quitter, so I decided to create a plan for success. Just like the foolproof plan I put together a couple years earlier. I went home and asked my mom to help me write another letter appealing to friends and family. In the letter, I asked again to earn money through odd jobs. As a disclaimer, the letter stated that my schedule was very limited, but I was determined to do whatever it took to stay on the cheerleading team.

At my next team meeting, I brought copies of those letters and humbly passed them out to my teammates, asking them to share the letters with their parents. I was openly admitting that my parents could not pay for my cheerleading costs and that I needed to pay my own way. That was very hard to do. But within a week, I was informed that someone had paid for my tumbling lessons. I couldn't believe it. That generous but anonymous donor had just saved me $120 each month.

Their generosity required a commitment from me to show up to practice every day and put forth my best effort. I chose to be accountable to my tumbling and cheer efforts to prove my gratitude for help. Using The Accountability Code in your life is proving that you value all you have been given.

Grateful, I continued to take other odd jobs to earn money where I could. A month later, I went to the cashier's window to make a payment on my cheer account, only to find that another anonymous donor had put $500 into my account.

This experience changed my entire life. Not only was I working harder than I ever had in my life, but I was being helped more than ever, too. "Giving is not just about making a donation. It is about making a difference." — Kathy Calvin

The point of this story isn't to tell you to find a poor person and give them money. It is about living your life in a way that allows you to be changed. I can only imagine what sort of life my donors were living and wonder, 'What about their situation compelled them to help someone like me?'

The first rule of being able to give to others is this: We need to be healthy. We need to be aware of what we put out to the world. The way that we show up for others comes back to us tenfold. But we have to start from a position of well-being to be able to do that.

Think about the times in your life when you were blessed by the generosity of others. Have you considered how they were able to make that contribution of time, money, or energy? What about the times when you have given to others? What about that experience enhanced your well-being?

The impact of being charitable creates a pattern that increases your awareness, but also deepens your mind/body connection. As the recipient of life-changing generosity, I have since made efforts to love and give —

sometimes in bigger ways than I was comfortable with. But each time I do, I feel more connected to God, the world, and to my best self.

Being charitable is a surefire way to increase your own well-being and awareness. How can you pay it forward today? When you give, both you and the recipient are blessed and more connected. I eventually found out the name of my generous donors, and today I think of them and their families with happiness and gratitude in my heart.

It begins with reflection. Count your blessings. Take a few moments each day to list what you have been given in life and to ask yourself, what can I give in return or in gratitude? At the very least, you can thank God for what you have been given and ask Him to provide that to others.
Your awareness of this blessing then extends to those around you. The only reason I received the generous gift during cheerleading was because some kind soul was paying attention and saw someone in need. Generosity asks you to observe and listen intently. To set aside your distractions and pay attention when others are seeking assistance.

Then look for opportunities to help. Connect the dots between having and giving. What you are most grateful for is the perfect gift to give to others. Grab a pen and paper and list a few people who could use more of what you have in abundance. Remember to look for opportunities to help, not to judge.

By developing the habit of connecting the dots between what you have and what you can give, that awareness breeds charity and the opportunity to be part of an amazing interaction. I know that I always have to strive to be in a position to give, in order to create the same or similar experiences that I've been blessed with. There is no lack of struggle in the world right now. Getting outside of your current life will boost your desire to show up in a healthy, happy way.

Remember, too, that you cannot pour from an empty cup. When called to give, is your response to say, "I don't have the time", "I have no energy for that", or "I have so little money myself right now"? Which excuse resonates the most for you? What then must be replenished, so that you can give in gratitude to others?

If you don't have time, you might be wasting time. I know that sounds harsh, but we have to dispel your expectation of what giving time looks like. Maybe it means putting away your phone while in the grocery store line to talk to an overworked cashier. Might it be helping your neighbor by watching their child while playing with your own? Is your problem really that you don't have enough time, or is it how you view the quality of how you spend your time? If it's time that you feel you don't have enough to give, write down the ways you might be wasting time.

If it is energy you're lacking, are you getting enough sleep, water intake, movement, and self-care? **By making your own health a priority**, you better prepare to give to others and enhance your life.

Having abundance is a sign that you can give more. Decide how you will be charitable with others. Money, energy, time: What do you have to give today? You have the opportunity and the means to change someone else's life right now.

In the children's movie, *Robots*, the great builder's mantra is, "See a need, fill a need." You know that you have something you can offer to others. Now it's time to get specific. On paper, match up opportunities with the resources you have available to share. I can give time to my sister, by taking her children to the park. I can give energy and assistance to my neighbor who is moving. I can give money to my kids' teachers for supplies.

I'm not asking you to donate your car or invite a homeless person to live with you. I'm asking you to give what you can and should, in proportion to what you have received. You know you've been blessed in many ways and if you haven't felt that generosity in a while, using The Accountability Code will help you get back to a place of ultimate gratitude that drives you to action.

If you need help making your health a priority, my Mental Strength Challenge is the perfect way to make sure your mind is the right place to move forward. It also comes with accountability to the basics of health: sleep, self-care, water intake, and movement.

Once the Gift Has Been Given

As a result of my baby being in the NICU, my first post-delivery hospital experience was less than stellar.

Because of that, I wanted to make sure that with future deliveries, my needs were communicated to loved ones. My mom helped me write a letter in advance of the next baby's birth. It asked visitors to refrain from bringing flowers to the hospital. My hope was that fewer people would show up to deliver gifts and visit before I was ready. And my mom also reminded me that receiving flowers means having to carry them out of the hospital when checking out. My hands were already full!

Years later, I read a post in an online mom's group where a woman was asking for feedback on her recent hospital stay with a new baby. Her husband gave her a bouquet of flowers, and they remained in the room while she recovered. Days later at discharge time, the flowers still looked beautiful and fresh, so she asked the nurse to give them to the new mom in a neighboring room.

But her husband got so mad at her for giving away the flowers he gave her. Her post online asked others if they thought her husband's anger was justified. The comments were overwhelmingly in her favor: "What a sweet gesture, to think of another mom! You really made a difference," and "Gosh, you saved your husband the hassle of carrying another item to the car. He should be glad he has such a kind wife!"

It was nice to see the support for this woman. and I commented, "Once you give something away, you don't get to choose what happens with it."

The gift of the bouquet served its purpose, not just once. But the impact was far-reaching. The reasons the husband was mad is open for interpretation, but the truth remains the same: Gifts are a thing given willingly to someone without payment. We should expect or require nothing in return for giving.

I didn't love my NICU experience, but because I went through that, I now have a deeper ability to relate to others who go through it, too. Every experience you are given is a gift, and you are free to choose what to do with that gift. I hate to break it to you, but it won't always be a bouquet of flowers. Sometimes your gift is a broken bone, a fight with a loved one, or getting sick. But when we get used to seeing every experience as a gift, it deepens our awareness and shows us how to respond. This process must be practiced, and it's, oh, so effective, at slowing down our fast pace, generating kindness to others, and even helping us master The Accountability Code.

Life is filled with good and bad. Many of my clients experience unhappy times in their marriages and while it makes me sad, we all know that marriage comes with a lot of hardship. But just because we're being tested doesn't mean we get a pass or fail grade. There are ways to reduce bad experiences and accept each interaction as a gift, to better develop our connections to our partners and others.

Do you know why they call the first two years of marriage the 'honeymoon phase'? Because phases end and new chapters begin. Many new couples think their honeymoon phase will be blissful, and last forever. But bliss isn't real life. I want you to say to yourself, as often as necessary, "I love and embrace real life!"

Don't let the end of the honeymoon phase in any relationship come as a surprise. Unpleasant surprises are often the result of unmet expectations.

Have you ever been shocked by receiving nothing from your husband on Mother's Day? Welcome to what seems like the rest of the world! I went through too many years being upset that my husband wouldn't treat me like a queen on my special day. That's because I expected bliss in the midst of real life.

"Look around at how lucky we are to be alive right now!"

— Eliza Hamilton from Hamilton, the Broadway play

I love that quote so much, I had it printed on a t-shirt! It's an affirmation to count your blessings and treat every imperfect day (and they're all imperfect) as a gift. We can find peace in what is.

After a few Mother's Days with no gifts and no royal treatment, I asked my mother-in-law what she wanted for Mother's Day. I was so taken aback by her answer: "I'm not your mom." I chuckled, then I realized that was why my husband didn't get me gifts for Mother's Day. It wasn't because he didn't care, but because he grew up believing you only gave Mother's Day gifts to your own mom, and I'm not his mom! That awareness allowed me to release the resentment I felt and to be open to a new interpretation of what that day could mean for me.

I no longer expect Mother's Day to include material gifts. I shifted my perspective instead, and I treat myself to something that actually feels blissful because I gift it to myself. I am responsible for my own happiness, and that is something I enjoy being accountable for now.

Every year around Mother's Day, I prepare to give myself a day filled with whatever I want. I even schedule it in my phone calendar, so I won't forget to treat myself like a queen. Gifting this day to myself releases any anger I might feel over not receiving gifts from others, or gifts I don't absolutely love.

Being grateful and accountable isn't about being perfect — It's about refusing to be numb. How can you reflect deeper on your own experiences and how they impacted you to become a better person? How can you be more open to change in order to experience more happiness? What day do you need to gift yourself with? Schedule it in your phone app *right now*!

If you want something to be different, you have to use your past anger and hurt to change your future. The hardest experiences, in fact, often teach the greatest lessons. The biggest lesson is to release your pain and anger. If you have enough information to be angry, you have enough to be grateful for, too. You don't have to engage in the same old patterns. Taking every single experience in life and choosing what to do with it, productively, is the greatest gift of all.

I wanted less resentment and obligation, and I wanted my future gifts to be genuine, not expected. Write down what you want your gifts to be and why you want to respond differently when you receive them.

The last thing is to give thanks, for every gift you receive. I no longer expect Mother's Day gifts, but I do give them – to my mom, to my mother-in-law (even though she's not technically my mom) and to other moms I know and respect. I also reach out at random times throughout the year, to say thank you to the moms (and the dads) I most appreciate. I don't wait for a greeting card day. I act in accordance with what feels right, to let my loved ones know I am thankful for them. That is my favorite way to demonstrate my accountability to whatever life throws my way.

Who in your life would you like to thank today? It's okay if it's yourself for right now. You deserve it. Use The Accountability Code to solidify this mindset:

Reflection — What experiences are you grateful for now?

Humility — How did those experiences help you grow as a person?

Planning — How would you like to extend your blessings to others?

Implementing — What must you do now?

Commitment — Don't let opportunities pass you by before it's too late.

Feedback — Let yourself feel edified, knowing you are improving others' lives.

Listen and Act

Life has a funny way of moving us forward, even when we don't feel like it. We experience another awakening, another day, another bedtime, and it starts all over again. There is absolutely nothing we can do to go back — and the sooner we accept that, the better.

The Accountability Code is such a vital tool that I hope you continue to use over and over as you sift through your struggles and goals. The process of continually waking up and showing up will prove you provide a level of happiness you never thought possible.

I am grateful for the understanding that the deep, challenging experiences are those that shape us into the person we are today. When life throws troubles and tests our way, we have to act in the moment. Hopefully, we choose growth and awareness.

I learned that there was no way to go back to the person I had been, once I appreciated the impact of my personal choices. They helped me understand how to wake up and show up, and I want to share that lesson with you.

In my church, I was given the assignment to be a part-time missionary for our local area. It was my responsibility to befriend others, introduce them to full-time missionaries when appropriate, and help everyone feel welcome. Perfect job for me, honestly! Even when I am not given the official assignment I still fulfill many of the duties.

As I was discussing the needs of our area with the other part-time missionaries, my leader told me the importance of stopping at the door of the chapel and praying for guidance on who needs me to sit by them, or who I should approach and try to connect with. That morning, as church was beginning, I decided to try this out. As I looked around the room, I asked our Heavenly Father, 'Where do I need to sit today?' Almost instantly, I knew my answer. 'Who was that cute redhead sitting alone? I haven't met her yet. I'll sit there.'

I sat beside the woman and introduced myself. I asked if she was visiting or if she was new, and I expressed my gratitude for letting me sit beside her. She told me she was just married and that this was her first time in this church. I don't recall why her husband wasn't there, but we began to chat, and then I sent her a friend request on Facebook, which she accepted.

Not one week later, there was an announcement at church that this woman's new husband had just passed by suicide. We were fully ready to love and support her during this hard time, especially because the next part of the announcement shared the news that she was also pregnant with her first baby.

My heart broke for her, and I immediately thought back to the week before. I knew exactly which woman they were talking about, and I began to cry as I thought, 'What if I hadn't asked and listened to the Spirit? What if I hadn't sat beside her that day?'

What if that woman had remained by herself during the entire service and left, feeling all alone, and then spent the next week in circumstances I could only imagine that would lead to the loss of her husband? I don't think I could have lived with the regret had I not followed through on approaching her, in answer to the question I had asked Heavenly Father. I hoped that choosing to sit beside her was a sign of God's love at that moment in her life.

I know the importance of listening to the Spirit and of practicing listening to it. How will I know how to serve God if I never listen to His answers to me through the Spirit? How would I have known to sit beside someone who needed a friend if I had just rushed into the chapel, sat where I normally sat, and gave no thought to where God wanted me to be?

This is an example of the Accountability Code in action. I was given directives on how to listen, I found surety in the message, I woke up, and I showed up. I'll go deeper into this experience to clarify just how effective The Accountability Code is perfect at helping you follow through with what you know you need to do.

There are specific steps you can take to experience a similar transformation in your own life. When we concentrate on certain matters, our abilities are challenged, but our trust becomes more solidified. Not only will you trust yourself with the message you get, but God will trust your desire and ability to follow through. Therefore, you'll receive messages more often and with greater responsibility and reward. What area of your life would you like to deepen your ability to wake up and show up?

Even when you don't see results immediately, the task of showing up cannot be ignored. Imagine adding up all the small steps you are taking. They do make a difference, and all great feats begin with one small choice. Take a deep breath and say, "My small actions matter. I am achieving my big goal now through my small actions."

Ask for guidance and opportunities. I now pray regularly for opportunities to serve and they are all around me. When you focus on something you want and you include God into your plan He will come through. He literally tells us: "Ask and ye shall receive!"

Here is how I continue to use The Accountability Code as I did in this story to multiply life changing experiences that help me become more like my Savior, Jesus Christ. That is my ultimate goal, and I can achieve significant progress toward that, now.

> **Reflection** — I showed up to my missionary meeting with the intention to follow through with my assignments. I was currently doing the best I could, and I put myself in a position to learn.

> **Humility** — I asked God where I should sit. He guided me and trusted me to make the best choice.

> **Planning** — My plan had always been to greet others, get out of my comfort zone, and to attempt a last connection.

Implementing — I had to physically show up to my meeting, I had to arrive at church with time to ponder. I had to physically pause and look around. After praying and listening, I had to now take action.

Commitment — I know that as I listen to the promptings and messages God sends I will be happier than if I only trust myself. I will never know when someone needs a helping hand so I must keep myself in a position to be open and ready.

Feedback — It was a tender mercy to receive reassurance that I was doing what was right, but by staying connected to this friend I realize just how much of an impact our meeting had that I wasn't able to realize at the time.

The Lord can work wonders with you if you let him. As you keep your mind and body in a connected space, you'll find immense joy from following through, and I hope The Accountability Code is the means to helping you develop the level of self-mastery you are searching for.

Now it's time to go ALL IN — and learn as you go! Mastery is impossible without levels of learning and application. Take the time to listen. We aren't always going to get answers really fast, but as we practice and apply the messages, we'll gain the ability to slow down and to hear more clearly.

Take a deep breath and say, "I listen to the lessons perfectly designed for me."

My eyes were opened when I physically sat by that new friend at church. This is the Accountability Code in action. You must be willing to put yourself in a position to get to the next step. You will never reach your goals by staying put.

So wake up and show up!

Be deliberate about what you are asking for, why it's important to you, and be willing to move in the direction you need to go.

There are so many helpers ready and willing to assist you, and so many helpful factors to discover. I am here for you, and I can't wait to see how your life transforms as you apply the goodness principles I share with you through this book.

I can't thank you enough for taking the time to read what's in my heart. The Accountability Code is merely a tool to help YOU change YOUR life and I would love the privilege to be involved in your progress and transformation. Please follow this final QR code and let's set up a time to chat and I would love to hear your thoughts on this book and what's next for you in life.

<3/ Marci